DATE DUE

AS LONG AS WE BOTH SHALL LOVE

KAREN M. DUNAK

*As Long as
We Both
Shall Love*

THE WHITE WEDDING
IN POSTWAR AMERICA

NEW YORK UNIVERSITY PRESS

New York and London

NEW YORK UNIVERSITY PRESS
New York and London
www.nyupress.org

References to Internet websites (URLs) were accurate at the time of writing.
Neither the author nor New York University Press is responsible for URLs that
may have expired or changed since the manuscript was prepared.

LIBRARY OF CONGRESS CATALOGING-IN-PUBLICATION DATA
Dunak, Karen M.
As long as we both shall love : the white wedding in postwar America / Karen M. Dunak.
   pages cm
Includes bibliographical references and index.
ISBN 978-0-8147-3781-1 (cl : alk. paper)
1. Weddings—United States—History. 2. United States—Social life and
customs—1945-1971. 3. United States—Social life and customs—1971- I. Title.
GT2703.D86 2013
392.50973—dc23
2013009421

New York University Press books are printed on acid-free paper, and their binding materials
are chosen for strength and durability. We strive to use environmentally responsible
suppliers and materials to the greatest extent possible in publishing our books.

Book design by Marcelo Agudo

Manufactured in the United States of America
10 9 8 7 6 5 4 3 2 1

CONTENTS

ACKNOWLEDGMENTS

When I was in my mid-twenties, my calendar began to fill with the weddings of friends and family members. Very suddenly, it seemed, weddings were a hot topic. As friends planned weddings or complained about weddings they were in, as I packed for another wedding weekend and my jaw dropped at items (and their prices) listed on wedding registries, I started to wonder how the wedding—which seemed so formulaic and old-fashioned to me then—had maintained the cultural power it had. A research topic was born. As critical as anyone else who had bought a bridesmaid dress never to be worn again, I expected I would conclude this project with a major indictment against weddings and their participants. Instead, as I dove into the wedding's past and continued to participate in friends' wedding presents, I was won over by the thoughtfulness and care so many brides and grooms showed toward their celebration, the communities of their choosing, and each other. My thanks to the many celebrants I have celebrated over the last several years.

Many thanks to Michael McGerr, who saw the potential in this project when I first considered it as a possible topic of study. He encouraged me to think big as I examined the motivations of Americans as they celebrated weddings over the course of the twentieth century. McGerr reminded me to remember the people of the past and to treat them with the respect they deserved. As I practice history—as a writer and researcher and also as a teacher—I regularly reflect on his advice. Other members of Indiana University's History Department, especially John Bodnar, Claude Clegg, and Wendy Gamber, likewise provided invaluable feedback and support during the time I spent in Bloomington. My thanks also to Joanne Meyerowitz and Elizabeth Pleck, who offered valuable advice during the very early stages of my research.

Before I made my way to Indiana University, my professors at American University shaped my development as a historian—and as a person interested in and fascinated by the world around me. Deborah Cohen, Peter Kuznick, Charles Larson, and Leonard Steinhorn especially encouraged me across their respective fields and introduced me to events and people and ideas of the past and present. I see a piece of each of them in my approach to the study of the past. I have often said that I wrote my way through college, and I would have been unable to do so without the guidance and instruction of Judy LaVigne and the late Edward Pigut. Mr. Pigut whipped me into shape upon my arrival at Neptune High School, and Mrs. Lav prepared me for life after my departure. I marvel at the books she dared to assign and think back often to her pedagogy and projects. My thanks to these teachers who taught me so well.

At New York University Press, Debbie Gershenowitz showed great enthusiasm for this project from the first. I am grateful for her encouragement and guidance. Clara Platter, Constance Grady, and Alexia Traganas moved me through the publication process with ease. Thanks also to the anonymous readers of the manuscript for their excellent suggestions and critiques. In the earlier stages of this project, the editors, staff, and anonymous readers of *Gender & History*, especially Michele Mitchell, helped me to think deeply about the possibilities the wedding afforded various populations in the postwar years. This book and this historian are better thanks to generous feedback and smart suggestions of others.

Research trips and time for writing would have been far more difficult without support from the Center for Communal Studies at the University of Southern Indiana; the Indiana University History Department; the Lyndon Baines Johnson Presidential Library; Muskingum University; and Smith College. During my many visits to libraries and archives, I was astounded—time and again—by the assistance I received and the enthusiasm shown by those helping me with my research. My sincerest thanks to the staffs of American Jewish Archives in Cincinnati, Ohio; the Archives Center of the National Museum of American History at the Smithsonian Institute; the Center for Communal Studies; the Center for the Study of History and Memory at Indiana University; the Herman B. Wells Library at Indiana University; the Iowa Women's Archives; the Kinsey Institute at Indiana University; the Lyndon Baines Johnson Presidential Library; the Muskingum University Library; the Sophia Smith Archives; and the Tamiment Institute at New York University. My thanks also to those archivists and librarians willing to deal with me long-distance: the Falmouth Historical Society of Falmouth, Massachusetts; the Library of Congress Prints and Photographs Division; the ONE National Gay and Lesbian Archives in Los Angeles; and the University Archives at the University of Missouri.

With each presentation of my work, I received comments, questions, and suggestions that served to enhance the way I thought about weddings and their participants. My thanks to co-panelists, commentators, chairs, and receptive audiences at the 2006 University of Illinois Urbana-Champaign Women's and Gender Graduate Symposium, the 2006 Conference of the Women and Gender Historians of the Midwest, the 2008 meeting of the Organization of American Historians, the 2010 meeting of the American Historical Association, the 2011 meeting of the Ohio Academy of History, and the 2011 meeting of the Midwest Popular Culture Association. I had the opportunity to present my research to students, faculty, and community members at Indiana University–Southeast and also at Muskingum University. The enthusiastic response I received at these events increased my own enthusiasm for the project—and its potential audiences.

I am lucky to have begun my professional life on Muskingum University's campus. Upon my arrival in New Concord, the History Department's collegiality far exceeded my expectations. My thanks to Amy Bosworth, Alistair Hattingh, Laura Hilton, Bil Kerrigan, and Tom McGrath. Other friends and colleagues in New Concord have made this tiny village feel like home, and for their fellowship, I am grateful. Friends made during my years in Bloomington have enriched my life and my trade with their intellect, generosity, and general love of a good time. My thanks especially to Ben Aloe, Brooke Aloe, Jennifer Cavalli, Bonnie Laughlin-Schultz, Bill Schultz, and Shannon Smith.

Kati Costar, Jamie Curtis, Liz Radel Freeman, Carly Irwin Keeny, Jason Maddux, Brian Smith, Mike Stefanski, and Laura Stets have celebrated milestones with me since the American University years. I thank them for their willingness to venture (mid)west to see an old friend and for putting me up (and putting up with me) during my many trips back east. Across both time and distance, friends from my New Jersey youth have remained steadfast companions. Love and thanks to Mary Margiasso Cafferty, Colleen and Vinnie Curto, Jeremy Dobes, Alana Duffy, Gina LaCour, and Rachael Rock.

One of my earliest memories is of sitting on the steps at my grandparents' house, next to my great-grandmother's chair, where she would read me story after story after story. My Na, the late Gertrude Schack, read me so many books and at such a young age that by the time I was three, I insisted that I should "read" these memorized tales to her. I've been reading ever since. Whatever natural proclivity for or enjoyment of learning I may have had as a kid was cultivated and celebrated by my great-grandmother, my parents, Carol Dunak and the late Tom Dunak, and my grandparents, the late John and Lucille Coyne. My dad rewarded perfect spelling tests with packs of baseball cards; my grandfather delighted in schooling me in all-night Scrabble sessions; my mother quizzed me for every high school history test; and no one ever boasted about a granddaughter like my gram did about me. It was only as I grew older that I realized not everyone grew up surrounded by such a sustained and unwavering network of champions and believers. Much has changed since I first embarked on this project, but I think of them all every day. Thanks also to my sister, Stephanie Dunak, and members of the Coyne, Paul, and Eberly clans for their support and encouragement.

Finally, I offer thanks to my husband, Keith Eberly, who has been with this project as long as I have. He showed great faith in its development—and in me—these many years. He is a constant source of encouragement, kindness, and strength, and I cannot imagine a life without him. As I lived with this book, as I thought about the couples in its pages and what they expected from married life, inevitably, I considered my own expectations. While they never married and ultimately went their separate ways, it was during Graham Nash's time of domestic bliss with Joni Mitchell that he wrote "everything is easy 'cause of you." I know just what he meant, and I could ask for no more.

Introduction

The 2009 film *Bride Wars* begins innocently enough. After a youthful sighting of a wedding celebrated at New York City's Plaza Hotel, best friends Liv (Kate Hudson) and Emma (Anne Hathaway) are smitten. They decide their weddings will be just as grand as the one they witnessed as girls. Childhood fantasy becomes adult expertise as they memorize and categorize the best in wedding styles, themes, and professionals. When the audience meets Liv and Emma as adults, they are attending a college friend's wedding, dissecting the celebration, point by point. Their verdict: "It ain't June, and it ain't the Plaza." When the bride announces that it is time for the bouquet toss, Emma and Liv join an excited (some might say manic) throng, jumping and straining so they might catch the bouquet and be the next to wed.

While we never learn who, exactly, caught the bouquet, we soon bear witness to two very different engagements. Liv finds a Tiffany's box amid her live-in boyfriend's belongings and proceeds to announce to friends that she is getting married—before the actual proposal has been made. When said boyfriend fails to act as quickly as she would have liked, Liv storms into his office and demands an explanation. Instead of being annoyed, he is charmed by his bride-to-be's impulsivity, and the engagement is officially on. As fate would have it, Emma receives an unexpected proposal from her homebody boyfriend at approximately the same time. When she calls Liv to announce her news, the immediate response is neither joy nor jealousy. Instead, a quick string of questions about the size and quality of the diamond are top priority. After ascertaining that the stone is worthy, the two share excited squeals.

As Liv and Emma prepare for their wedding days, they meet with the best wedding planner in Manhattan, Marion St. Clair (Candice Bergen). St. Clair schools them, unnecessarily, on the importance of their impending celebrations as she states, "The wedding marks the first day of your life." Punctuating her point, she continues, "You have been dead until now." Improbably, both Emma and Liv are able to book June wedding dates at the Plaza. When asked if they would like to check with their grooms on the dates, the two quizzically respond in unison: "No." With dates firmly set and St. Clair contracts signed, they have approximately three and a half months to plan their weddings. Delighted at their good fortune, they begin the requisite wedding shopping. The first stop is clearly meant to be an upscale wedding boutique. Here, Liv decides on a "perfect" gown, designed by Vera Wang. While the audience never learns a price (for the gown—or any other part of the weddings), they do learn a vital fact about wedding gowns, and Wang gowns, in particular: "You don't alter Vera to fit you. You alter yourself to fit Vera." Ultimately, this process of alteration will serve as a guide for all things wedding-related.

Of course, some amount of conflict is necessary to make the movie pop (the film is called *Bride "Wars,"* after all). St. Clair reveals that she has booked the women for the same day at the Plaza, and if they plan to be in each other's weddings, one will need to change her date and venue. What begins as a civilized agreement to give consideration to who will alter her plans quickly escalates into an all-out cat fight, pre-wedding style. Emma endeavors to make Liv fat by sending her food bouquets. She sneaks into Liv's salon to swap out her normal hair color for a blue hue. Liv gives as good as she gets. She spreads rumors that Emma's is a shotgun wedding and, in another kind of salon attack, she replaces Emma's light spray tanning colorant with a color called "Blood Orange." Even before the full battle begins, Emma's fiancé, Fletcher, wonders why women get so "worked up" and "crazy" when it comes to weddings. The audience marvels not only at this level of crazy but also at the power of a wedding to destroy a friendship that had spanned decades.

Ultimately, after a cathartic wedding day wrestling match, the two best friends realize how silly they have been. Only once the months of wedding preparation are over does Emma see that Fletcher is not the right man for her, and she cancels her wedding. Conveniently, this allows her to attend her once-again best friend's nuptials. In a rapid-fire sequence of events, Emma and Liv's brother, Nate, get together, and when the two friends meet a year later, after Emma and Nate's destination wedding, they reveal to one another that they are pregnant and due on the same day. The end.[1]

Critics savaged the film. From its negative female stereotyping to its blatant and excessive materialism to its near erasure of the groom's import, reviewers agreed: the film highlighted the worst of American wedding culture. Manohla Dargis of the *New York Times* zeroed in on the flatness of the main characters. They are, she wrote, "deeply unreasonable because they are female stereotypes: unreasonableness is built into their character arcs." Elizabeth Weitzman of the *New York Daily News* went even further, suggesting the film indicated that women (not just Liv and Emma) are "'obnoxious,' 'overbearing,' 'crazy,' 'pathetic,' 'bitchy,' and 'basket cases.'" Dargis identified the character inconsistencies brought on by Liv and Emma's weddings. Trading their identities as "putatively sharp, savvy, seemingly capable modern women" for a turn as "fairy tale princesses," the women allowed the wedding to distract them from their careers, their friendships, their fiancés, and, one might add, reality. The very selection of the Plaza as wedding venue, particularly for a New York City public school teacher (like Emma), rankled those with a sense of fiscal realism. The material assumptions of *Bride Wars*—the use of an exclusive wedding planner and the self-conscious references to Tiffany and Vera Wang—gave the film, particularly in the midst of an economic recession, a "sense of upper-middle-class privilege," wrote the *Chicago Tribune's* Michael Phillips, that "feels smug." The grooms, Weitzman observed, wedding day props of little importance, "hover on the sidelines, fully aware of their own insignificance."[2] Audiences likewise were unimpressed—or, perhaps, more accurately, they were uninterested. The film grossed $58,715,510, ranking 56th of all 2009 releases.[3]

From *Runaway Bride* to cable television channel TLC's *A Wedding Story* to the celebrity celebrations featured in *InStyle Weddings*, weddings saturated American culture during the 1990s and early 2000s.[4] But somewhere along the way, the celebration got a bad rap. The critiques waged against *Bride Wars* mirrored critiques made about real weddings and wedding celebrants. Rather than a day of meaning, commitment, and partnership, the wedding had become the province of the selfish, the catty, the overindulgent. Eye-rolling and whispers over wedding excess were as typical as misty-eyed sentiment. Complaining about weddings became as common as weddings themselves. Friends shared anecdotal tales about brides who had gone over the edge, or couples who had taken their demands too far. Guests increasingly were directed to several expensive registries, invited to an array of showers, and expected to attend a wedding "weekend" at a destination far from home. Television shows such as MTV's *My Big Friggin' Wedding* or WE TV's *Bridezillas* delighted in the bad behavior of wedding participants (especially the brides, who, like Liv and Emma, typically had lost any semblance of sanity). Indeed, tales about brides who made bridesmaids sign contracts, vowing they would not gain weight or get pregnant before the wedding, cemented what everyone knew: weddings were out of control.[5]

At a time of heightened prosperity (real or imagined), celebrity veneration (and imitation), and unabashed willingness to accumulate consumer debt, the wedding became a site of justifiable overspending. In a 2007 examination of "20 Most Expensive Celebrity Weddings," Forbes. com described the celebrity wedding, "the Super Bowl of event planning" and declared budgets to be a "non-issue." The excess of spending and the seeming joy this excess brought to spenders marked the wedding as another site where Americans had gone horribly astray. By 2005, Americans spent $125 billion a year on weddings, an estimated average of just under $27,000 each, even as public perception held that 50 percent of marriages ended in divorce. Everyone, it seemed, knew someone who had spent a small fortune on a wedding, only to be divorced before they could celebrate their fifth (and sometimes, first) anniversary. If couples focused more on their marriages and less on their weddings, many believed, the state of American marriage surely would improve.[6]

Intellectual investigations of the wedding echoed the messages of popular media and the experiences of so many wedding attendees. Critiques of the consumerist impulse associated with weddings suggested they were nothing more than extended shopping sprees or wasteful indulgences. Feminist texts charged that in their acceptance of wedding excess, couples not only participated in consumer overindulgence, but strengthened the patriarchal nature of the existing heterosexist culture. Blindly following the path laid before them, grooms and, even more, brides bowed to convention and kowtowed to conformity as they unquestioningly engaged with the rules of the vilified wedding industry. Some texts targeted "alternative" brides, with essays and anecdotes from women who had consciously negotiated wedding territory, uncomfortable with the expected path. These sources, while seeing the possibility of what weddings might be, marked themselves as guides for those who were the exception rather than the norm. Conservative and conventional, the white wedding seemed to perpetuate and highlight the worst characteristics of the American people and the worst elements of American culture.[7]

This book does not continue in that thread. Instead, it argues for an alternative investigation of the American wedding and its evolution in the years since World War II. While many elements of the wedding, from the symbolic meanings behind its "traditional" components to the way it is marketed, deserve questioning and critique, too many evaluations have ignored the possibilities the wedding offered its celebrants. Re-evaluating the modern American wedding's postwar progression reveals a far more complex and even contested history than first imagined. Brides and grooms have not and did not merely follow a well-trod path. During the second half of the twentieth century, many couples embraced the familiarity of the wedding celebration and then used the seemingly safe and staid location of a wedding to challenge expected cultural norms and behaviors. Many couples approached their weddings with thoughtfulness and care. The wedding is an ideal site for historical inquiry because its actual evolution differs from what many people, confident because of their assumed knowledge of the celebration, imagine its historical development to have been.[8]

Admittedly, the wedding is rooted in a patriarchal history in which women were "given" from one man to the next and vowed to "obey" their husbands, but for many years, many celebrants have rejected or amended these elements of the celebration to reflect a more egalitarian view of their impending marriages. Rejections and amendments of this kind marked multiple components of the ceremony and celebration—as seen most obviously, perhaps, in the increasingly widespread celebration of same-sex weddings. Over the last several decades, participants have reclaimed the celebration, and, in the process, have used the wedding to challenge traditional expectations of men and women, masculinity and femininity, and marriage and commitment. Rather than forcing people into cookie-cutter sameness, the celebration has provided couples with the possibility of individual expression, personal authority, and cultural reinterpretation, all hallmarks of the cultural shift that occurred in the decades following World War II. While this book is a history of the wedding and its celebrants, it is also a book about the nature of post–World War II American culture, its changed understandings of individuality, its complicated blend of public and private life, and its shifting notions of American civic participation and belonging.

Certainly, men's and women's personal expression and cultural negotiation occurred through varying degrees of participation in the marketplace, thereby demonstrating the continued power of the consumer economy. The fact that the marketplace influenced and continues to influence the wedding has been established. But the relationship between couples and the market is not that of one-sided influence. Critics bemoaned the commercialization of American holidays and celebrations long before the marketplace exerted the cultural influence it has in the years since World War II. Historian Vicki Howard has uncovered the history of the wedding industry, demonstrating how celebrants alternately led and were led to various trends, how the business allowed women an outlet in professional life, and how the changing shape of American consumerism indelibly influenced the shape of the American wedding. Contemporary observers, those who wish the wedding could be simple, or be "as it used to be," Howard proves, rely on a mythic past, which never truly existed. Since the nineteenth century, for better or worse, a version of a wedding market has shaped and has been shaped by wedding participants.[9]

More than the wedding industry or wedding consumption, this book is interested in the personal motivations of the celebrants who have contributed to the wedding's continued cultural power. What has driven generations of brides and grooms to celebrate in the familiar style that has been criticized as outdated, rehearsed, and seemingly incapable of distinction or true personal meaning? If it were only about spending, men and women could find other sites, likely with more lasting returns, in which to invest their consumer and cultural capital. If the celebration were so unyielding to social and cultural change, most modern women (and many men) would pause before submitting to the wedding's gendered roles and regulations. If the wedding allowed no possibility of uniqueness or personal expression, in an American culture that so values the individual, it would have fallen out of favor years ago.

While postwar American weddings followed a fairly standard format—some degree of reliance on the marketplace, adherence to prescriptions of gender, declaration of religious belonging, and self-conscious embrace of "traditions" such as formal dress, proper vows, and a post-ceremony reception—the truth is that each wedding could be as unique as the celebrating couple wished. At the heart of the wedding's longevity was its basic flexibility. "Tradition" may have been the keyword for weddings, but like other American traditions, those associated with the wedding proved malleable. Men and women could embrace the traditions that fit with their image of the ideal celebration and ignore the rest.[10] They could share community ties with brides and grooms who had wed before them, but still feel confident in their celebration's distinctiveness. The flexibility of the wedding guaranteed its survival in a nation marked by social and cultural diversity. As a creation of the late nineteenth century, limited visions of an American population that was distinctly raced, classed, and sexed initially shaped the white wedding. White, middle-class, heterosexual celebrants were the expected and targeted population (and this book focuses primarily on their story), but those outside the imagined group likewise celebrated weddings that demonstrated their visions of both public and private life.[11]

In the decades since the end of World War II, the American population found that the promised postwar standard of living allowed for a greater focus on individual expression and personal fulfillment. The wedding, with its emphasis on romantic love, provided brides and grooms with an avenue for such expression and fulfillment.[12] As the rise in personal authority challenged more traditional political, religious, communal, and familial influences, men and women exerted greater authority over their private relationships and romantic partnerships—and, by extension, the ways they wed. Couples shaped their weddings to reflect their values and beliefs. While they relied on a standard format, they discovered they could vary the standard just enough to satisfy personal desires while fulfilling public expectations.[13]

This blend of public and private has been a hallmark of postwar culture—and of postwar wedding celebrations. In the years after World War II, understandings and demonstrations of citizenship increasingly intertwined with private life and rewards. Citizens expected access to a home, a decent standard of living, and family membership as fundamental rights. Facing the massive size and bureaucracy of modern American government and politics, individual efforts to find personal fulfillment and demonstrate citizenship often took a more cultural and less traditionally political cast. Organization of home life and personal relationships helped Americans negotiate and define their place in a rapidly changing nation. As personal and political life became increasingly intertwined, the wedding served as a site where the interchangeability and overlap of the two could be tried and tested.[14]

Even before World War II, the U.S. government historically promoted marriage among its population as a means of social organization and stability. Various rights and privileges of American citizenship were (and continue to be) extended through marriage, seemingly the most private of personal relationships. And yet, state intervention and promotion of the institution marked this private relationship as a public concern.[15] The wedding, as the starting point of the majority of American marriages, was thus tied to the interpretation and articulation of citizenship. As a public celebration of private life, the wedding blurred the boundaries between the two realms. Men and women expressed expectations of their independent, individual relationship while joining a broader community of those who likewise had celebrated in a similar fashion and were partnered in relationships that, on a surface level, were similar to their own. Beneath the surface, of course, no marriage was quite the same. This, too, factored into the shape of American weddings. Across the postwar decades, this distinctiveness and, even more, the recognition and celebration of this distinctiveness became a celebrated part of the American wedding.[16]

In the face of familial pressure, communal expectation, and market-place suggestion, the couple decided the shape of the celebration. The various interpretations of modern weddings revealed the ways men and women used their weddings to respond to larger social, economic, and political trends. Seeing their celebrations as representations of themselves and their relationships, modern brides and grooms infused their weddings with personal sentiment, be it a commitment to postwar consensus, the counterculture, or efforts to achieve full civic equality. Putting personal views into practice made brides and grooms instrumental to the development of social, cultural, and political trends as they lived their ideals via their weddings.[17]

Certainly, women took the lead in the celebration, particularly in the first two decades following World War II, when the view of the wedding as "the bride's day" prevailed. By the late 1960s and early 1970s, reflecting amended understandings of gender, men increasingly played a role—of their own desire or as a conscious demonstration of expected marital partnership. Even if grooms joined in wedding planning only incrementally, expectations of male participation became more common as ideas and understandings of romantic relationships increasingly focused on marriage as a shared partnership.[18] As same-sex couples embraced the wedding, the division of labor, of course, was less determined by sex. Indeed, same-sex unions highlighted how commonly wedding responsibilities were navigated on a couple-by-couple basis rather than under an umbrella of universal expectations.

Convention had its place, and prescriptive literature proliferated throughout the postwar years. But the messages of the prescription did not remain static. Even tried and true rules of etiquette and good taste could be shaped to fit alternative visions presented by brides and grooms. The familiar format of American weddings reveals the pressures of cultural expectation. Still, those pressures only held so much sway. If wedding "experts" rejected an emergent style or trend, a new wedding guide could be (and often was) added to the ranks. Celebrants shaped the market even when they were no longer its target audience. Critics of consumerism might charge the market with co-opting and de-radicalizing transformative ideas, but an alternative view might highlight the power of men and women to shape not only the market but also broader cultural trends.

Couples' decisions obviously affected the experience of their personal celebrations. But even more, their willingness to engage with or reject the pressures of wider social influences determined the form the "white wedding" as institution took. A focus on personal expression and a commitment to individual desire pushed men and women to embrace wedding day authority as their own. Shaped as it was by average men and women, the wedding revealed the power and practice of postwar cultural change. Through their celebrations, participants revealed the shift from the privileging of community and familial expectations to the emphasis on the desire for and increased legitimization of self-expression and personal fulfillment. In this capacity, interpretations of the wedding as conformist, staid, or conventional are misplaced.

This book traces the emergence, acceptance, and evolution of the white wedding as it became the celebration so familiar to so many today. Chapter 1 evaluates the shift from a variety of wedding forms, shaped by the diversity of the American population, to a single, recognizable celebration style in the years following World War II. Demonstrating the growing importance of the national market, media, and peer influence, the white wedding, despite industry claims of "tradition," reflected a modern turn. Rather than bowing to the authority of their extended families and local communities, postwar brides and grooms followed a national wedding model and thereby demonstrated their commitment to modern visions of married life and civic belonging. Chapter 2 examines the white wedding at the pinnacle of its popularity when First Daughter Luci Johnson's 1966 wedding illustrated not only the dominance of the celebration style but also ongoing public concerns about the power of individuality, community, and cultural authority in American life. Chapters 3 and 4 evaluate the white wedding at its most vulnerable time, when observers believed it might fade from prominence: the 1960s and 1970s. Reluctant to follow a standard path and critical of previous generations' seeming conformity, couples of and aligning with the counterculture changed American wedding culture as they built upon the fluidity allowed by assumed wedding traditions. Even as a relatively small population celebrated with alternative weddings, media coverage of unconventional celebrations, with their focus on individual expression and personalization, attracted even the more conservative members of the population and shaped the ways in which the wedding industry pitched its product. By the late 1970s and 1980s, as style makers declared a "return to tradition," couples found they could shape their weddings to communicate any number of personal or political perspectives. The white wedding, assumed to be on its last leg at the start of the 1970s, was reinvigorated by celebrants who infused the event with individual significance. Chapter 5 demonstrates how same-sex couples built upon and embraced the political potential of the wedding in their battle for marriage equality. Just as celebrants in the 1960s and 1970s used the wedding to communicate alternative viewpoints of love and marriage, queer couples embraced the familiar language and performance of the wedding to stake their claim to equal rights of citizenship and national belonging. Building on the flexibility of postwar wedding tradition, same-sex couples used their weddings both as public celebrations of private life and as political demonstrations against civic inequality.

Throughout the postwar years, the importance placed on the wedding celebration communicated the forethought and sensitivity with which couples approached married life. When critics pushed for a focus on marriage rather than on the wedding, they overlooked the fact that many couples used their weddings as a time to think about what their marriage would mean to them and what marriage meant more broadly. Whether it was based on the couple's dedication to a newly accessible nuclear family model, their faith, or political persuasion, the wedding consistently said something about the couple being wed and their expectations of their union. In the process of shaping their weddings, couples contributed to the evolution of Americans' expectations of intimate relationships, understandings of sex and gender, and relationships to public and political life.

1

"Linking the Past with the Future"

ORIGINS OF
THE POSTWAR
WHITE WEDDING

In the midst of the planning for Kay Banks's 1948 wedding, her father Stanley mused to himself: "It should have been so simple. Boy and girl meet, fall in love, marry, have babies—who eventually grow up, meet other babies, fall in love, marry. Looked at from this angle, it was not only simple, it was positively monotonous. Why then must Kay's wedding assume the organizational complexity of a major political campaign?"[1] Stanley's bewilderment at the wedding process indicated the changing nature of the celebration in post–World War II America. Edward Streeter's *Father of the Bride* chronicled the events leading up to the wedding of Kay Banks and Buckley Dunstan. The book gave readers an in-depth account of a newly democratized style of wedding celebration: the increasingly typical white wedding. A national best-seller, Streeter's 1948 novel struck such a chord among the American public that it soon became a Hollywood film starring Spencer Tracy as the ever-baffled Stanley Banks and Elizabeth Taylor as his daughter, Kay.[2] Although told from a father's perspective, *Father of the Bride* resonated with readers and viewers alike, regardless of previous wedding role or experience. Americans learned that in order to achieve an ideal white wedding, the newly requisite style of postwar celebration, no detail could be spared. As the 1940s and 1950s progressed, a series of requirements marked the white wedding: acceptance of idealized gender roles, market participation, religious expression, and industry-approved traditions. As the white wedding took its place as the seemingly agreed-upon ideal, *Father of the Bride* suggested that the path to the altar was often far from smooth.

Even while her parents supported her and paid for the celebration, from the first moment of her engagement, Kay continually insisted the wedding was her day. She would have the final say on all decisions. As such, she believed that her personal desires should be fulfilled and her opinions should carry the most weight. The views of others—including her groom-to-be—were secondary. In one representative scene, Stanley reported that a friend, having "married off" four daughters, indicated that a wedding was "either confined to the bosom of the family or held in Madison Square Garden." There were either "thirty or three hundred" guests, no in between. Kay rejected this notion out of hand:

Pops, if you mean that you're *crazy.* I know what you and Mom want. You want every old fogy in town so that you can hear them say, "Yes, she really was *too* lovely. And the *most* beautiful dress, my dear." Well I just won't *have* it. This is *my* wedding and it's going to be *my* friends.[3]

In Kay's mind, her personal relationships, particularly those with her peers, superseded her parents' relationships with members of the community. No longer privileging the family and community participation that had long marked the wedding celebration, Kay's wedding vision represented a departure from past tradition and a move toward a modern celebration style.[4] In Kay's view, parents were necessary for financial and moral support. They could help with the planning and the logistics, but in major wedding-related decisions, their opinions ranked behind the bride's.

Kay's parents had other ideas for the wedding. They were determined to have a voice in the planning. Both the book and film featured scene after scene in which Stanley Banks struggled to understand the seeming necessity of the white wedding, while his wife, Ellie, embraced the chance to host the ultimate in wedding celebrations. Mrs. Banks,

Streeter wrote, "looked at the matter more from the point of view of a stage manager. How long would it take to prepare the costumes, build the scenery, and collect the props? She concluded that, working day and night, the production might be staged in three months—not a minute earlier."[5] Attempts to limit the guest list failed as Stanley, Ellie, and even Kay realized that they "had too many dear, close, loyal, lifelong friends, to all of whom they seemed to be indebted."[6] For the modern bride, a small wedding seemed an impossible feat. Multiple publics had to be considered. In spite of Kay's assertion of the wedding as her day, various interests still had to be taken into consideration.

Kay inhabited dual roles during her three-month engagement: she was Stanley and Ellie's daughter, but she was soon to be Buckley Dunstan's wife. On the one hand, she relied on her parents to support her until marriage and to finance the wedding that would mark her entry to married life. But, at the same time, she had started to shift her alliance to Buckley. She increasingly agreed with Buckley's points of view and defended these points to her father. Kay struggled to establish independence from her nuclear family as she planned to start her own. The wedding provided Kay with a trial run at demonstrating personal authority and the newly achieved maturity associated with married life. Other brides of the time, and throughout the late 1940s and 1950s, would embrace their weddings in a similar style. For the most part, grooms of the time, like Buckley, played second fiddle. They accepted their supporting role in wedding planning and on the wedding day.

The larger struggle was between the generations. Kay and her parents consistently butted heads over their conflicting views of what the wedding should be. While Kay insisted on the prominence and preeminence of her role, she felt pressure from various sources that undermined her independence even as she attempted to exert it. On Kay's wedding day, Stanley found her crying. He insisted that she should be happy; no girl should cry on her wedding day. Kay despondently replied, "Oh, I know it, Pops. That's just the *trouble*. It's my wedding day, but it *isn't*. It's everybody *else's* wedding day but it just isn't mine."[7] Other brides of the time—and in the future—would find themselves in similar predicaments as they fought for the wedding as a day they could call their own.

While Stanley believed he was providing his daughter with an elaborate celebration, Kay and Buckley's wedding was but a hint of what was to come. The Bankses presented Kay with a substantial trousseau, and friends and family contributed numerous wedding gifts. Kay wore a white, sweetheart wedding gown and her bridesmaids wore matching dresses.[8] The wedding took place in a church, filled with flowers. The reception, however, was held at the Bankses' home, and while catered, it was not a sit-down meal.[9] An orchestra played but there was little dancing. In the decades following World War II, home weddings would become less common. Dinner and dancing would become key parts of the white wedding style. Kay Banks's wedding demonstrated how postwar brides negotiated the modern and the traditional. She included elements of wedding celebration that were growing increasingly common, and, according to the growing wedding industry, increasingly necessary. Simultaneously, she made room for wedding elements insisted upon by her parents and designed to satisfy the broader expectations of family and community.

Kay Banks's wedding represented—in a primitive form—the new white wedding that became the standard style of wedding celebration in the decades following World War II. Like other brides in the booming postwar economy, Kay Banks stood at the center of the newly democratized white wedding and held unprecedented authority over its direction. Her wedding preparations showcased the influences that would inform the shape of the wedding for the rest of the twentieth century and into the twenty-first: desire for personal authority and autonomy, increased participation in the consumer marketplace, and the influence of an ever-stronger peer culture. The overlap and interrelationship of these components further enhanced the white wedding's power and appeal as brides and, to a lesser extent, their grooms, used the wedding to express their views about modern American life and their place within it. The astounding popularity of *Father of the Bride*, both as novel and film, suggested the growing influence of mass media as a wedding model for the celebrations of young couples. From the late 1940s on, the white wedding would be the wedding style against which all others were measured. *Father of the Bride* predicted the growth of the white wedding's popularity. The tale likewise foreshadowed contests that would mark this new wedding style and postwar American life more broadly.

* * *

While a wedding such as Kay Banks and Buckley Dunstan's would be described as "traditional," their celebration marked a sharp departure from weddings of the American past. During the late nineteenth and early twentieth centuries, Americans wed in a variety of celebration styles. Some men and women enjoyed the splendor of the white wedding, but for many Americans, the wedding day was just another day. It was rare for a ceremony to have been planned months in advance or that wedding planning would consume the majority of one's time and focus in the months prior. When Inez Chase married in September 1941, she recorded in her diary, "Rainned morning & evening. Will & I were married."[10] The weather, not the wedding, merited first mention. As Mrs. Banks recalled her own wedding, she described a front parlor ceremony during which she wore a simple blue suit. The white wedding, for a variety of reasons, had been beyond the grasp of many Americans just several decades before.[11] Affected by Americans' cultural affiliations, social views, and economic status, the white wedding's path to prevalence was marked by a series of stops and starts.

White weddings had long been the province of the American elite and upper-middle class. Elaborate celebrations signified wealth and social distinction. The rich showcased their connections via their wedding celebrations. Those with the economic means and social status had celebrated in this elaborate style since the mid-nineteenth century, when merchants began to play an important role in wedding ceremonies. Specially designed gowns, professional catering and wait staffs, and expertly arranged flowers and wedding décor were luxuries enjoyed primarily by the urban upper-middle class and elite. Postwar couples of privileged backgrounds could claim a link to the white wedding as they embraced such goods and services in their own celebrations. But those of middle-class, working-class, or rural backgrounds were unlikely to have had parents or grandparents who celebrated with the kind of wedding that rose to prominence in the 1940s and 1950s.[12]

During the nineteenth and early twentieth centuries, variation in region, ethnicity, race, and class differentiated one wedding celebration from another. Weddings ranged from inauspicious visits to a county justice of the peace to quiet home ceremonies to festive communitywide ethnic celebrations. Families and communities passed along celebration styles and helped young couples as they prepared to celebrate their weddings in ways familiar to those of similar background and social standing. "Traditional" weddings linked participants to a variety of shared ethnic or regional pasts. As couples followed diverse practices handed down by family or community members, no single American tradition emerged.[13]

Upper-middle-class and elite weddings might be marked by lavish consumer expenditure, but weddings of middle-class, working-class, or rural men and women were more likely to be a blend of carefully selected purchases and home craft or entirely homespun affairs. Essie Simmons's Arkansas wedding demonstrated the importance of the family's willing participation to a successful rural celebration. Married at 4 p.m. on Sunday, October 16, 1921, Simmons celebrated her wedding with the help of family, in a simply decorated home. "Jim had four nieces," Simmons recalled, "and they had gone out and found autumn leaves and flowers and decorated the whole house. The women of the family had cooked a wonderful wedding supper, and they had invited some of the family. . . . The girls had decorated the fireplace with all this beautiful foliage. And that was my wedding."[14]

Emphasizing the importance of family and place, Simmons remembered, "Jim's father said to me after the marriage ceremony, 'Jim was married on the exact same spot he was born.'"[15] Essie Simmons's father-in-law's emphasis on the home and local community suggests just how strong a role region and background played in a couple's relationship during the first decades of the twentieth century. Family and community influence and approval weighed heavily on prospective brides and grooms.[16] While couples of the postwar years often would experience a different relationship to place and extended family, during the first half of the twentieth century, the bride and the groom served as a link between or a demonstration of strength within a community.

Ethnic communities likewise used the wedding celebration as a time to demonstrate the strong connection between the couple and their respective backgrounds and kin. During the first decades of the twentieth century, extended family, community, and ethnic association all played important roles in the Romanian-American weddings of Lake County, Indiana. Local influence created a standard of celebration, one that future generations might follow in their weddings. Receptions featured typical ethnic fare, often prepared by women of the neighborhood or church. Emilia Apolzan indicated that this trend was common, as she noted of her own wedding, "The women prepared sarmale [stuffed cabbage], different salads, flat cakes, with apples, cheese and farina fillings." Traditional community practices that involved many members of the extended family and community helped a couple to prepare for their wedding day. Elizabeth Drag remembered, "They used to have a basket that they carried and each house used to give you a couple of eggs. When they came back to the bride's house the eggs were used in baking for the wedding. They baked the colac [sweet bread], nutroll and whatever else needed to be baked."[17] The willing assistance of friends and family—and the expectation that they would assist—made the commercial services of a baker or caterer unnecessary. Guests were not incidental, but rather, were a fundamental part of the wedding planning and the wedding celebration.

The beginnings of the modern wedding industry developed during the 1920s with the first wave of mass American consumption. Business promoted the white wedding as a standard to which all Americans could aspire. Department stores, jewelers, florists, photographers, and the growing field of "wedding experts" attempted to convince (often with great success) engaged men and women that their weddings should follow a "traditional" format, one that imbued their union with the sanctity it and they deserved. The business of weddings participated in a clear "invention of tradition," a process designed so businesses might profit from a couple's desire to make their special day as special as they could afford. As with other manifestations of the emerging consumer society, the wedding industry shaped the wants and needs of the population. Wedding practices formerly relegated to fantasy became commonplace. Those with an eye to fashion, in particular, relied on the advice of the burgeoning wedding industry to learn how they could arrange to have a perfect "traditional" wedding.[18] While the industry maintained some power even during the Great Depression and war years, many couples faced financial and material obstacles that prevented the white wedding style of celebration. While large celebrations were considered improper during wartime, circumstance beyond a couple's control just as often prevented a white wedding celebration.[19]

Wartime weddings, by their very nature, were often rushed affairs. In the early years of World War II, June Lundy's fiancé, Herbert Boyd, was stationed in Denver. Learning he had wanted to marry her on his last furlough home to Iowa, she found a substitute to teach her grammar school class and hopped a train to take her to Denver. Arriving on Saturday, Lundy did a whirlwind round of wedding preparation: she visited a doctor to procure a statement testifying to her health (a legal requirement), found "a light blue, two-piece, polka-dot dress" to wear to the ceremony, and joined Herbert to buy wedding rings. After finding a Methodist minister, "Herbert had dashed out to the nearest USO and drafted a fellow he worked with at the hospital to be best man." His first choice was unacceptable—a Catholic friend who could attend the wedding but whom the minister refused to allow as a participant in the marriage service. Even in a quickly arranged wedding, the minister required that the bride and groom respect and adhere to the authority of the church. June and Herbert's willingness to follow this direction demonstrated their belief in the power of the religious officiant. If one wanted a religious wedding, one bowed to religious authority. Protocol could not be compromised. At long last, after finding a suitable witness, the wedding proceeded. Finally, before the fireplace in the hastily procured minister's home, Lundy and Boyd were wed. As June Boyd recalled her 1942 wedding nearly sixty years later, she noted, "Ours, of course, was a war wedding. You couldn't call it a stylish wedding, but it suited us and we had plenty of love."[20]

The circumstances of World War II influenced the world of postwar weddings and marriage in spirit more so than in practice. The uncertainty of war time allowed for the sanctioning of quickly consummated courtships and short engagement periods. While few postwar couples would marry as June Lundy and Herbert Boyd or other World War II-era newlyweds had, the desire for romance and individual satisfaction spilled over into the postwar years. In a break from previous generations of brides and grooms, men and women might choose a mate with far less consideration for the person's background or the thoughts of either family. Of course family approval remained an important consideration for most marrying youth, and marriage across religion and, even more so, race remained taboo.[21] However, the mood of wartime opened up and even sanctioned new possibilities in mate selection that did not mandate or privilege familial consent. For soldiers heading overseas and women remaining on the home front, practicality did not always serve as the first priority in the decision to marry.[22] One marriage counselor in 1945 recognized the already existing power of romance in young couples' consideration of marriage. As "romance" became an increasingly justifiable reason for entry into marriage, society recognized and affirmed "the right to personal satisfaction." Over the next several decades, this newly identified "right" would influence the trajectory of the wedding and of American life more broadly.[23]

By no means was the power of the white wedding assured. The circumstances of the postwar years, however, created an environment in which this wedding style could thrive. Even as it had varied considerably across the population, the wedding still served as a recognizable component of American culture and symbolized home, marriage, and stability. As fighting forces returned to the home front, a wedding, marriage, and a family seemed an ideal trifecta for domesticating war-weary veterans. As the white wedding became ever more popular, and increasingly was identified as the American way of wedding, differences in wedding style became less prominent. During the postwar years, the white wedding provided a safe, and in some ways natural, vehicle for experimenting with the many social and cultural changes on the horizon. At the same time, the celebration served a more conservative purpose as it reinforced traditional and idealized notions of gender, sexuality, and family life.[24]

* * *

After years of duty and sacrifice, a growing focus on legitimization and fulfillment of individual desire marked the postwar decades. Newly expanded national influence on government, culture, economy, and media undermined what had been the localized control of individual communities. Modern interpretations of life and love, previously confined to urban centers, reached men and women in small towns across the country. Local authority came into question as Americans, particularly those of the younger generation, realized they might pursue a life beyond the town limits. Wartime and postwar mobility introduced a world where individuals could escape the sometimes stifling gaze of their local communities. Exposure to alternative behaviors and cultures opened up the possibility for great changes in American life. The development of the postwar white wedding reveals the tremendous changes that marked 1950s culture as anything but staid or predictable: the growing focus on the personal rather than the communal, participation in an expanded consumer economy, and the rising authority of peer culture over family culture.[25]

The market and the media contributed to the shift in the American mind-set. The rapidly expanding consumer economy presented Americans with a vast array of consumption opportunities as they returned to a peacetime world. Response to the housing crisis of the immediate postwar years spurred numerous consumer possibilities. The home—and the suburban home, in particular—became a staple adult fantasy. A couple would marry, find a home, and fill that home with children and goods. As early as 1943, marriage preparation texts, intended for a national audience, promoted the suburban lifestyle that would come to define postwar expectations: "It's a fine thing if you can establish your home at some place in which you can be part of a real community instead of a city-block-dweller. A garden, a pup of your own, a doormat with 'Welcome' on it, a live interest in your community—these are the kinds of things which make people really happy." Couples imagined a life of individual satisfaction in their married relationships. They also imagined a life of communal solidarity in their new neighborhoods, populated by like-minded, like-married peers rather than the neighbors of various ages, occupations, and persuasions who might occupy a city block. Beyond buying a house, a car to drive to and from the house, and appliances and furnishings to fill the house, a man and a woman who dreamed the suburban dream would first spend money on the event that inaugurated them into domestic bliss: the wedding. As an event that played to more traditional, conservative notions of home and family—and celebrated the domestication of American men and the harnessing of American women's sexuality—the white wedding served a number of different masters.[26]

The circumstances of World War II directly informed the elevation of the wedding to a position of importance, and even necessity. The massive disruption of the war and mobilization of the American people brought widespread change and, as a result, produced widespread anxiety. The war displaced social norms and regulations as workplaces were integrated, both racially and sexually, and female breadwinners led—albeit temporarily—many families. But the war altered the social landscape even beyond work and family life. Young women—young, *single* women—who lived and earned on their own operated beyond the constraints of family and community control. Their independence threatened the American family—a central tool for the organization and reproduction of social values.[27]

The immediate postwar years were witness to efforts to regain a measure of stability. The disruption caused first by the Great Depression and then by World War II permitted some flexibility in gender behaviors, but upon return to peacetime, such inversion no longer was acceptable. Women's newly achieved independence had to be harnessed as men made their way home. As women returned to domesticity, popular advice suggested they defer to their husbands' wishes and allow the men to lead the household. This deference would help facilitate veterans' reacclimation to peacetime life, a primary goal of the immediate postwar years. Further, this deference would help facilitate the return of proper social and familial order.

Soldiers encouraged to fight for God, country, and family returned to a postwar America where their wartime motivations intersected. The idealized return to the home front involved interwoven public and private rewards. A man who had fought for his country would be rewarded not only by the public provisions of the GI Bill or Federal Housing Administration veteran mortgage; he also would reap the private rewards of a marriage celebrated before family and friends, under the blessing of a religious official. A return to traditional morality and social stability informed the national promotion of the values associated with the wedding celebration: family, gendered behavior, submission to religious authority, and containment of sex within the boundaries of marriage.[28]

The 1946 film, *The Best Years of Our Lives*, indicated the importance of a stable private life to the soldier's reintegration into peacetime living. After his wartime service, Homer Parrish (played by World War II veteran, Harold Russell) returns home to Boone City, USA, his family, and his high school sweetheart, Wilma (Cathy O'Donnell). Having lost both his hands in the war, he maintains a jaunty optimism, having been trained to use the hooks the military had provided. As a double-amputee, however, he worries about his relationship to Wilma. "Wilma's only a kid," he notes. "She's never seen anything like these hooks." In his first few weeks back from the war, Homer distances himself from his family, his community, and Wilma. Solitary and often sullen, he is hardly the idealized postwar veteran. As Wilma persists in declaring her love and devotion to Homer, even in the face of his daily challenges, she reveals herself as the kind of domesticating force ideally suited to helping veterans transition back to peacetime life.

Demonstrating their union's importance to their future happiness, the film concludes with Homer and Wilma's wedding. On the surface level, the wedding appears to reflect fairly traditional views of the American family, home, and matrimony, but closer inspection reveals a shift in focus. While a public celebration, designed to be witnessed by family, friends, and community, the wedding served as a site where the private marital relationship of one man and one woman was celebrated as the preeminent relationship in one's life. Indeed, it was not Homer's family, his veteran buddies, or figures of religious or institutional authority that brought him back from the self-imposed isolation of his war injury. It was Wilma, his eventual bride-to-be. The wedding celebration that marks Homer's return—to his family, to his community, to American society more broadly—privileged the marital relationship above all others. The private rewards of military service began with the wedding and created a link between the celebration and civic belonging.[29]

The war experience, which had been so universal, ideally would be followed by a universal peacetime experience. As Homer uses his hooks to place the wedding ring on Wilma's finger, viewers learned that postwar opportunities extended across the population. But even as his experience suggested that those injured or altered by war could have full access to the idealized rewards of postwar private life, the presumed universality of this experience was flawed, of course, by the fact that the experience was explicitly middle-class, heterosexual, and white. And yet, the public vision assumed that all Americans would once again embrace a shared vision and lifestyle, just as they had during World War II. This time, the shared experience would be the private joy of nuclear family life.[30]

During the early postwar years and throughout the 1950s, marriage was both the "normal" and the "desirable" state for adults.[31] As exemplified by Homer and Wilma, the marital relationship took on new significance. Marriage literature and the wedding itself celebrated the married couple as an independent unit, separate from extended families. As one popular textbook used in 1950s marriage courses claimed, Americans "believe that marriage must serve one basic purpose: the satisfaction of deep personal needs, such as affection, security, emotional warmth, companionship, and sexual satisfaction."[32] Another 1957 text expressed a similar sentiment: "Marriage permits spouses . . . to form a close community, marked by companionship, mutual loyalty, sexual gratification, and parenthood, and quite unlike, therefore, any friendship or other association." Couples learned that the relationship between husband and wife was the primary relationship in one's life and should provide total emotional fulfillment.[33] The postwar white wedding, with its emphasis on defined gender roles and distinction of the couple from other wedding participants, reflected modern views of American family life and marital relationships. As the likelihood grew that men and women would find a partner previously unknown to his or her family and community, the distinction between the couple and the community increased. The importance of local approval diminished as fulfillment of personal desire grew in importance.[34] No longer was the home community's sanction or advisement a prerequisite in mate selection. Instead, new sources of authority became paramount, just as a new sense of personal motivation or individual decision-making became acceptable.

National media and a renewed wedding industry shaped the wedding and standardized the white wedding style of celebration, further cementing the "normalcy" and indicating the desirability of the marital state. Such influences often replaced the authority of ethnic, familial, or local culture. For example, *Bride's* magazine, founded in 1934, initially served as a guide for East Coast elites in New York, New Jersey, and Connecticut. During the postwar years, the publication expanded its circulation to reach a broader range of American brides. Young women across the country now had access to advice on how to achieve the most modern of wedding fashions and practices. Ironically, brides learned of traditions they should aim to follow in their weddings through a modern method of advice distribution.[35] Rather than relying on the wisdom of traditional outposts—parents, older family members, or ministers—women looked to advertising, peer groups, media, and popular prescriptive literature that crossed regional boundaries.[36] With modern advice, they could be confident that their celebrations matched the expected wedding and relationship ideals.

As items once scarce due to the Depression and then rationing and war production became available, Americans felt no need to practice restraint, especially on a day that allowed for excess and celebration.[37] Freshly minted members of a growing middle class found, for the first time, that they might celebrate with an elaborate ceremony and reception. In an increasingly affluent and optimistic time, young men and women embraced consumerism and fulfilled personal wants rather than contributing to the fulfillment of familial needs or communal expectations. At the same time, young spenders performed a national civic duty in their spending, feeding a growing economy. Personal expression might be accomplished through any number of consumer expenditures, but the white wedding stood out as a reward for wartime service, a demonstration of postwar prosperity, and proof of national belonging. Weddings became sites where couples could fulfill personal desire and express a newly modern outlook, particularly as they found themselves with more time to plan their nuptials.[38] Where couples of the past had sacrificed autonomy as their parents and families weighed in on the style of wedding celebration, modern brides and grooms increasingly asserted their own point of view.[39]

While couples celebrated in increasingly similar wedding style across the nation, their ceremonies emphasized not only belonging to a national community of citizens with shared goals but also a personal, individualized acceptance of modern life. The nature of American culture, particularly during the early postwar years, put "pressure on increasingly self-aware individuals to harmonize what they understand to be what they themselves want with what they understand to be the social prescription for people *like* themselves."[40] Young men and women negotiated the still ongoing tension between the individual and the community, the actual and the expected.[41] Personal desire might be expected to match with prescriptions of their locale as well as with increasingly national expectations of modern American youth. The local and the national, even in the postwar years—and to some degree, *especially* in the early postwar years—might be at odds.[42] As couples struggled to satisfy personal wants while still pleasing their families, they found in the wedding an opportunity to connect tradition (however mythologized) to modernity. They could fulfill local and national moral objectives while celebrating their marriage in a modern style. Through the white wedding ritual, they negotiated their relationships to the past as well as the future.[43]

As such, "tradition" once again became a watchword among jewelers, department stores, and wedding literature, even as the white wedding clearly deviated from the celebrations of past generations. Despite the wedding industry's effective use of "tradition" as sales pitch, the newly popular, newly accessible white weddings represented not so much a connection to a personal history as a connection to an idealized past, one unmarred by economic hardship, family conflict, or war. Weddings became sites of attempted compromise where couples negotiated a relationship between personal, familial traditions and the idealized "traditions" they wished to replicate in their modern white weddings. A newly popular, "modern" tradition, one encouraged by the marketplace, marked a couple as unique within their family or local community and as fashionable among peers. Further, the concept of tradition melded seamlessly with desires to restore stability to American families, and the nation as a whole.[44]

Prescriptive literature and the expanded wedding industry created a notion of tradition that could be shared across demographic differences and worked in connection with a couple's dream of distinctiveness. As Marjorie Binford Woods opened her revised 1949 edition of *Your Wedding: How to Plan and Enjoy It*, she wished for every bride to have a wedding that would "graciously follow the time-honored dignities and fine traditions of the past . . . yet be as individual and precious in expression as your own romantic love."[45] Couples could fulfill their desire to belong as well as their desire to be unique. They were modern even as they embraced the requisite traditions. The growing consumer economy, ever malleable, helped young men and women meet multiple goals. As they prepared their weddings, brides and grooms accepted the language of tradition, emphasized by the market and media. It was through this embrace of tradition they found they could justify their adoption of some of the more modern aspects of American life—consumer expenditure, individuality, and personal authority.[46]

Mrs. Wells Ritchie, a well-known Chicago wedding consultant, directed hundreds of weddings in the postwar years and well understood the audience to which she catered. Ritchie knew the proper etiquette for any and every wedding situation. At the same time, even with her attention to prescriptive detail, she recognized the desire for distinction when she remarked of weddings, "No two are ever alike, I assure you!" Weddings allowed "plenty of leeway for personal tastes and prejudices," Ritchie maintained. Whenever in doubt, however, she would always return to the "genuinely traditional." But even Ritchie, expert that she was, allowed that "tradition" was a concept open to some maneuvering. "Many wedding traditions have evolved through the ages, linking the past with the future," she said. This evolution of tradition provided brides and grooms of the late 1940s and 1950s with wedding options: they could choose elements of the traditional that fit their personal style even as they contributed to the evolutionary process by altering less appealing traditions.[47]

Tradition, of course, was to be navigated carefully. While a white dress might be deemed "traditional" in style by department stores and dress designers, the possibility that a bride-to-be might wish to wear her mother's wedding gown was a tradition not to be encouraged. Marguerite Bentley advised women against following through with this bit of tradition, a stance likely earning her the devoted thanks of dress manufacturers nationwide. Bentley described the practice of wearing a mother's dress as "the bête noire of this era." Mothers and daughters, likely to see the old gown through eyes tinted with sentimentality, should consider the view of the rest of the world, she urged. While the bride and her mother might find the gown stunning, Bentley suggested others likely would disagree: "Unfortunately, the bride will be viewed realistically by the guests and will fare badly in comparison with her bridesmaids in their becoming dresses—an unfair role for a bride to have to play on her wedding day." The bride, the star of the wedding, should never, under any circumstances, be outshone by the wedding's supporting cast. Tradition had to be negotiated so that it was charming and complimentary to contemporary styles and standards. To be out of date was out of the question. As Bentley concluded, she advised young women to "use the lace, if it is good and looks well on a model you would choose; otherwise, consign it all to the past and the realm of mementos."[48] As a nod to what must have been an increasingly popular opinion about the inadvisability of wearing mother's dress, the 1948 print version of *Father of the Bride*, in which Kay wore her mother's made-over dress, was changed for the 1950 film, as Kay wore a beautiful, newly purchased gown.[49]

The wedding, tied to the values of matrimony and domesticity and constantly identified as "traditional," provided a respectable venue for pushing the boundaries of conventional behaviors. Even as couples used the language of tradition to describe their wedding and thereby connect to the past, they focused on the fulfillment of their individual wants, a modern notion. Thus, tradition justified modern behaviors and views.[50] A couple fit with contemporary notions of social morality even as they fulfilled individual desires. The postwar white wedding challenged and even altered the intention of the wedding. Rather than celebrating local or familial belonging, the wedding increasingly focused on the bride and the groom as a separate entity and served as a celebration of their personal interests and expectations.[51] In so doing, the white wedding challenged understandings that connected marriage and community, even as the wedding continued to mark marriage as a sacred bond through a familiar public celebration.[52]

While men and women embarked upon a new class status and a new view of marriage, they embarked upon a new way of wedding. And for many young couples, this way of wedding was very new. It was likely that no one in either party's respective families had married in this way. As couples celebrated the white wedding, they imbued the ceremony with idiosyncrasies and personal touches, even as they aimed to match an idealized style.[53] Seeing the growing popularity of the formal, white wedding, and identifying a ready and willing audience, market and media forces contributed to the notion that there was but one way to be wed. A long-established prescriptive literature and, eventually, an ever-stronger peer culture contributed to the white wedding's cultural cachet. Bit by bit, white weddings became more familiar. As more and more young people celebrated in the increasingly standardized form, the white wedding gained national popularity.

* * *

Just as the white wedding received more attention in the postwar years, American youth likewise experienced a surge in visibility during the 1950s. The newly sanctioned fulfillment of personal desire combined with the growing power of peer influence among American youth contributed to the wedding's enormous popularity. Kay Banks and Buckley Dunstan served as fitting middle-class representatives of 1950s' young America. Identified as a kind of transitional generation, other fifties-era brides and grooms, just like Kay and Buckley, viewed their move to adulthood in a distinct way. Given the young age at which brides and grooms tied the knot, youth culture and wedding culture inevitably overlapped. In 1955, the average age of the American male at the time of marriage was 22; the average age of the American female, 20. Nearly half the population of brides married when they were still teenagers, a trend both documented and seemingly encouraged by popular media.[54] Kay Banks matched her peers. In the novel, she lived with her parents, despite her rather advanced age of 24. The film altered this detail, making Kay 20 years old, closer to the average bridal age of the time.

Youth of the 1950s, instructed to embrace maturity, contained sexuality, the nuclear family, and a newly idealized domesticity, often used the wedding as their first attempt at establishing independence from their respective families.[55] The dominant culture, the world overseen by adults, instructed middle-class teens that "social leadership, decision making, individualism, [and] creative problem solving" characterized maturity.[56] Marriage course books and various marriage guides likewise emphasized maturity as a necessary prerequisite to a successful union. A wedding, sociologist Ada Hart Arlitt assured young couples, would change their relationships instantaneously: "After the ceremony the parents and friends are ready to release the couple from adolescence and to welcome them into the young married group."[57] As couples prepared for their wedding, they could emphasize their maturity as they claimed their authority to shape their wedding day plans. The wedding provided a perfect opportunity for youth to display and even co-opt these "adult" attributes.

Young brides and grooms were not always interested in receiving the sanction of American adult authority. Given the growing independence of American teens—fostered by their size, their prosperity,

and the American marketplace's savvy recognition of these two characteristics—youth believed in their power to create their own views of
adulthood, maturity, and marriage. The idea that they could shape the
ceremony that seemingly began all three—the wedding—was a natural
connection. Youth found they could question not only the characteristics that defined maturity; they likewise could question the sources who
created the definition. Expressing a view that lived experience constituted a kind of maturity, Alice Gorton wrote in her diary, on the day of
her wedding, September 11, 1954, "May I profit by the mistakes recorded
here and increase the joys by my own labor and by my love."[58] Adulthood no longer was a prerequisite for marriage; marriage and even the
decision to marry conferred adulthood.

Couples-to-be-wed received advice from their parents, older siblings,
and community members as they planned for wedding celebrations
that were beyond the scope of these advisors' personal experiences.[59]
Before their official "release" from adolescence, brides and grooms-to-
be looked for advice, but they looked to sources of authority beyond
their parents as they prepared for their weddings. As young men and
women coped with the incompatibility between the expectations of
the past and those of the present, they created a cultural phenomenon.
They embraced the newly accessible form of the white wedding, influenced by etiquette and prescription but shaped by personal preference.

As the white wedding grew increasingly prevalent on the national
stage—in books and movies, among celebrities such as Grace Kelly
and Elizabeth Taylor, and in advertisements intended to sell a variety
of products—the white wedding style became normalized among the
marrying population.[60] Sexual education specialist Lester A. Kirkendall
connected the early marriage trend to cultural forces that highlighted
the satisfaction associated with marriage and family life. He wrote, "One
has only to see the movies, watch television, read current newspapers
and magazines, and listen to conversation to realize the importance
given marriage and family life. Youth can hardly escape the conclusion
that entering marriage is achieving a state that is worth attaining as
early in life as possible." As young Americans saw other young Americans wedding in the white wedding style, they knew they had to match
their friends and the idealized brides and grooms that peppered the
pages of bridal magazines and other popular print media.[61]

Ellie Banks, in the 1950 film version of *Father of the Bride*, recognized the importance of the peer group as she insisted to Stanley that Kay must have a wonderful wedding—or suffer shame in front of girlfriends already wed.[62] Kirkendall's 1956 Public Affairs pamphlet, "Too Young to Marry?" looked beyond cultural influence and pointed to peer influence as a factor contributing to young marriage: "In some communities a wave of early marriages may occur, like an epidemic. The experience of seeing many of their friends marrying and of hearing many discussions about marriage undoubtedly causes some young people to marry who might otherwise have waited."[63] The desire to remain a part of the group, to share experiences with friends, led many young men and women to youthful marriage. Joyce Purvis, a young African American woman from East St. Louis, Illinois admitted, "I do think I got married because everyone else was getting married. All my friends were doing it, or so it seemed. I was the last single woman in my group."[64] As young men and women heard friends discuss their wedding plans, they absorbed expectations of what a modern white wedding might be and frequently used these expectations in their own decision-making. In the June before her September 1954 wedding, Alice Gorton received a thank you note from a recently married friend, who used her note to extol the virtues of married life. Knowing of Gorton's impending nuptials, her friend Gretchen teased, "Oh Ally, do find a man and get married! Try September. That sounds like a good month!!!" More seriously, she went on to describe the benefits of marriage: "Really—what a feeling! You know they always say that your love changes from physical to being deeper as you grow older. Well, even in these few weeks it has changed. But it's better, because the physical side is still there also. But it really is different after you are married."[65] With such an endorsement, married life appeared a desirable state.

"Epidemics," such as those identified by Kirkendall, were especially prevalent on college and university campuses. Following the cultural standards of the 1950s, many young women married by the time they reached their early twenties. Those who attended college often left before graduating or they finished their education as one-half of a married duo. A 1956 *Chicago Tribune* article reported that approximately 25 undergraduates left Northwestern University during the scholastic year so that they might wed. Others planned to marry immediately following graduation. The social status associated with college attendance and the potential social networking to be achieved on and between campuses created an environment that many young women found desirable. In 1956, 80 percent of the engaged female students on Loyola University of Chicago's campus were engaged to current or former Loyola students. [66] Alice Gorton, a recent Smith College graduate, found herself in a similar position as she married a former Yale man in the September following her 1954 graduation.[67] Female undergraduates were thus in a prime position to meet and marry eligible young bachelors who were likewise upwardly mobile.[68]

The Hillel director at the University of Wisconsin was forthcoming in the role of the university in mate selection. "Let's face it," he said. "Jewish parents send their daughters here to meet nice, bright Jewish boys." A girl who reached junior year without having found a "steady" began "to mourn her lost youth." Jewish co-eds at the University of Wisconsin were known to transfer after their sophomore year if they had not yet met a potential spouse.[69] Although young men and women experienced a measure of freedom while attending university, they still experienced pressure to defer to cultural and religious expectations. The authority to choose a potential spouse's religion or social standing remained limited, which, in turn, may have pushed young couples to demand authority over the wedding day—a battle more likely to be won.

Young women attended a flurry of weddings throughout their college years. The scrapbooks of Templecrone, a cooperative housing unit at the University of Missouri, indicate that the college community played an important role in wedding ceremonies. Dozens of wedding announcements, invitations, photographs, and mementos are scattered across the scrapbooks, and it was not uncommon for the house to host a pre-wedding celebration in honor of the bride-to-be.[70] Brooklyn College, an urban commuter school with a predominantly Jewish student body, likewise witnessed a wave of young marriages through the 1950s. The House Plan Association—a system of social clubs at the College— was described as a "teeming marriage mart." Brooklyn College's newspaper, the *Kingsmen*, sold space to various house plans, fraternities, and sororities who wished to announce good news of their members. The paper listed "box announcements of watchings, pinnings, ringings, engagements, and marriages in a carefully graded hierarchy of felicity

('Witt house happily announces the engagement of Fran Horowitz to Erwin Schwartz of Fife House')." When women planned to wed someone from out of town, the young man's credentials were given in full detail.[71]

Especially in a collective living environment such as Templecrone, college friends often got to know a housemate's boyfriend or girlfriend in a more intimate way than would either of the couple's immediate families. Peer endorsement of a potential spouse might serve as a replacement for family approval. One invitation from the 1950s suggested the Templecrone women's friendship with both the bride and the groom-to-be. The handwritten note expressed the bride and groom's joint desire for the Templecrone housemates to attend their wedding: "Templecroners, Tom and I are to be married on Monday, June fifteenth 8pm at the Park Baptist Church. Brookfield, Missouri. We want you to be with us both at the ceremony and for the reception. Please say if you can come. Affectionately, Shirley Ann."[72] The peer community's influence then might extend to include other areas of a young woman's decision-making, including the wedding planning process. And while undergrads at Brooklyn College, often living at home with their parents, could maintain closer family ties during their college years, their marriage goals matched those of middle-class and aspiring American youth: marry early and marry well. Even in a community still marked by local familial influence, peers played an important role in affecting the shape of the wedding.[73]

As men and women planned to face their adult lives, they increasingly took advice from modern sources. Beyond their peers, men and women viewed media, advertising, and self-proclaimed experts on wedding and married life as better equipped to provide advice in the postwar landscape.[74] No longer was mother's word good enough. Times had changed since her wedding. Men and women of marrying ages during the 1950s encountered a world far different from that of their parents a generation before, or even their older siblings just a few years earlier. The older generation's courtship rituals, marked by localism and group dating, were foreign to a generation of daters who had started "going steady" sometimes as early as middle school. Parents might control the household, but their knowledge of the world of youth often was regarded as sorely lacking.[75] Youth often considered the newly designed system of dating and engagement as beyond the grasp of their parents.

During the prewar and wartime years, it was not unusual for young men and women to consult directly with their parents as they planned their weddings. After a fairly extended separation, Frances "Frankie" McGiboney and Robert "Zuke" Zulauf married on June 7, 1944. Both from Missouri, the two married in Columbia, South Carolina where Zulauf waited for his overseas departure. In a series of letters sent by McGiboney, she detailed her pre-wedding plans, from meeting Zulauf's parents to purchasing her wedding dress. McGiboney's mother played an important role in the planning process. In a May 28, 1944 letter to her fiancé, she wrote:

> I've misplaced those books you sent me on the *Etiquette of the Engagement and Wedding* and now I don't know what to do. Mom knows quite a bit about everything—but since I've never been married before—and never paid much attention to formality etc. (planning to be an old maid) it's a trifle hard for me. All will have to be as proper as necessary, though.[76]

McGiboney indicated that the rules of etiquette were to be taken seriously for a "proper" wedding. Her mother's participation was essential for wedding day success and even might serve as a stand-in for the missing *Etiquette of the Engagement and Wedding*. McGiboney's mother was a trusted advisor and friend, an authority beyond Frances herself.

In just a few years, however, this relationship between mother-of-the-bride and bride changed. Women continued to rely on their mother's assistance and guidance, to be sure, but new expectations for the white wedding created new expectations for the kind of advice necessary to host such an event. Many mothers were ill-equipped to handle such a responsibility. And so young women often encountered advice such as that found in the *Good Housekeeping's Complete Wedding Guide*, which warned the bride-to-be that she and her mother might "feel overwhelmed by all that needs to be done." While few brides could afford to have the wedding entirely directed by a professional planner, the *Guide* suggested relying, at least in part, on expert advice: "almost any wedding will be easier in the arranging and smoother in the performance if some of this professional know-how is utilized."[77] A long-time guide for middle-class American women, *Good Housekeeping* served a national audience and suggested that a national wedding style existed.[78]

While couples' immediate families aimed to maintain some measure of authority, brides and grooms received advice against relying too heavily on parental guidance. A January 21, 1950 article in the *Washington Post*, "Mother Isn't Best Authority on Weddings," directly advised brides to seek the counsel of others. Emphasizing the fact that weddings had changed, the article suggested that a mother's experience with weddings was dated and could not be trusted to live up to "modern ideas and methods." Relying on the expertise of Kathleen Brown, the Nation's Dean of Bridal Consultants, the article insisted that couples should aim to please themselves in their wedding planning. The couple's desires were of primary importance. While still insisting on regard for the feelings of others, Brown suggested that wedding planning called for "acts of polite brutality."[79]

Other periodicals made similar suggestions to various audiences. This type of advice crossed both race and region. The *Post*'s advice mirrored that articulated in a 1947 issue of *Ebony*. Drawing on the potential anxieties and insecurities of young black men and women (and possibly creating new worries), the cover article suggested the use of a professional wedding planner, noting, "She takes all the details off the family's hands and saves the harried and sometimes socially inexperienced mother from making mistakes."[80] The fact that publications for different audiences predicted similar social anxieties, goals, and behaviors underscored the growing homogeneity of the white wedding celebration. But this new white wedding power was better understood and more readily accepted among those about to be married rather than their extended families. Even before marriage, couples negotiated a tenuous balance as they considered their relationship to their respective families while also aiming to assert their autonomy as an independent couple. Young people struggled to satisfy both familial expectations and individual desires, or they faced the daunting task of following through with their own wishes, practicing Kathleen Brown's "polite brutality."

Some traditions suggested by older family members struck modern brides and grooms as unnecessary relics of a past age, revealing a generational divide. American women of the past traditionally began preparing for weddings and marriages in girlhood. For years it was common for women to collect silverware, linens, and china during their youth and store these items in hope chests. Upon marriage, they would be ready to outfit a home. Increasingly, as the home became a site in which to display consumer prowess, the items long-ago acquired in a hope chest appeared out of date, mismatched, or unstylish. Likewise, the practice of maintaining a hope chest seemed outdated.[81] Young women were sometimes irreverent in their dismissal of formerly widespread customs. After Eleanor Eyestone's relationship with Merle Trummel became increasingly serious, her grandmother asked her if she had a hope chest prepared. Eyestone good-naturedly responded, "No, but I would rather have hopes and no chest than a chest and no hopes!" Her grandmother found her response amusing, but promptly sent pillowcases to help her start on acquiring necessary items for setting up a home.[82]

Eyestone's grandmother was not the only member of an older generation to place value upon the hope chest tradition. Her future mother-in-law likewise agreed on the importance of a hope chest. After Eyestone and Trummel became engaged, his mother suggested that he give Eleanor a cedar chest, a practice not uncommon at the time. Eyestone, a home economics teacher, had long had her eye on an electric sewing machine. Knowing she coveted this modern appliance, Trummel asked his fiancée her preference: a chest or a sewing machine. For Eyestone, the answer was obvious: "I told him I'd rather have the sewing machine, so he purchased the one of my choice. Ah! An electric sewing machine! No foot pedaling to do."[83] Eyestone and Trummel married in 1942, but even during the war years, modern convenience trumped tradition. Further, and just as important, personal desire triumphed over familial suggestion.

In the years following the war, the preference for modernity over long-held custom became even more pronounced. Anticipating an audience uncertain about what to buy ever-more-modern brides and grooms, periodicals offered advice on desirable wedding gifts. The practice of gift giving, still a relatively new "tradition," remained. Gifts, however, had changed with the times. For the most part, articles highlighted young married couples' attention to practicality. The marketplace likewise emphasized 1950s' brides and grooms as a new generation of just-marrieds. Financial stability, which had long been a prerequisite for marriage, became less important during the early marriage craze of the

1950s, in part because of continued parental financial support.[84] Additionally, newlyweds could depend on the generosity of friends and family as they embarked upon furnishing their new homes or transitory apartment dwellings.[85]

Indicating the extent to which couples received assistance from family and friends, scrapbooks collected by Myrtle Keppy featured dozens of invitations for linen, kitchen, and other miscellaneous showers—including invitations to her own celebrations. Throughout 1946 and 1947, these events, both pre-wedding and wedding celebrations, served as highlights in Keppy's social life. Following a long-standing tradition, women helped other women prepare for marriage. Focusing specifically on the home, and thus highlighting the idealized domestic focus of a woman's married life in postwar America, showers provided women with the opportunity to share their knowledge of necessities for establishing and keeping a home. Brides were not expected to come to a wedding already prepared for marriage. They could and would depend on networks of female friends and family members.

However, even showers—traditionally female-only events—received a modern twist.[86] "Mixed showers," for the bride and the groom, called for gifts such as "records, bar accessories, ash trays," and other such gender-neutral or more masculine offerings. The items presented at a mixed shower were meant for both the bride and the groom-to-be. Mixed showers became popular in the postwar years, as these parties increasingly were given in the evening to accommodate the schedules of the growing number of working brides-to-be. The blend of workplace experience and domestic focus led to the modernization of the traditional wedding shower.[87] Beyond accommodating the bride's schedule, these mixed showers also reflected the privilege that was bestowed on the marital relationship. The modern relationship between husband and wife was meant to be a person's primary relationship, closer even than those between and among women.[88]

Modern practice likewise affected other elements of gift-giving. Wedding registries, formerly meant for those who might request cut-glass, china, and silver, became accessible to young men and women who were getting their first taste of middle-class life.[89] Demonstrating the

Wedding shower invitations, 1946–47, from scrapbooks compiled by Myrtle Keppy. Courtesy Iowa Women's Archives, University of Iowa Libraries, Iowa City.

growing popularity of the white wedding across social and economic lines and the growing popularity of the registry, John Wanamaker of Wanamaker's Department Stores opened his wedding gift registry "to assist the one-room apartment bride as well as the one more generously endowed . . ."[90] "Home-keeping" was streamlined to limit time devoted to housework and increase time for casual entertaining. Practical gifts trumped the traditional. While couples still received sterling silver with which to entertain, the preference increasingly was for the more practical stainless steel.[91] According to a 1958 survey commissioned by *Bride's* magazine and conducted by National Analysts, Inc., nearly half of all surveyed brides indicated gift preferences to their family and friends before the wedding.[92] If families were unwilling to accept this modern turn, brides and grooms found ways of infusing unwelcome gifts with practicality. In 1949, receiving a cornucopia of silver and china designed for a traditional style of entertaining, Betty and Paul Fussell, unbeknownst to Paul's mother, "sold most of the silver to a secondhand shop in Boston as soon as the honeymoon was over."[93]

Iowa native Beverly George found herself witness to a slightly more dramatic struggle between a bride and her family's conflicting views of tradition and modernity. Newly engaged, George had left home for a summer employment at George Williams College Camp in Lake Geneva, Wisconsin. Between her camp responsibilities and leisure time with coworkers, she still found ample opportunities to correspond with her fiancé, Larry Everett. Letter after letter indicated George's preoccupation with the future: her thoughts on the proposed layout of their future home, her desire for the Everett family to like her and the George family to like Everett, and her general eagerness at the prospect of being married. Mixed in with her excitement over her own pending nuptials was news about George's friend Fran DeForest and her experience as a likewise newly engaged woman. While DeForest's engagement was fraught with more tension than her own, George seemed to consider the similarity between their two circumstances as she kept Everett abreast of her friend's predicament, particularly in regard to the DeForests' response to Fran's engagement and wedding plans.

While parental approval helped a marriage to get off to a good start, a point unanimously agreed upon by wedding literature and marriage educational materials, the necessity of approval regarding other components of the marriage process, including a wedding, seemed open to interpretation.[94] DeForest was relieved to find her parents increasingly accepting of her fiancé, Marlow, especially since their approval at first had seemed unlikely. However, when DeForest mentioned that she and Marlow planned to hold the wedding in Ames, home to Iowa State University, rather than her hometown, her mother "pressed a firm foot downward & said absolutely not." As she relayed the situation to Everett, George considered the situation:

> I feel this way about it—that the girl should decide whether the value
> of having the ceremony exactly where she wants it overshadows the

keen pleasure that her parents derive from being able to share in it. The fact that a son or daughter is leaving home for good is hard enough for parents to take without allowing them to have a part in engineering the activities—adding insult to injury.[95]

George admitted to having considered Ames for her own marriage but calculated that the majority of her friends would have left town by the time of her wedding. Ultimately, even as she recognized the hurt a girl's family might feel at her selection of wedding location other than her hometown, George deemed the choice the bride's alone. While George realized that there would be consequences to such a decision, she believed awareness of the consequences was all that mattered. Embracing a modern and increasingly popular view, George supported the authority of the bride above the authority of her family.

George self-consciously identified the familial disruption caused by a child's marriage, a circumstance long recognized, particularly by the family of the bride.[96] While a son or a daughter's departure might be equally heart-wrenching, George emphasized that the female should have the final say on where the wedding ceremony should be held. In this way she reflected the popular understandings of the gendered nature of the wedding planning and decision-making, which privileged the bride's wishes over the groom's. She likewise demonstrated the tension many couples felt as they encountered the traditional (following family wishes) and the modern (focusing on individual desire). Neither, it seemed, could be achieved without a cost. A white wedding required that young men and women negotiate a common ground between their past and their future: the local, familial relationships of youth and the newly emphasized national, peer relationships of early adulthood.

This tension between the modern and the traditional, felt even in 1946, foreshadowed a move in an increasingly modern direction. While parents of engaged couples might fail to grasp the newly modern style of celebration, it was just as likely that they might fail to understand the nature of youthful courtship. Elizabeth Stewart Weston, bridal editor of *Good Housekeeping Magazine*, edited the 1957 *Good Housekeeping's Complete Wedding Guide*, which highlighted generational differences in its pages. Years ago, the engagement was "as clear-cut an event as a marriage," but changed standards in dating had complicated understandings of the engagement process, especially for older men and women unfamiliar with the new rules of courtship. "Generally relaxed rules of chaperonage, the custom of going steady, the practice of pinning (girls wearing men's fraternity pins) or of exchanging class rings, have all served to leave the world, and particularly the older generation, in some doubt as to exactly what constitutes an engagement."[97] Many members of the late 1940s' and 1950s' youth population did not worry about their parents' ignorance of popular social customs. Adult society no longer served as their only source of authority. They had the media, the market, and each other.[98] Parental views looked out-of-date. Stanley Banks's indignation that Kay would dare marry a boy whose family he and Ellie did not know, and his subsequent desire to have a discussion with Buckley about his earning ability and financial stability, struck Kay as hopelessly old-fashioned.[99] The newly conceived white wedding, with its legitimization of individual wants, reliance on consumer expenditure, and focus on personal and peer authority, was on its way to becoming the standard style of American wedding celebration. Stanley Banks was not the only father uncomfortable with the white wedding's growing power. Even as the white wedding's popularity became clear, discomfort with the nature of the celebration remained.

* * *

The white wedding, despite the alleged connection with tradition, was new, as was what the wedding represented. With its focus on the bride and groom, the wedding legitimated and even sanctified a kind of selfishness rarely condoned in American life. Business, media, and the growing national community encouraged grooms and their brides, especially, to look upon the wedding as their special day. Marguerite Bentley assured brides that while expected wedding customs existed, the wedding held special individual significance for the girl being wed: "You are the bride and this is your wedding; therefore, it is for *you* to choose what you desire most to do."[100] The focus on the bride and groom as the starting point of their own nuclear family, the unit so highly prized during the early postwar years, indicated the primacy of their relationship above all others.[101] On the wedding day, that relationship was celebrated by friends, family, and members of the various communities to which the bride and groom belonged. Their presence, of course, was highly desired. But those witnesses often believed they had a right to an active form of participation rather than a role of passive observance, an idea not quite in line with the modern wedding approach.

In the first decade and a half after World War II, marriage was a key component of adult life.[102] For men and women of various ages, classes, and ethnicities, marriage was something they could agree upon. The wedding, however, became a site for conflict. While the white wedding became the standard style of postwar wedding celebration, couples quickly learned that Stanley Banks's simple view of "Boy and girl meet, fall in love, marry, have babies" was an antiquated view from a long-distant past.[103] A wedding required planning, negotiation, patience, and tact—a combination of qualities that was, indeed, rare. Efforts to please various parties sometimes resulted in the pleasing of none. But brides and grooms cleverly picked and chose from traditions, those passed from generation to generation as well as those advocated by modern media and industry. Through their careful negotiation of these seemingly contradictory traditions, men and women justified increasingly modern ideas of married love and postwar American life and expressed these views in their wedding celebrations.

In later years, the weddings of the late 1940s and 1950s would be criticized as "cookie cutter" or "conformist." Yet, although they may have conformed to stylistic suggestions or idealized concepts of gender performance, these weddings represented not so much a placation of expectations as a challenge to long-held beliefs about a wedding's importance and meaning. The white weddings of the 1950s demonstrated a testing of, and, more significantly, a commitment to new views of American life. Challenges to traditional forms of authority and assertion of the acceptability of fulfilling personal desire—hallmarks of future weddings—marked white weddings of the 1940s and 1950s. But even as this wedding style became the predominant way in which Americans wed, questions over the nature and meaning of the white wedding remained.

2

"The Same Thing That Happens to All Brides"

LUCI JOHNSON,
THE AMERICAN PUBLIC,
AND THE WHITE WEDDING

The bride-to-be sat in the center of a circle of friends. The first of several wedding showers to come, this particular event was hosted by a close friend and bridesmaid. Most of the young women in attendance were close in age to the 19-year-old guest of honor. The year was 1966, and these young women had yet to embrace the increasingly casual style that soon would dominate American fashion. Dressed in knee-length shifts of various summer hues, the guests had spent time preparing for this party. Each woman's hair was styled and her face made up. They looked like junior versions of their mothers, eager to join the grown-up married world. The young guests, and some a bit older, sipped punch and nibbled on small cakes as they watched the guest of honor open fairly typical shower gifts—placemats, casserole dishes, potholders, scouring pads, and kitchen towels. Yellow was her chosen color, and gifts matched this request. As a tribute to her southern roots, someone had given the bride a Texas-shaped cookie cutter. The day's events were caught on film—but film of a quality higher than the usual home movie. A narrator noted, "Some of the guests were momentarily transported back to the day when they were brides at showers given for them and to some of the bridesmaids, it was a heart-quickening reminder of an engagement just ahead."[1] This bride-to-be was deemed typical, a young woman other women could relate to, a woman with whom they shared or would share a common experience. The wedding—specifically the white wedding, this bride's style of celebration—and the events leading up to the wedding had become universal experiences in the lives of American women.[2]

From the moment she accepted Patrick Nugent's proposal of marriage, Luci Baines Johnson, daughter to President Lyndon Baines Johnson and this particular shower's guest of honor, insisted that she was just like any other girl. And like any other girl, she would have a white wedding. Despite her fame, Luci saw herself as a typical bride-to-be. On the night of her engagement, December 24, 1965, Luci requested that Liz Carpenter, Press Secretary and Staff Director to the First Lady, make a late-night announcement of the engagement. Luci, a recent convert to Catholicism, and her husband-to-be planned to attend Midnight Mass, and Luci wanted to wear her new engagement ring. As she told Carpenter, "There may be reporters there. I'm not going to take off my ring. And I don't want the story to leak. I want to announce it like any other girl."[3] Her quest for normalcy continued throughout her engagement. At her July 1966 press conference, Luci emphasized her typicality to the gathered reporters. When asked to describe "her reaction to this moment, less than three weeks before her marriage," she drew upon the common feelings that might be expected of any bride. "I am very excited, a little anxious, and a little nervous," she said. As she continued, she noted, "I don't think that I am that much more nervous or that much more excited or that much more anxious than any of the friends that I have . . . who have gotten married. I think it is the same thing that happens to all brides."[4] The White House wedding press corps, led by Liz Carpenter and Social Secretary Bess Abel, dutifully followed Luci and the Johnson family's lead. Their line for the entirety of the engagement remained unchanged: Luci was just like any other girl, and her wedding would be just like any other wedding.

Of course, not just "any girl" warranted a press conference to detail her courtship, wedding, and plans for married life. Few brides received thousands of letters and greeting cards from the American people. A typical girl did not have to guard the secret of her wedding dress from hoards of investigative journalists, unwilling to accept the fact that Luci—like any bride—wanted her gown to be a surprise for her groom.

It was rare for other girls to have protesters march at their weddings.[5] Beyond the Johnson family's political and public renown, they were a family marked by substantial wealth. This affluence, as much as the family's celebrity, informed the shape of the wedding. Luci's wedding followed in the steps of the dominant white wedding style, but hers was the ultimate celebration—a specially designed gown, a long row of bridesmaids, the biggest church in the country, and a reception at the most famous home in the nation. If Kay Banks's wedding represented the white wedding in its primitive or burgeoning form, Luci Baines Johnson's celebration represented the white wedding at its zenith.[6]

To some degree, Luci Johnson was not inaccurate as she empha-sized her typicality. While some letters to the White House criticized the amount of money spent on the wedding (most were fearful that American tax dollars paid for the bash), the majority of correspondence accepted that Luci would marry in the most popular postwar style: the white wedding.[7] By the mid-1960s, the white wedding had become so popular and, to some extent, so accessible, that "any girl" might cele-brate in this way. Luci Johnson's 1966 wedding highlighted, in an exag-gerated way and on a very public stage, the popularity and power of the white wedding celebration. As the first postwar White House white wedding, Luci's nuptials demonstrated just how typical this wedding style had become. When it came to the president's daughter, the Ameri-can public accepted—and even expected—a grand celebration.[8]

Despite its popularity, the white wedding's ascendancy was not without conflict. As this wedding style matured into something of an American institution, it became vulnerable to critique. Correspondence between the American public and the White House demonstrated that the white wedding's preeminence had not eliminated questions about the appropriate way to celebrate the event. Misgivings born in the 1950s came to fruition in the 1960s as Americans became increasingly uncomfort-able with the white wedding's size and scope. With its mix of individual and communal, modern and traditional—topics of constant debate, par-ticularly in the later 1960s—the wedding inevitably presented a poten-tial site of conflict. Older interpretations of what a wedding should be clashed with the newness of white wedding ideas, particularly regard-ing the primacy of the couple, especially the bride, above all other par-ticipants. Men and women argued over whose authority should prevail in white wedding planning and celebration. While often publicized as a day of romantic fulfillment and familial bliss, the ceremony also served as a location where generations engaged in a tug of war over understandings of religion, sex, gender roles, family, and the nature of modern marriage.[9] Americans may have accepted and even anticipated the white wedding, but expectations varied when it came to questions about who might have the final say on the wedding's appropriate shape, meaning, and audience.

Wedding experts and the wedding industry endorsed the wedding day authority of the bride, but the general population remained unconvinced. Like other brides-to-be, Luci received advice and fielded suggestions from those who had gone before her. But instead of several aunts and cousins, neighbors and coworkers, Luci Johnson experienced the pressure of an entire nation who believed they might weigh in on her wedding decisions. Most brides enjoyed the luxury of a wedding public they had selected through the narrowing of a guest list (and even this chosen public often produced conflict), but Luci was subject to the scrutiny of a public she had no hand in choosing. Every move was reported, and often in staggering detail. Americans seemed convinced that the wedding of a First Family member was a topic on which they could advise, and with as much ease and often as much candor as they would advise one of their own friends or family members.[10] Conflicting views over the distribution of wedding day influence exposed broader questions about the nature of modern American life and culture.

As Luci Johnson prepared for her ceremony, she attempted a delicate balance of satisfying public opinion while designing a wedding that matched the ideal she imagined for herself and her future husband. While debate over the nature of Luci's ceremony was exaggerated due to the special status of the bride, the question of what a wedding should be and mean reflected a conflict that influenced the trajectory of the wedding's development—and personal life, more broadly—in the decades to follow. The white wedding had become the standard wedding style, but how it should be celebrated, what it should represent, and who should have a voice in these decisions was not entirely clear. Much of the debate over Luci's wedding focused on disagreements over whether a wedding should satisfy public or private goals. Many observers were anxious about a wedding shaped by notions of individualism and personal authority, as opposed to a wedding formed by more traditional influences, such as family and community advice. Others believed public, political responsibilities trumped bridal desire. Such a contest reflected ambivalence about the move from the traditional to the modern in the broader scope of American life. The "traditional" descriptor applied to postwar white weddings only went so far. Brides like Luci Johnson, who embraced the "traditional" style of wedding, still navigated a sea of opposing viewpoints.[11]

* * *

By the early 1960s, the white wedding was *the* American wedding style, driven not only by the era's prosperity, but also by an increased comfort with the idea of consumer expenditure and fulfillment of personal desire. Former luxuries had become necessities.[12] Like their counterparts of the late 1940s and 1950s, couples—and especially brides—of the 1960s carried on the newly accepted tradition of imagining the wedding as their day. When Gloria Emerson of the *New York Times* visited a Brooklyn bridal show in 1960, she interviewed some of the 2,000 women gathered for the event. Declaration of the wedding day as the most important day of one's life was, among brides interviewed, "a refrain that never ceased." Wedding experts reinforced this notion. Barbara Wilson of the *New York Tribune*'s Brides' School advised prospective brides that they "might well compare the wedding—and its planning—to a big-time theatrical production in which she acts as producer, director, stage manager and star, all in one." Luci Johnson was like other brides who imagined themselves as stars in their wedding productions. She believed she had a right to celebrate as she saw fit.[13]

A generation brought up with the image of the white wedding as their ideal, young adults of the 1960s cemented the white wedding's cultural power. Young women in particular grew familiar with the white wedding though multiple forms of consumer culture and mass media, from bridal dolls to popular films to the pages of their *Seventeen* magazines, where they learned early lessons on topics related to courtships, engagements, and weddings. Even more than their predecessors the decade before, these women lived in a world of weddings. For brides having grown up in a time of postwar prosperity, the culture of American consumerism was often the only one they had ever known. Spending money on a wedding was as natural an act as spending money on any number of products deemed indispensable during their teenage years.[14]

In 1962, J. A. Livingston of the *Washington Post* estimated that wedding rates would increase with baby boomers' coming of age. His predictions proved accurate.[15] The U.S. Department of Health, Education, and Welfare calculated that in 1966, the year of Luci Johnson's wedding, an estimated 1,857,000 marriages took place, a figure 2.2 percent higher than the previous year. Of these marriages, approximately 85 percent would be celebrated "in a showy, formal, ritualistic, once-in-a lifetime wedding complete with bridesmaids, flowers, ushers, the whole traditional kit and caboodle."[16] Nearly 1.5 million white weddings would take place. According to the U.S. Department of Commerce, by 1967, Americans spent approximately $7.2 billion on weddings, with $3 billion allotted for the wedding day in particular.[17] While not every bride and groom married in the white wedding style, enough did to make the wedding big news and big business. More significantly, popular perception held that all brides and grooms celebrated this way.[18]

Weddings across the United States served as sites of comparison, even as they varied in size and scope. Married at the Calvary Baptist Church in The Dalles, Oregon on May 22, 1965, Harry Smith and Doris Lewis celebrated their marriage with a wedding not so different from the wedding of Luci Johnson and Pat Nugent. Engaged on January 2, 1965, the couple, like Johnson and Nugent, waited several months before getting married. The bride, like Luci Johnson, was feted with a number of showers before her wedding day. Doris and Harry, she in a white dress and he in a dark suit, each had four attendants and were married before approximately one hundred guests. Like Luci, Doris adhered to the popular tradition that required the bride to have something old, something new, something borrowed, and something blue on her wedding day. A post-ceremony reception followed the wedding, after which the couple enjoyed a week-long honeymoon on the Oregon coast. Even as the religious, geographic, and economic details of the Smith-Lewis wedding differed from the Johnson-Nugent wedding, the celebration contained many similar elements. The white wedding had become typical.[19]

Kitty Hanson's contemporary investigation of the white wedding in 1960s America reported the power of the wedding's appeal. Caterers, banquet managers, and bridal consultants agreed that brides of the 1960s

Harry and Doris Smith, 1965. Courtesy Shannon Smith.

play a much more aggressive role in planning their weddings than did the brides of fifteen or twenty years ago. Those girls did little more than choose their gowns and their attendants (and their bridegrooms, of course) and let the family handle the rest of what was, then, purely a family affair. The bride of the sixties, however, has her own ideas on how things should be done—ideas nourished in great measure by Hollywood movies, movie-star weddings, and what her friends did when *they* got married.[20]

Of course, even in the 1950s the wedding had ceased to be "purely a family affair," as brides and grooms tested their independence through celebrations informed by personal tastes rather than familial suggestion. The full maturation of the white wedding occurred in the 1960s when it became the most familiar form of celebration among young brides and grooms-to-be. Hanson's findings point more to the recognition of

Luci and Pat Nugent cut their wedding cake. Photo by Yoichi Okamoto. Courtesy Lyndon B. Johnson Library, Austin, Texas.

change. This recognition raised concerns about the white wedding's meaning and power.

As couples of the 1960s built upon the patterns and practices set by those before them, weddings became increasingly elaborate. The prosperous sixties allowed for the competitive spirit, begun in the 1950s, to continue among brides and grooms as they planned their wedding celebrations.[21] Couples and their families participated in a contest to see who might have the most extravagant wedding. A grand wedding demonstrated a family's social and economic standing and indicated a sense of closeness among its immediate members. Parents, especially those who might have wed in more meager celebrations, saw their children's nuptials as a time when they, too, might shine. The wedding marked the union of a bride and the groom, but couples' families frequently viewed the wedding as a time to celebrate social and economic success.[22]

Hanson's *For Richer, For Poorer* paid special attention to the role of the engaged couples' respective sets of parents, focusing particularly on the mother of the bride:

The mothers of today's brides were themselves married during the do-without years of World War II. Their weddings were simple, hurried, often drab; set in the context of war, urgency, and short leaves. Weddings in those days came without honeymoons, and often without any members of the family present. Certainly few brides had wedding gowns and veils and attendants, much less receptions with champagne, sit-down dinners, and live music.[23]

Periodicals suggested that Lady Bird Johnson was one mother living vicariously through her daughter's nuptials. Whether a trope emphasized because of its familiarity or authentic regret (or regret she thought necessary to express), accounts of Lady Bird cast her as a fairly typical mother of the bride.[24] The First Lady, wed in 1934 by a pastor she had never met, with a hastily procured $2.50 ring from Sears, Roebuck, remarked wistfully of her daughter's wedding, "The wedding day will be something beautiful to remember, and I want Luci to have it."[25] In reporting about Luci's dress, a California newspaper noted that Mrs. Johnson confessed her regrets of "not having had a wedding gown herself that she could let her daughter wear."[26] Since her own wedding had been a modest event, Lady Bird seemed determined that her daughter's celebration would be an affair to remember.

Even as the wedding established a couple's independence, attention to the bride's and groom's respective families demonstrated the continued influence of extended family. As much as brides and grooms aimed to express modernity and personal authority in their celebrations, parents regularly insisted on having their voices heard during the wedding planning process. In the ideal situation, the bride and her family would find their plans perfectly in sync. Fortunately for the Johnsons, Luci's wedding plans typically coincided with her parents' expectations or met their approval. Luci indicated the harmony in her family relationships when she spoke of her mother's understanding of the growing seriousness of her relationship with Pat. Luci noted, "Mothers and daughters are always so close that mothers can sense those things."[27] This closeness allowed for relatively smooth wedding planning, at least within her immediate family.

Not every family fell into such happy agreement. Some brides and grooms engaged in a tug-of-war with their family members as they planned their weddings. Numerous women interviewed by Kitty Hanson suggested that the wedding had been out of their hands before their engagement. As one woman recalled of her wedding, "It was that Big Party mother had always wanted to give. I figured it was her wedding, somehow, not mine."[28] Even when couples advocated personal expectations for their weddings, they were not guaranteed a receptive audience. Popular ideas from the 1950s and 1960s about the secondary pace of the family in wedding planning did not mean that parents immediately acquiesced to a lessened role. Newspaper announcements of engagements and wedding plans pointed to continued parental involvement, particularly the participation of the bride's parents, who were often cited as having announced the news of their daughter's impending nuptials.[29] As such a pivotal event in a family's life, parents of the bride and groom believed they had a very real right to make suggestions. They further expected that these suggestions be taken seriously.[30]

Family relationships were particularly complicated just before and upon engagement. Couples learned that they should tread lightly. Joyce Jackson, an author advertised as a teenager able to advise other young women about dating and romantic relationships, recognized the tension between traditional and modern ideas. She wrote, "Up until very recently in our history, it was customary for a young man to ask a girl's father for her 'hand in marriage.' We no longer regard this as obligatory in the strict sense of the word, but times have not changed to the extent that we completely ignore the custom either." Instead of speaking with the father, a couple might "talk it over" with both parents, thereby demonstrating respect for each parent. As Jackson noted, "Times have changed in that both parents should now be consulted instead of just the father, but times have not changed with respect to the manner of consulting. You don't *tell* them that you plan to become engaged—you *ask* them if you may."[31] Jackson's advice suggested placation rather than deference. Couples still would decide on their marriage before discussing the subject with parents. Parents were brought into the discussion not for advice, counsel, or permission, but so as not to feel excluded or ignored. Prescriptive literature demonstrated remarkable savvy in its recognition of the struggle for wedding day control. Brides and grooms could manipulate traditional expectations in a way that soothed parental ego while simultaneously maintaining personal wedding authority.[32]

Despite the picture of Johnson family accord painted by the First Family and their bevy of PR professionals, Lyndon Johnson was one such father who refused to take a back seat in his daughter's engagement process. As multiple media sources reported on Luci and Pat's increasingly serious relationship, LBJ demanded an explanation. Reports surfaced that during an October 1965 trip to the Johnsons' Texas ranch, Pat planned to speak to the president about having Luci's hand in marriage.[33] Some reports speculated that LBJ preferred the two wait before an official engagement.[34] As Luci shared the tale with the journalists at her press conference, she indicated that LBJ, having learned of the alleged meeting between himself and his future son-in-law, was perplexed when no such meeting occurred. Some weeks later, "in a very jovial way" he asked, "What is all this stuff I have been reading about in the paper?" Luci, Pat, and her father discussed the situation at length. As she recalled, LBJ suggested the three sit down and discuss the pros and cons of the situation. As their meeting concluded, Johnson said, "Well, I want what you want to make you happy. I trust your judgment and I approve."[35]

While Luci's telling of the tale—some months after the event had occurred, just a few weeks before her wedding—suggests a gentle, good-natured exchange between LBJ and the couple, one wonders if the moment was slightly tenser than suggested by the bride-to-be.[36] Lady Bird remembered the weeks before the discussion somewhat differently. Media reports affected LBJ, recovering from gallbladder and kidney stone surgery, more than Luci knew or indicated at the time. As Lady Bird recalled, "I could tell—though he had been out of the hospital a little over a week—he didn't yet feel really fit." The media reports, she noted, "had eaten into him."[37] *Time* magazine took the president's reaction one step further as it speculated that LBJ had "vetoed" the initial request for permission, thus delaying Luci and Pat's engagement.[38] While the media may have played a role in causing some of Luci's personal pre-wedding drama, her experience points to the potential for conflict and confusion in the weeks and months before a wedding. The struggle for wedding day authority seemed as universal as the white wedding itself.[39]

The Johnson clan may have resolved its issues, but unfortunately for Luci Johnson, she also faced the expectations of those beyond her immediate family. In an issue that featured Luci and Pat on the cover, *Time* magazine reported that the breadth of the wedding and the popular interest "could hardly be otherwise in an age of ubiquitous journalistic surveillance and omnivorous curiosity about the day-to-day doings at 1600 Pennsylvania Avenue."[40] Louise Hutchinson noted the complexity of the celebration in her syndicated column: "[The nuptials] are not a state occasion, and therefore in the public domain, but a personal event, though not necessarily a private one."[41] Even on the day of his younger daughter's wedding, the president remained a public official, open to comment from the American public.[42] Johnson could rightly expect to enjoy his personal life, but he was not guaranteed privacy. His family shared this burden. As a representative of the American public and of American brides, Luci was subject to a larger, more public argument over wedding day authority than were most of her peers. She answered not only to her immediate family but to the "immediate country" as well.[43]

* * *

White House weddings had long been big news. When Alice Roosevelt Longworth wed in 1906, the press received no details about the wedding or post-wedding travel plans and had thus fabricated ludicrous stories to satiate public desire for news. Carpenter prevented the distribution of misinformation by providing reporters with a steady stream of information. But the appeal of the Roosevelt wedding differed from that of the Johnson wedding. Roosevelt's white wedding was a spectacle, a sharp contrast to the front parlor weddings of rural America and the middle class. "Princess Alice" walked down the aisle in her cream satin, princess style gown with 18-foot-long train as the Marine Band played the march from "Tannhauser." Refusing to share the spotlight, Roosevelt chose not to have a maid of honor, bridesmaids, or a flower girl. Approximately 680 guests remained after the ceremony for a wedding breakfast where the bride cut the wedding cake with a sword offered to her by her father's military aide.[44] Unlike Roosevelt's celebration, which was truly extravagant and even exotic, Luci Johnson's wedding shared elements familiar to weddings many Americans in the 1960s had attended or even celebrated themselves. The white wedding's popularity and near constant presence in the culture fed desire for news about Luci's wedding. Modern media exposure produced a sense of familiarity with the First Family that stimulated the American public's interest as well as their sense of entitlement to details about and even artifacts from the wedding. Americans wanted—and expected—immediate and up-to-date knowledge about the Johnson-Nugent white wedding.

Upon learning the wedding date and the decision to hold the ceremony at the National Shrine of the Immaculate Conception, television networks made plans to televise the entire wedding day, from pre-ceremony preparation to the newlyweds' honeymoon escape. Without consulting Carpenter, Abel, or any members of the White House staff, reporters traveled to the Shrine to investigate potential camera positions and lighting.[45] Ultimately, Luci decided that she wanted the ceremony to be as private as possible. She and Lady Bird Johnson came to agree that television cameras would not be allowed to film the wedding from inside the Shrine. After several months of speculation, a May 31, 1966 announcement declared that the ceremony would not be televised or broadcast. Carpenter delivered the news: "the couple indicate that the service will have deeper meaning for them if television cameras are not inside the church."[46] Television stations would have access to footage of the wedding party leaving the White House, arriving at the Shrine, leaving the Shrine, and then returning to the White House. Further, the Johnsons eventually agreed to allow taping of a segment of the reception for evening airing.[47]

The decision to prohibit cameras from the ceremonial proceedings inside the Shrine instantly became a point of controversy. As harmless as the decision might have seemed, the choice to ban cameras produced endless turmoil for Carpenter. Letters poured in. The public, associating Luci's wedding with her father's office and assuming she should fulfill the responsibilities of her public role even on her wedding day, voiced discontent with the bride's decision to limit public access to the ceremony.[48] Many read her choice as an expression of disregard for the public support she had received throughout her engagement. By putting her personal desires above community preference, Luci Johnson was not unlike many 1960s brides. Public unhappiness with her decision indicated that many Americans still questioned elements of the white wedding, particularly the authority often assumed by the bride.

Those who had followed Luci and Pat's courtship and engagement were devastated to learn they would not be able to see the culmination of all the wedding planning, and they wrote to the White House to express their displeasure. As a member of the First Family, Luci was a "kind of rare public property," one writer suggested.[49] Indeed, writers corresponded to Luci as though they knew her personally. Men and women responded to Luci as though she *were* any girl—from their church, their family, their neighborhood. People advised her as they might advise their own.[50] Through their correspondence, writers revealed personal views that indicated acceptance of and an eagerness for the wedding—and specifically the white wedding. However, letters also revealed discomfort with elements of this white wedding style, most notably the wedding hierarchy that placed a bride and the groom at the very top and members of the surrounding community at the bottom.

Luci Johnson's wedding struck a chord in the American public because it was an event with which they could identify. Rituals serve as symbolic acts, reaffirming a sense of interconnectedness among a community. Because broader cultural forces shape the wedding, interest extends beyond the direct participants to include other members of the shared culture. Given the extraordinary nature of the First Family's life and lifestyle, the familiarity of a wedding celebration provided the general population with a point of common interest and a way of relating to the president and his family.[51]

The understanding of the First Family as a public entity rejected the notion of a family as a private group and emphasized the communal rather than the individual. While not an elected official in her own right, Luci represented both her family and the national community as she planned her wedding. The trappings of a famous family were exaggerated, but not entirely novel or atypical. The First Family, given something of a celebrity status, might serve as the embodiment of what "average" American families experienced in their own lives. Americans felt they could identify with the family and, therefore, could offer advice on a topic with which many were familiar.[52] Even as popular media suggested that the wedding was the day when a woman left the family of her youth and began the family of her adult life, Luci Johnson continued to be identified as her father's daughter and remained tied to her role in the First Family. The public rejected Luci's wedding authority.

Instead, she remained linked to the president. Power remained in the hands of an older, established male rather than a young female.

While business, media, and peers affirmed modern brides and grooms' plans to personalize the wedding and focus on individual desires, many Americans clung to the traditional notion of the wedding as a time of communal celebration.[53] Luci Johnson's wedding allowed for this argument to be waged on a public stage. Even those who believed that a wedding was an important celebration disagreed about the nature of its significance. Ideas about the individual authority of the bride and groom clashed with traditional expectations of family and community influence. Even traditional views, however, reflected a modern turn. The creation of a national community and culture had changed the nature of cultural exchange within the United States during the years following World War II. As part of a larger community, those who believed in active community participation in the wedding—and thus believed they had a voice in Luci Johnson's celebration—merely fulfilled their role in the now less remote national community.[54]

Joy Starr, a recent bride from Escondido, California, criticized Luci's decision to ban television cameras at the Shrine. While Starr realized Luci was in a position not of her own choosing, she argued that Luci still owed the public gratitude, if only on her father's behalf. A bride of just one year, Starr viewed her recent trip down the aisle as license to counsel Luci about the wedding day experience. The filming of the wedding would not even affect the young bride since, as Starr recalled, "you don't notice a thing" during the wedding. Starr chided the First Daughter: "You had better think a little more of your responsibility and of all us millions that supported your father and how we'd like just a small return . . ." In Starr's view, responsibility trumped desire. Selfishness—even on one's wedding day—was unacceptable. Starr suggested that "millions" of Americans had a vested interest in the wedding celebration, and their interest deserved consideration. Rejecting Luci's presumed focus on individual happiness, Starr wrote, "Try to think of us and not all of yourself."[55]

Starr disagreed with the growing notion of a wedding as a bride's day of particular individual importance.[56] Instead, she viewed the wedding as a day of significance also for guests and well-wishers. The wedding was a time to express gratitude to the community who had supported the couple and befriended their families. Starr's dissatisfaction with Luci Johnson's wedding highlights the tension between the traditional focus on the community and the modern privileging of the individual.[57] The battle between the privileging of the individual or the community would continue to mark negotiations over the nature of the wedding celebration and American culture more broadly. For Starr, a wedding should cater to the desires of the audience as much as to those of the couple being wed.

Many believed that Luci, as the president's daughter, might provide a service to the American public by sharing footage of the nation's capital and largest Catholic Church. Those who had followed the wedding planning throughout the duration of the engagement viewed their inclusion in wedding information as an unofficial invitation. Many people indicated that they would feel tremendously let down were they not able to "attend," even if by television, the actual wedding ceremony. Laura Kilbane expressed her belief that Luci should have a "truly national wedding." Kilbane used language increasingly associated with the wedding, noting the event as a "once in a life time occasion." "You have many friends in this nation," Kilbane reminded Luci, as she indicated that the televising of the event provided "the only way we can attend."[58] In the instance of Luci Johnson's wedding, the uniqueness of the ceremony might extend beyond the bride and groom and to the American public as a whole, particularly for those who had never traveled to Washington or seen a Catholic mass. Luci's wedding, many believed, was not only her wedding. It was a historic event and celebration of national significance, and citizens felt entitled to experience it. "After all," Marsha Wiedler mused in a June note to President Johnson, "it is probably the only White House wedding we will ever see."[59] Any bride marrying in a grand or unique ceremony might receive similar pressure to include extended family or community members in their wedding celebration.

People living far from Washington, DC, unlikely to visit the nation's capital in the near future, emphasized distance in their requests that the Johnson family reconsider the television ban. A young Betty Jo Miller of Kettering, Ohio appealed to the president in this way. Having never been to Washington, Miller wished for the wedding to be on television so she and her family could "see it on our new color set." She represented not just herself, but her grandfather as well, who, she wrote, would enjoy watching the wedding from Green Bay, Wisconsin.[60] Luci, it seemed, might use her wedding as a fulfillment of civic duty. As much as the wedding was a private affair, an event to celebrate Luci and Pat, it also became a public affair due to Luci's celebrity, her choice of venue, and the sense of audience a wedding created. The national audience created by coverage of Luci Johnson's wedding asserted its significance to the celebration.[61]

The decision to host the ceremony in the National Shrine of the Immaculate Conception raised eyebrows immediately. Some wondered just how private the family intended the wedding to be. The tradition of the time was for a Catholic couple to wed in the bride's parish church, but Luci opted not to celebrate at St. Matthew's, just six blocks from the White House. Some speculated her decision was related to the church's association with the funeral of President John Kennedy. As Luci described it, she and Pat had attended the Shrine during their court-ship and engagement. Thus, the location held a special significance for them. But never before had a bride been married within its walls. For a woman claiming a desire for a small, personal wedding, the selection of the Shrine seemed an incongruous choice. As much as Luci may have desired privacy on her wedding day, she also expressed a desire to be like any bride. Like most brides of the 1960s, she would marry in a site of religious significance. Like these other brides, she likely wished for a way to make her wedding unique and personally significant. Choosing the Shrine for the wedding accomplished both tasks.[62]

Luci, by this time familiar with the trappings of celebrity, did not attempt to deter public interest in choosing such a wedding venue. The Shrine's enormity—its 400-yard aisle and seating for up to 3,500 guests—prompted speculation over Luci and Pat's sincerity in their espoused desire for a "family affair" and surprise at the extent of national interest. *Time* described the Shrine, the largest church in the United States, as a "great hilltop edifice in northeast Washington, with its mosaic domes, 30 satellite chapels and ornate, still-incomplete inte-rior that has had to be cleared of scaffolding for the occasion." Not for want of size was the guest list limited or cameras banned. Rather, Luci wished these measures taken. Bowing to the bride's desire, they were carried out.[63]

Luci and Pat Nugent exit the National Shrine of the Immaculate Conception. Photo by Yoichi Okamoto. Courtesy Lyndon B. Johnson Library, Austin, Texas.

Catholics across the nation had eagerly anticipated Luci's marriage in such a sacred site. In one of the many letters begging the Johnsons to reconsider their decision to ban television cameras from inside the Shrine, Charles L. Sponseller of Baltimore appealed to Luci's Catholicism as part of his plea. Not only would Luci be the first member of the First Family to be wed in a Catholic ceremony, but were she to televise her wedding, she would "give countless thousands of poor but devout Catholics a free 'visit' to Mary's Shrine."[64] The wedding could have religious meaning for the bride and the groom, but this meaning also would be shared with others around the world. Given that she had emphasized her religious devotion—and Pat's as well—throughout her engagement, Luci's Catholicism seemed an effective way of appealing to the young bride-to-be.[65] A Catholic nuptial mass often was open to an entire congregation. An open church followed by a closed reception was not uncommon. Luci instead adhered to her own desires. Tradition as interpreted by the modern wedding industry here clashed with long-held practices among Catholics.[66]

Citizens suggested that they shared a relationship with the First Family, and as such, could comment upon private matters. Representing this feeling of closeness to the president, Mrs. Johnson, Lynda, and Luci, Minerva B. Kasper of Reading, Pennsylvania wrote to express her support of a televised ceremony. Citizens, she asserted, enjoyed a personal relationship with the president. "The joys, sorrows, or ill health of his family are of immediate concern. . . . His family is like a member of our own family." The decision to keep television cameras from the ceremony because, as White House representatives noted, it would make the ceremony "more meaningful" enraged Kasper. The wedding, even as it became standardized, still held tremendous meaning among those attending and those observing. "Little does it matter how meaningful it will be to the nation who," she wrote, "banded together in a landslide vote made it possible for Miss Luci to be a White House bride, the first in many long years." For Kasper, Luci's wedding had personal as well as direct political implications.[67] While she emphasized her familial feeling for the Johnsons, she likewise emphasized her due as a citizen and Johnson political supporter.

Kasper appealed specifically to Lady Bird Johnson, indicating a belief in the power of the bride's family over the wedding plans. Having celebrated her own daughter's wedding, Kasper knew "the disappointment friends can feel who cannot be invited." Friends and family always wanted to share in the joy of the celebration, and it was an awful feeling to be left out. Kasper, given her experience as part of her daughter's wedding, felt qualified to correspond with Lady Bird on this matter and, further, felt qualified to advise the First Lady. Given Luci's widespread appeal and the possibility for national inclusion, no one needed to feel excluded from her celebration. All citizens should be guests of Luci's wedding. Referring to the United States as a "nation of friends," Kasper pleaded for a public ceremony and urged that the public "should not be ignored." The wedding as a national celebration was an idea expressed by many who contacted the First Family. Kasper referenced the televised wedding of Princess Margaret and pleaded that the Johnsons not allow the wedding of England's princess "be more important to the nation than the daughter of our own dearly beloved President." "Are we not FIRST among nations?" she asked. "The greatest nation of all?"[68]

Marriage and family life contributed directly to notions of American citizenship and national belonging. Americans felt free to express publicly their views of these seemingly private enterprises, even for those they had never met.[69] But as Luci prepared to marry, it was not her ability to fulfill wifely duties or her future plans for motherhood that drew public attention. Instead, the wedding was the real point of public interest. The American public's response to the celebration revealed the typicality of the white wedding. Most writers accepted the white wedding and thus demonstrated just how widespread it had become. The letters expressed views of what a wedding might be and do, proving that even the most popular style of celebration remained open to interpretation. As much as Luci Johnson's wedding fit the "traditional" model advocated by the wedding industry and experts, the modern twist of these traditions did not go unchallenged. Public expectations revealed the overlap between the traditional and the modern, the community and the individual, and the tensions that affected their increasingly muddy dichotomies. In her counsel to young brides, Mary Williams highlighted the public nature of the event: "A wedding is a significant action performed to express the giving and taking of love . . . an acknowledgement that the marriage is more than a private affair, and a public declaration of your love and faith in each other."[70] Many Americans agreed with this view of the wedding as "public declaration" and further believed the public nature of the event invited even more public comment.

* * *

While some citizens expressed their disappointment or anger at the First Family for denying television coverage, individuals expressing such opinions ultimately supported the wedding. Their unhappiness stemmed from limited input on and access to the event. Other objections to the wedding and the First Family related more directly to presidential politics or the perceived ostentation of the celebration style. As she prepared for the wedding, Lady Bird Johnson noted that the Johnson family had lived with constant protest outside the White House since 1965. The First Lady feared that protesters would pepper the streets outside the White House on the wedding day. Lady Bird recalled, "A peace organization has already requested from the National Park Service a permit to picket in Lafayette Park that afternoon." The Shrine would also be a site of protest. Lady Bird wrote, "The Student Nonviolent Coordinating Committee, I think it is—led by Stokely Carmichael—has expressed its intention of picketing as close as possible to the Shrine of the Immaculate Conception." While many American citizens cheered the wedding and wished for even greater access to the celebration, others saw the public nature of the event as an invitation to air their grievances with the politics of the father of the bride and American culture more broadly.[71]

While the protesters were not invited guests, many were Luci Johnson's peers, members of her generation. During the 1960s, more vocal critics of the American Dream, of which the white wedding was a significant part, began to challenge the values that allegedly characterized American society. Unfailing loyalty to American government and unquestioning patriotism were no longer representative of the nation's youth, many of whom expressed growing unhappiness with their country's domestic policies and international actions. Even if this shift in youth culture was most pronounced among a few, the influence of the burgeoning Left eventually expanded to include many young Americans, no longer deferential in the face of age or established authority. Much of the protest was directed at President Johnson, but Luci Johnson was not immune to the public criticism her father faced in his final years of office. Luci's decision to wed in an elaborate ceremony was called into question, especially as racial tensions grew and the United States became more and more embroiled in the war in Vietnam. No matter if a wedding was taking place; in politics, nothing was sacred. As the personal increasingly became recognized as political, a wedding seemed an ideal place to make political statements or air political grievances. Critics saw the wedding as a public performance and a public relations coup for a presidential administration. Seeing the value of such public attention, they seized the opportunity to reach a national audience.[72]

Pat's parents, Gerard and Tillie Nugent, first traveled to the White House to meet the Johnson family on February 14, 1966. At this time the families decided upon August 6 as the wedding date.[73] Considering the travel plans of out-of-town guests and knowing the inconvenience of a weekday wedding, they likely selected August 6 because it was a day agreeable for all wedding participants. For peace activists, the selection of this date was a blatant disregard for the anniversary of the 1945 dropping of the atomic bomb on Hiroshima. Upon the decision of the August 6 wedding date, the Hiroshima World Friendship Center, an organization of Japanese and American pacifists, issued a direct protest. Another organization, the Ad Hoc Committee for the August 6 Protest Against the War in Viet Nam, announced its plan to host a protest at the National Shrine and the White House during the wedding celebration.[74] Carpenter recalled, "The American Embassy in Japan notified the White House Situation Room (home of the Hot Line). Bromley Smith of the National Security staff called me, nervously wondering if we could change the date." Carpenter was irate: "'Yes,' I replied hotly. 'We'll change it to December 7, the day the Japanese bombed us.'" The August 6 wedding date expanded the community of potential protesters to include members of the international community. Carpenter ultimately told Smith, "'Don't you know that a girl sets her wedding date for reasons quite apart from politics. And you tell our ambassador that!'"[75] But just as those imploring Luci to televise the wedding reminded her of her special role, protesters rejected the idea of Luci Johnson's typicality. As the president's daughter, she had responsibilities she could not set aside, even on her wedding day.

Writing on behalf of the World Friendship Center, founder Barbara Reynolds corresponded with both President Johnson and Luci about her objection to the August 6 wedding date.[76] Like those who wished to have Luci's wedding televised, Reynolds emphasized that the "daughter of the President of the United States is not just another girl. She is a symbol." Reynolds moved beyond Luci's national importance and encouraged the First Daughter to consider her influence on the international stage. Reynolds argued that Luci's public role was accompanied by a public responsibility, and she should consider how her decisions might affect those around the world. Were she to ignore that influence and go ahead with her plans to wed on August 6, widely recognized as "Hiroshima Day," Luci would "inflame the resentment of others in Asia and all over the world, resentment which will inevitably be directed against you, your family's official position, and the country you represent."[77] Luci might desire a private family affair, but her choice to celebrate in the popular white wedding style meant that her wedding—an extremely public event—represented more than just a union of a young bride and groom.

Reynolds suggested that Luci might not realize the importance of the date she had selected, being part of the "postwar generation." But this was no excuse. Suzanne Williams, a woman who identified herself as being about Luci Johnson's age, argued that Luci should not, under any circumstances, wed on August 6. Even if Luci was not familiar with the significance of August 6, Williams wrote, "the citizens of Boston, Massachusetts, the U.S.A., and the rest of world are." Imagining herself in Luci's bride-to-be role, Williams noted, "I would not want to go through a ceremony such as marriage on the twenty-first anniversary of the greatest mistake in the history of our country." Imagining her future wedding, Williams saw the date's political significance and expressed an increasingly popular viewpoint that private events represented a political perspective. Williams argued that a bride should look beyond her own desires when planning a wedding. Williams reinforced Reynolds's view of Luci as an international figure and public representative of the U.S. population. She insisted that Luci should consider the American image above and beyond her own desires and remember that her actions had consequences.[78]

Carpenter sent Reynolds and Robinson similar letters, which stated, "I am sure you can appreciate the fact that each young girl selects her wedding date for personal reasons, quite apart from historical considerations."[79] But the two women's letters argued against the idea of Luci as any "young girl." Being in such a public position, they contended, it was selfish for Luci to indulge personal desires over the public image of the American people and government. Each woman highlighted Luci Johnson's responsibility as First Daughter, but in their correspondence, they moved beyond Luci's national importance to emphasize her global significance. Further, the two women rejected the acceptable selfishness allowed in modern weddings. The conflict between personal desire and public responsibility highlighted the growing tension between understandings of public and private life. The wedding, as a combination of both public and private, provided an ideal location for questioning which might take precedence, or if it was possible to separate the two.

Reynolds and Williams emphasized that were Luci to change her wedding date, she would be making a "gesture of peace and goodwill" and would "further world friendship."[80] Luci's wedding stood for more than just a wedding. Its importance moved beyond the couple being wed to affect, Reynolds and Williams suggested, citizens of the United States and people around the world. The public nature of the ceremony was inherently political to many of those who protested the event.

With the nation engaged in an undeclared war in Vietnam, others used Luci's wedding as an opportunity to critique the time and energy dedicated to a wedding during wartime or as a chance to critique the war itself—or both. Jacob Liebson, in a letter to the editor of the *New York Times*, criticized the First Family for spending so much time and money on the wedding planning. "In view of the trouble and turmoil in this country and the seemingly endless war in Vietnam," he wrote, "where so many of our young men are suffering wounds and death, it appears to me the elaborate preparations for the wedding of Luci Johnson are not exactly in good taste. This extravagant display should have received the President's veto."[81] Some citizens likewise chose to rebuke Carpenter for her decision to exclude *Women's Wear Daily* from the ceremony because of the publication's violation of release deadlines. About letters she received, she wrote, "Much of the mail berated me for making such a fuss over a small thing 'when our boys are fighting in Vietnam.'"[82]

Some critics brought attention to Pat Nugent's fairly minimal military service in the Air National Guard, particularly as the number of soldiers serving in Vietnam continued to increase. *Time* noted, "After completing basic training at Lackland Air Force Base in Texas, Airman Third Class Nugent became vulnerable to further criticism by arranging a transfer to Andrews Air Force Base near Washington, to serve the balance of his four-month active-duty tour less than an hour's drive from 1600 Pennsylvania Avenue." When questioned, the Pentagon insisted that such transfers often were granted when possible.[83] Luci's sister Lynda Bird was linked romantically to actor George Hamilton at the time. Hamilton, who had received a draft deferment because he claimed to be the sole financial support for his mother, did nothing to help accusations or assumptions of favoritism as bestowed upon the Johnson daughters' beaus.[84] One angry letter berated Lynda and saw fit to remind her "that every young American male owes it to his country to give a little time to protect the rights and freedoms we now enjoy. And anyone who tries to weasel out of this duty doesn't really deserve to live in this country or call this country his own."[85] With so many young men serving in Vietnam, the Johnson family's seeming avoidance of such hardship invited accusations of hypocrisy or indifference to the plight of the average American.

An anonymous writer from Oak Park, Illinois sent a particularly angry letter. He or she claimed to write on behalf of the "average American citizen" and criticized Luci for her wedding's extravagance and her perceived indifference to those serving in Vietnam. "When you walk down the aisle in Aug.," the letter read, "think of all those 18, 19, 20 year olds sacrificing their lives to make the country safe for the slacker who waits at the other end." Included with the four-page letter were two letters to the editor, presumably from the local newspaper. A. Tarsi from Melrose Park angrily pointed out the inconsistency of the administration's call for thrift and sacrifice and the Johnson family's indulgence in the "huge wedding of Luci's." The other letter, from Mrs. Mary Jalovec, highlighted Nugent and Hamilton's escape from overseas service. "You'll notice that Pat Nugent and George Hamilton," she wrote, "aren't suffering from combat fatigue, jungle rot, ringworm, or the new species of malaria with which hundreds and thousands of boys are afflicted."[86] The letters used the private relationships of the Johnson daughters to highlight their opposition to presidential policies, most specifically, the war in Vietnam. The publicity afforded the wedding created an environment in which citizens could voice their frustrations about the private decisions of this very public family. The cultural significance of the wedding provoked critique about the broader culture in which it existed.

On the day of the wedding itself, war protesters lined up at the National Shrine and the White House. People began gathering at the

Shrine at 7:30 a.m., and by 11:00 a.m., several thousand spectators had arrived. Among those gathered were approximately 30 peace picketers who marched on the sidewalk between the Shrine and the Benedictine Hall. One sign, painted in red, white, and blue letters, read "L.B.J.'s Great Imperialist Society." Nearby were two children's coffins covered with Japanese and North Vietnamese flags. As reported by the *New York Times*, "A white boy wearing a 'Black Panther' button carried a box of rice and a sign saying 'Wedding Rice for Starving Vietnamese.'"[87] The tradition of tossing rice upon the bride and the groom as they departed from their wedding presented protesters with a convenient and timely prop.

Sponsored by the Washington Ad Hoc Committee for August 6 Protest Against the War in Vietnam, the protesters focused on both peace in Vietnam and observance of the atomic bombing of Hiroshima as they advocated a pacifist stand. William Higgs, a man identified as a lawyer for "various radical causes," communicated that the protesters had been horrified to learn of Johnson and Nugent's plan to wed on August 6. Protesters saw it as well within their rights to object to a decision that, to them, was made in such bad taste. Like the letters of Barbara Reynolds and Suzanne Williams, activists believed that August 6 "should be a day not for celebration but for mourning." Later in the afternoon, after the wedding was over, the group joined other protesters for a peaceful demonstration outside the White House. Some chanted a taunt that would become increasingly familiar to President Johnson during his final years in office: "Hey, hey, LBJ! How many kids did you kill today?" Approximately 300 individuals joined to protest the choice of wedding date, presidential policies, and, of course, the war in Vietnam.[88]

Marked by displays of Vietcong flags, posters denouncing the Johnson administration, and folk songs, demonstrations from Hollywood to New York protested the wedding and the war. The *Chicago Tribune* estimated that 21 other cities were also sites of protest. One member of the Student Non-Violent Coordinating Committee theorized that Johnson had had a strategic hand in the selection of the August 6 date. The spokesperson suggested Johnson chose the date as a way to divert international attention away from the peace protests scheduled for the day. Presuming that Johnson used his daughter's wedding for political motives gave protesters free license to use the day for political gain.[89] This view, much like the views expressed by those in support of the wedding, questioned the privileging of bridal authority. Protesters' challenge to authority was twofold: they rejected the authority of the most powerful political figure in the nation, and they rejected the bride's authority to act without regard for public concern.

The protests surrounding Luci and Pat's wedding hinted at heightened protests yet to come. Most Americans in 1966 were war supporters. Only a handful of anti-war groups existed. Veteran political activists and pacifists joined with members of civil rights and New Left organizations to protest the war. To them, the war represented just another example of American imperialism, a distraction from domestic problems that more greatly affected Americans' lives. These views would not have widespread support for several years.[90] Still, this small population was vocal. As President Johnson walked into the Shrine for the wedding rehearsal the night before the actual wedding, someone in a crowd gathered across from the church shouted, "Murderer!" although Johnson appeared not to hear or chose to ignore the taunt.[91] Such protests would become increasingly commonplace during the remainder of Johnson's term of office. Even in 1966, however, the publicity afforded the wedding invited those disagreeing with Johnson's policies to use the wedding as a site where they might voice their opposition.

Coverage of the wedding concluded that Luci's wedding had not been ruined by protesters. Lady Bird, whether determined to ignore the protesters or too busy to pay attention, regally noted in her *White House Diary*, "I myself did not see the pickets. I understand they were there somewhere."[92] Protesters were, in fact, in attendance at the wedding, and others protested more subtly, sending critiques to the White House, writing letters to the editor, or simply refusing to read or watch coverage of the well-publicized event. The wedding, as a public expression of private ideas, invited response and criticism from the American public. Citizens refused to accept or defer to the wedding day authority of the bride. The lines between the personal and the political, the public and the private appeared increasingly vague and likely to overlap. In the decades to follow, men and women would use the intersections of those seemingly competing ideals in their arguments against the white wedding. At the same time, many of those embracing new conceptions of the "political" would use the intersection of public and private life to infuse their own weddings with changing interpretations of gender, sexual relationships, and marriage.

* * *

When all was said and done, to anyone looking in from the outside, Luci Johnson's wedding might have been the wedding of any prosperous American woman. Dressed in a gown created especially for her by renowned designer Priscilla Kidder, the 19-year-old bride glided down the aisle. Flanked on either side by pews filled with family, friends, and the professional connections of her parents, she moved toward an expectant groom who admitted before the ceremony that he was "nervous and excited."[93] Her father, a full foot taller than his young daughter, guided her slowly, "subdued, serious and formal," reluctant to part ways with his soon-to-be-married child. At the end of their walk, the bride hugged her father and moved on to recite her vows and begin married life.[94] Newspaper coverage of the wedding indicated that this might be any wedding of any bride in any church across the United States. But the story ran in papers across the nation, unique because of the bride's role as First Daughter.

Ultimately, Luci Johnson wed with little disruption on August 6, 1966. Lady Bird fondly remembered her feelings of the wedding day. As she sat in the church, she recalled, "I felt a warm tide of love as I walked down the aisle. So many were there who had meant so much in Luci's life from the moment she entered the world!"[95] The wedding allowed those who had known her since birth to witness Luci's transformation into an adult. The day, as captured on film and described in print, was magnificent, a truly resplendent celebration. Networks set up television cameras outside the Shrine, and the arrivals of the First Family, the wedding attendants, and Luci and Pat were captured on film. More than 200 reporters and photographers lined the 36 steps leading to the Shrine's entrance.[96] The American public, while unable to see the wedding ceremony itself, was treated to many scenes of the wedding day pageant. Of course, the unexpected did occur. A hurried wedding day press release contained a typographical error: "Priscilla of Boston taught the bridesmaids how to sin in the car" read the release, when, in fact, Priscilla had instructed the women how to *sit* comfortably while wearing their bridesmaid dresses.[97] Lynda Johnson became faint and nearly passed out from the sweltering temperatures inside the un-air-conditioned Shrine.[98] Following a 42-minute ceremony, the wedding party returned to the White House for the wedding reception. Luci and Pat left for their honeymoon shortly after six o'clock. When the day came to a close, Luci Baines Johnson was married to Patrick John Nugent.[99]

But the seeming ease with which the wedding progressed masked the months of planning that went into the celebration. The idyllic nature of the wedding and the goodwill showered upon the bride and the groom drew attention away from the drama that had engulfed the wedding from the earliest engagement announcement. And while the wedding might look familiar to outsiders, the planning had required tremendous personal investment by those given the task of seeing it prepared to perfection. As she recorded her memories of Luci's wedding, Liz Carpenter identified August 6, 1966 as the climax of "some of the most exhausting, nerve-wracking months of my life." "I managed to live through [it]," she wrote, "but that is all I can say."[100]

Many Americans expressed their desire for greater inclusion in the wedding as public recognition of their affiliation with the First Family. Others saw the wedding as the embodiment of an American lifestyle they found hypocritical and insincere and immoral. Some saw the veneration of the white wedding form as the ultimate insult to those who suffered from war, poverty, or discrimination. Luci and her family may have seen the wedding as an escape from the realities of their daily lives, as a way to flee, albeit momentarily, from the constant pressures of political life accepted as an occupational hazard of Lyndon Johnson's presidential role. But Americans, both those in support of and those in opposition to the wedding, refused to allow the First Family a moment's reprieve from their political position. Luci Johnson's wedding, in fact, legitimated the public discussion of private debates. The wedding highlighted questions about the nature of the communal, the familial, and the individual; who counted among what group; and what influence one population might have on the other.

Young radicals were considering the idea that the personal might also be political. Increasingly, they articulated this vision to raise vital questions of social policy and institutions of power.[101] Unknowingly, mainstream Americans seconded this notion as they identified Luci

Luci and Pat Nugent pose with their wedding party in front of the White House. Photo by Kevin Smith. Courtesy Lyndon B. Johnson Library, Austin, Texas.

Johnson's wedding as a transcendence of the boundaries of public and private. Disagreement over the roles of modernity and tradition in American culture stimulated correspondence with and comment on a political official's family. During the 1960s, at the height of its popularity, the wedding experienced the pressure of a population who debated what the ceremony should be and mean. Luci and Pat Nugent argued for the privacy and primacy of the bride and the groom, while others emphasized the public nature of the ritual. The couple believed they were celebrating in a traditional style, one that the public would recognize and affirm. But tradition remained open to interpretation. Personal fulfillment clashed with what were perceived to be personal responsibilities and valid public suggestions. Even those who agreed on the importance and necessity of the wedding disagreed about how it should be performed, what it should signify, and for whom. Other, more blatant charges against the wedding likewise threatened to undermine the ritual's strength. Challenges to the American way of life and all its components created a landscape in which the white wedding very well might fall from its unofficial position as the standard celebration of American youth. While Luci Johnson and Patrick Nugent's marriage ultimately would end in divorce, the wedding that celebrated their temporary union held great symbolic value during a time of tremendous social and cultural shifts. In the decade to follow, the dividing lines over the wedding's role and import in American life would be drawn more clearly. The celebration's strength would be put to the test.

3

"Getting Married Should Be Fun"

HIPPIE WEDDINGS AND ALTERNATIVE CELEBRATIONS

On June 29, 1971 *Look* magazine, the general-interest American publication based in the tradition of *Life* magazine's photo essay, published an article entitled "Marriage the New Natural Way." In a multi-page spread, *Look*'s middle-class, middle-American readers were treated to a vibrant vision of a wedding celebrated on a daffodil farm in the Virginia countryside. While just a dry run put on for the benefit of *Look*'s readers, the simulation replicated plans for the actual wedding day. A group of young, attractive men and women, bathed in sunlight, celebrated in a field full of trees and flowers. Dressed in colorful garments that reflected contemporary styles and hip fashions, the wedding participants basked in the beauty of nature, untouched by human development.

Designed to reject the conspicuous consumption and empty rituals that some members of American youth increasingly associated with the American Dream and, thus, also with the American wedding, the wedding of Laura Jones and Carl Cummings appeared to be the opposite of the standard white wedding. Guests stood or sat on the ground as the couple recited their vows. A group of college friends provided the musical entertainment. Rather than a catered sit-down dinner, the couple arranged a spread of "pre-technology foods, unpolluted by artificial colors, flavors or preservatives." A variety of honeys, breads, and cheeses covered a picnic table dressed with a patchwork tablecloth. Instead of a tall, white "frosting skyscraper," guests were invited to satisfy the sweet tooth by enjoying a cake composed of dates and nuts. Two Japanese wines served as the celebratory libations. The sake the couple chose to serve held a special significance. "Symbolizing luck, wealth, and longevity," the drink fit perfectly with traditional wedding wishes, even if this new, natural wedding seemed in no way similar to the traditional white wedding that had become the American standard.[1]

This trend to the alternative form of celebration, *Look* reported, was "decried by the makers of bridal veils and mothers-of-the-bride dresses."[2] Beyond manufacturers within the wedding industry, mothers of the bride also might have cause for concern. Neither the bride's nor the groom's parents appeared in the article or the accompanying images. Given the formerly central roles parents, particularly the bride's parents, had played, parental absence suggested a drastic change to the wedding form. While businesses and services within the expanding wedding industry might worry about a narrowed market, *Look* subtly hinted that parents across America might fear exclusion from their own child's wedding. As journalist Marcia Seligson noted in her evaluation of the new wedding, "Mother is but another guest."[3] The guest list did not privilege the relationships of the couples' parents or families. Instead, the attendees represented the relationships the bride and groom had developed, independent of their families and without regard for what might be considered standard wedding etiquette.

The new, natural wedding seemingly created a more egalitarian environment for the wedding guests. No one person was more important than the next. *Look*'s coverage made no mention of bridesmaids or groomsmen, a marked difference from Luci Johnson and Pat Nugent's 24 attendants. The Jones-Cummings's wedding consisted of witnesses ranging from "an attentive Irish setter" to "five children and a six-week-old baby." The bride and groom, students at Virginia Commonwealth University (VCU), used the guest list to reflect the relationships they had developed at the university as they had matured into adulthood. VCU Professor Casey Hughes was in attendance, and a local group, the VCU Combo, provided the wedding's country and western music.[4]

The new wedding celebrated the natural environment, natural food-stuffs, natural fabrics, and, most important, a natural and honest relationship between a bride and groom. A focus on honesty and authenticity pervaded the ceremony as the bride, groom, and their friends aimed to shed association with what a growing number of American youth increasingly regarded as an uninspired, conformist mainstream.[5] The presiding minister of *Look*'s featured wedding, Reverend William Gold, expressed approval of the couple's choice of wedding celebration. To prove his countercultural credibility, *Look* indicated the minister's preference for "rock music instead of the old wedding march."[6] Even religious officials, it appeared, could support this new wedding style.

All elements of this new, natural wedding seemingly pointed to a rejection of the status quo, a rejection of the old, "traditional" style of wedding celebration. Still a wedding style embraced by only a minority of brides and grooms, the "new natural way" of wedding, *Look* suggested, had the potential for great popularity. This "untraditional wedding" was a celebration in direct opposition to the expected form in which a be-gowned bride and an expectant groom exchanged vows, celebrated with formally attired friends and family in a hotel or club or banquet hall, and escaped for a romantic honeymoon getaway. Given the strength of the white wedding ceremony throughout the 1950s and 1960s and the language of "tradition" attached to this wedding style, readers of the mainstream *Look* would understand the implication of the "untraditional" descriptor attached to the ceremony. No doubt they would shake their heads and wonder what American youth was coming to. The white wedding, it seemed, might soon be a relic of a past age as brides and grooms used their weddings to express alternative views of life and love, shaped by beliefs in individualism, the emergent counterculture, and the politics of liberation. Generational divisions, begun in the preceding decades, became more pronounced as the authority assumed by couples led to weddings that looked very different from the postwar standard.

* * *

The Jones-Cummings 1971 celebration reflected a growing trend in wedding celebrations, begun the decade before. Hippie weddings, as unconventional weddings initially were called, reflected a direct connection

Picnic Wedding, from *Look*, June 29, 1971. Courtesy Library of Congress, Prints and Photograph Division.

with the alternative lifestyle embraced by a tiny fraction of American youth, described as "hippies."[7] So named because of the group's derivation from the "hip" culture of the 1950s, hippies had been living in the Haight-Ashbury district of San Francisco since the early 1960s. Pockets of countercultural groups—some identifying as hippies, some rejecting the terminology—lived across the nation, but media paid little attention to this relatively small population before the mid-1960s. Following the January 1967 Human Be-In, news of hip living sparked intense curiosity in the straight world. The idea of hippie culture exploded after the 1967 Summer of Love, when thousands of young Americans traveled to San Francisco to "turn on . . . tune in . . . and drop out." Following the attention given the Haight-Ashbury scene, hippie living became more common beyond the Bay Area as American youth aimed to replicate hip style. Depicted as disciples of experimental drugs, free love, rock music, and a do-your-own-thing approach to life, hippies embraced values considered to be in direct opposition to the values of 1950s Cold War America. As middle-class youth proved susceptible to the hippie allure—even if only in dress and mind-set rather than actual daily living—hip culture became big news.[8]

Personal appearance and style of dress indicated membership in the early hippie community, especially for those in the "straight world," for whom hippies remained something of a puzzle. Appearance likewise served as a marker of alternative weddings, which first grew popular in the mid-1960s as couples aimed to imbue their weddings with a sense of artful simplicity. Like the rest of hippie culture, hippie weddings gained greater national exposure following the 1967 Summer of Love. A move from the expected white gown and tuxedo in favor of the homemade frocks, costumed styles, or colorful dress of the hip scene marked a "hippie wedding."[9] The 1965 wedding of folk singers Roberta Joan Anderson and Chuck Mitchell provides an early example of one such alternative celebration. Held in the front yard of Chuck's parents' Detroit home, the wedding was "rural and rustic." Joni, as Roberta preferred to be called, had made her own dress. Recalling the wedding on a radio program a year later, then-named Joni Mitchell recalled, "There were trees and birds and streams and folksingers and baroque trios hiding in the bushes." Joni and Chuck's wedding represented an earlier 1960s' approach to a different kind of wedding celebration, one that predated the expansion of the counterculture but demonstrated that a change was under way.[10]

Hippie weddings came to appear more performative, especially in the eyes of a public who viewed the hippie as something of a spectacle. The 1968 San Francisco wedding of Francine Nelson and Thomas King fulfilled public expectations of a hippie ceremony to a tee. Nelson chose a short, white gown and bare feet for the ceremony, while King opted for a white Nehru jacket and beads. After the 18-year-old bride and 22-year-old groom were wed in Golden Gate Park, they "kissed and ran dancing through the grass to their communal hippie home in the Haight-Ashbury."[11] Ideas of hippie weddings of the late 1960s continued to conjure up images of barefoot brides and grooms, and a sense of silliness often accompanied this vision. The public viewed these ceremonies as harmless, and jokes about hippie weddings, particularly the difficulty of identifying which participant was the bride and which the groom, peppered the pages of small-town newspapers across the American heartland.[12] The local Pennsylvania newspaper that reprinted news of the Nelson-King ceremony represented the levity with which hippie weddings were regarded, as the paper wryly recounted the presiding reverend's statement that the wedding had been "reverent and digni-fied."[13] Like early visions of hippie culture more broadly, the peace and love espoused at the weddings of flower children seemed a preferable alternative to an angry youth characterized by political demands.

Hippie culture and hippie weddings received disproportionate national exposure, suggesting a larger following than that which existed in reality. But this media caused the population aligning with hippie views to grow.[14] No longer could one assume "street people" to be the sole celebrants of alternative weddings. "Middle-class youths who want something different or find traditional weddings hypocritical or bor-ing" might also find the new style of celebration attractive.[15] In 1970, Roberta Price and her husband-to-be, David, 1968 graduates of Vassar and Yale, respectively, headed out to join Libre, a commune in Huer-fano Valley, Colorado. Before leaving Buffalo, where they had been enrolled as graduate students, they hosted an outdoor wedding celebra-tion. Roberta described the May event as a "mini-Woodstock." Justify-ing their decision to exclude their parents, David told Roberta, "If we're going to get married, we should do it our way, a revolutionary way." Price herself knew that her parents' "angry disapproval" had no place at the wedding they had planned. Held outdoors, the wedding was a communal celebration. As Price recalled, "People arrive[d] in a steady stream, carrying platters of food, bottles of wine, guitars, drums, and flowers." After a friend ordained by the Universal Life Church declared them husband and wife, Roberta and David shed their clothes, swam across a small stream, and embraced under a small waterfall. Guests cheered. After the ceremony everyone ate, drank, and played music by the light of campfire. Even "The Blades," a motorcycle gang that had stumbled upon the wedding, were welcomed as part of the wedding celebration.[16]

The new wedding appealed to members of hip or activist youth pop-ulations as well as those who sympathized with an alternative lifestyle or leftist political vision.[17] One man from Wisconsin recalled his initial view of the hippie wedding: "The first I heard about personal weddings was those kids in California, back in the sixties. I thought it was pretty strange at the time." After seeing several hippie weddings, however, he had a change of heart. As he considered his personal experience with weddings and the planning that occurred the months before, he noted,

"But, then, I also liked the idea. They all seemed to be having a good time, and in my family, everyone gets worried and short tempered for a good month before a wedding. In a way, I thought those kids had the right idea. Getting married should be fun."[18] Other couples agreed. In the eyes of new wedding celebrants, the big wedding and the work and stress involved drew attention away from the most obvious, most important part of the wedding: the union of the couple being wed.

Look's coverage of the new, natural wedding indicated that new approaches to weddings and marriage had attracted "average" American youth, well beyond the urban centers of the East and West Coasts, the alleged bastions of radical behavior and politics. Joined by their peers on their wedding day, Virginia natives Jones and Cummings represented the growing appeal of the untraditional wedding among members of the American youth population. The *Tucson Daily Citizen*'s coverage of a 1968 hippie wedding—"intended not to shock but to inform"—warned readers that the wedding being reported took place "not in San Francisco's Haight-Ashbury or New York's Greenwich Village East, but here in Tucson." The first reported hippie wedding in Chicago was celebrated in 1968 with an early morning service in Lincoln Park and a subsequent "honeymoon" walk through the Lincoln Park Zoo. Two years before *Look*'s coverage, Pennsylvania's *Delaware County Times* published a full-page report of a local hippie wedding.[19] The expanding influence of new wedding styles suggested that new ideas about sex and marriage were reaching typical American brides and grooms rather than solely attracting cultural radicals. *Look*'s middle-class audience could examine the Jones-Cummings wedding in the pages of their *Look* magazine and see a nice young couple, not so different from the young people in their own neighborhoods or families.[20]

Media may have used chronicles of hippie life and behavior as diversions from the seriousness of tense contemporary issues: the war in Vietnam, racial divides on the domestic front, and general political turmoil.[21] The largely student-propelled, politically oriented New Left was never entirely separate from the alternative culture of hippie living, but especially during the late 1960s and early 1970s, the two became progressively more intertwined. As hippie culture became identified as a full-on national counterculture, young activists found they could participate in a politics of group empowerment as well as a politics of personal liberation.[22] While *Look's* coverage of the new wedding focused primarily on the materiality of the celebration and its difference from the expected elements of a wedding ceremony, the natural wedding of Laura Jones and Carl Cummings represented a trend identified by journalists and those chronicling the effects of the youth counterculture as the 1960s became the 1970s.[23] Increasingly, alternative weddings often had a quite serious side. They represented perspectives that allied closely with the social movements of the 1960s and 1970s—both politically and culturally. Unconventional weddings—still called hippie weddings, but often referred to as personal weddings, new weddings, or alternative weddings—reflected an alternative view of American life and values.

* * *

Inspired by their attendance at a personalized wedding celebration of two friends, scholars Howard Kirschenbaum and Rockwell Stensrud conducted an investigation of the trend toward alternative styles of celebration. The two sociologists collected hundreds of interviews for their 1974 analysis of new wedding forms. Based on their findings, Kirschenbaum and Stensrud asserted that many couples rejected the idea of the "traditional wedding" but not the institution of marriage. Couples embraced what Kirschenbaum and Stensrud called the "personal wedding," a ceremony that meant to "affirm new values and new hopes in marriage." Through this alternative form of celebration, brides and grooms showed their individuality and cultural independence as a contrast to the traditional expectations of the ceremony. Many couples interviewed by Stensrud and Kirschenbaum found, "The old way of marrying simply did not meet enough of the needs people felt. . . . By rejecting traditional forms many couples found they could become more personally involved in all parts of the wedding—rituals, vows, prayers, readings, and music." American youth challenged the forms or goals of traditional relationships, but marriage and the wedding, clearly identified as the starting point of marriage, remained important to this generation. Relying still on the sanctity of ritual, couples used the ceremony to declare publicly their expectations for married life. Young men and women of the late 1960s and early 1970s shaped their weddings to communicate a number of personal views: the value of individuality, the belief in countercultural ideals, and alignment with the politics of women's liberation and second-wave feminism.[24]

While the decades following World War II ushered in a singular view of the white wedding ceremony, couples embracing the new wedding had different ideas about the nuptial celebration. Rejecting the call to conformity they believed had influenced so much of 1950s culture, new wedding brides and grooms embraced personal expression over cultural alignment. Schooled to play by the rules and follow direction, children of the postwar baby boom generation likewise had been encouraged to achieve individually and distinguish themselves from their peers.[25] As they moved into adulthood, many young Americans aimed to express their unique individualism in their personal styles and private relationships. As noted of the interviewees featured in *The Wedding Book*, "Each couple wanted a ceremony that was part of them in all ways, that used a new or modified ritual, and that met their expanding human awareness and needs. They weren't interested in the form of the wedding as much as they were in what the ceremony meant to them and their guests." The new wedding provided an opportunity to express both the style and the substance of the couple's relationship.[26]

With the growing focus on and celebration of individuality, the idea that one style of wedding celebration could fit all couples seemed outdated and unrealistic. Not surprisingly, Kirschenbaum and Stensrud's interviews indicated that many brides and grooms abandoned the view that weddings should follow a standard form. Young men and women rejected the notion that couples should be married in the same ritual format in order to maintain social or religious bonds. The decision to have a wedding could be the connection among married couples. The weddings need not be identical. Couples focused on themselves, their connection to one another, and the authentic relationships they shared with their individually selected wedding community.[27] Bill and Kris, a couple from Massachusetts, highlighted their individuality as well as their link to other celebrants in the text of their wedding invitation: "Our wedding is both common and unique—common in that the ceremony is a public affirmation of our values and ritualistic. It is unique in that it is happening to us at this time in our lives and we have our own personal expectations for it."[28] Brides and grooms had specific ideas about what a wedding should be, but only as it pertained to their personal experience. Changes to the ceremony might be minor, but they were essential to preserve the individuality of the couple being wed.

Robert E. Burger, author of the 1973 text, *The Love Contract*, provided men and women with ideas about how to apply the legal concept of a contract to daily living. In his mind, doing so might liberate a relationship and help to preserve the marital bond. Like Kirschenbaum and Stensrud, Burger believed that men and women might imbue their unions with any number of personal touches. This applied to daily rituals as well as larger, more celebrated rituals, such as the wedding. Burger wrote, "The wedding ceremony . . . allows pent-up feelings of exuberance, tenderness, or spirituality to be released. The same ceremony focuses the aspirations and desires of the betrothed, in a sense restricting them. What is most impressive in the lives of most young people, however, is the *liberating* quality of the wedding rites." While Burger suggested that the liberating quality related directly to the liberation of children from the authority of their parents, he went on to emphasize the importance of personal development of the celebration. As he noted, "the rites of love, generally symbolized in the wedding ceremony, are worthwhile and worth cultivating just for themselves and not for their exact significance." Beyond the wedding, couples might remember that "rites of love go on endlessly in the life of a marriage—in many different forms." Once the wedding was over, invention, authenticity, and personalization remained important. Burger's points reflected views of leftward-leaning youth. For many new wedding participants, making the celebration representative of the values that would influence the relationship *beyond* the celebration was a primary goal.[29]

New wedding brides and grooms viewed the wedding as an opportunity to share their individual vision of their relationship. In the eyes of these couples, celebrating in the standard style, without any personalization or variation, suggested complicity with the standard American vision of married life. One woman from New York reflected this view:

> When Gary and I got engaged, we wondered what we would really be saying if we had a traditional wedding. What would it mean? That our life is going to be like everybody else's life? That Gary will go to work and I'll just have kids and stay at home and raise them? And we'll have a

house in the suburbs and live happily ever after? That isn't what either of us wanted for ourselves.[30]

Celebrating in the traditional wedding style indicated alignment with traditional notions about marriage and family life. Believing in the uniqueness of their relationship, this couple required a wedding that was equally unique. Ultimately, the couple settled on a celebration that represented their personal vision of love and marriage and incorporated the ideas and participation of close friends. Describing the ceremony, the bride reported, "We wrote most of our own ceremony with the help of a minister friend who suggested different passages from the Bible. Another friend chose and played the music. We really created our own little world there. . . . We wanted to achieve a very special feeling for ourselves and our guests, and we did it."[31] Religion remained an important component in the wedding celebration, but the religious emphasis came from the couple rather than any institutionalized authority. Spirituality trumped organized religious belief. Personal selection and contribution were paramount.

More assertive about their roles than previous generations, new wedding celebrants embraced the idea of the couple as the central participants of the wedding ceremony and as full partners in wedding planning. While the contest for wedding authority had long existed, new wedding participants were more forceful in their exertion of authority. If spiritual growth and self-realization were the goals, then submission to mainstream notions of expertise, authority, or propriety were the obstacles. Couples would be married by ministers, rabbis, or friends of their choosing rather than the officials of the faiths selected by their parents. Location would be a site of personal significance. The bride and groom would determine the celebration's details. Just as members of American youth culture challenged adult, established authority, so did new wedding celebrants challenge the standard wedding authorities.[32] What many of these brides and grooms failed to realize was that through their contests for and assertions of wedding day control, they were carrying on a postwar wedding tradition.

Brides and grooms placed particular importance on the witnesses to their unions. Couples insisted that the guest list be populated by people close to the couple, not business associates or friends of their parents.

The bride or the groom, not their respective families, provided the link among wedding guests. Each guest should share a personal connection to either the bride, the groom, or, ideally, both. Just as with the marital relationship, brides and grooms believed their relationships outside the bounds of marriage should be authentic and immediate rather than artificial and removed. These guests, seen as contributors to the couple's relationship, might participate in the celebration that made the union official, just as they participated in the couple's lives before marriage. Brides and grooms privileged the uniqueness of their personal relationships, just as they celebrated the individuality of their own relationship.[33]

Some members of the counterculture desired membership in more permanent alternative communities. Several thousand Americans of various ages rejected the "straight" society altogether and embarked on the adventure of creating new communal settlements. Following the 1967 Summer of Love, especially, such settlements popped up throughout the United States. For these men and women, creation of a strong, meaningful community was essential to personal development and, upon coupling, romantic relationships. While outside perceptions of sexual relationships on "hippie communes" ranged from frequent partner swapping to full-blown orgies, the reality was that most romantic relationships more closely resembled "serial monogamy," albeit sometimes without the full acceptance of the marital title, per se. But many couples initiated and then celebrated unions in a manner not so different from their hip peers who remained a part of mainstream American society.[34]

From the time of its 1971 founding, weddings on the Tennessee commune, The Farm, often followed Sunday Meditations. Under the religious leadership of Stephen Gaskin, Farm founder, couples embraced a lifestyle that privileged honesty, spirituality, and love. Inspired by countercultural ideals and a desire to go "back to the land," members of the commune aimed to live a purposeful life marked by cooperation. Gaskin learned, upon arriving in Tennessee, that under state law, he could serve as a preacher to Farm dwellers. Within the first year, Gaskin wed 46 couples. While entirely devoid of the consumerist element of American weddings and hosted without much fanfare, the weddings were still important events. In contrast to widespread ideas of communes as hotbeds for unchecked sexual activity, the Farm privileged monogamy and promoted life-long commitment. Thus, celebrations conducted in front of all community members held special significance. As Ina Mae Gaskin recalled, couples "were promising certain things—commitment being a basic one no matter whether you were sick or healthy, rich or poor. There was a lot of respect, too." As described by Michael Traugot, in his history of The Farm, "The combined attention of two hundred folks in a worshipful mood, after meditating silently for 45 minutes and singing a long 'om' together, all paying close, minute attention to the couple, feeling with them, wish them well, was like bonding with the entire community." Every Farm resident was a part of this very different style of wedding celebration.[35]

Alternative brides and grooms continued to privilege the public function of ritual and community witness in their celebrations. But they demanded acceptance of their life choices, no matter how unconventional. Robert Burger used the example of a young couple who "walk up the aisle with a baby in their arms." As Burger noted, the couple might assert that their "marriage" or "contract" began at the time they first started living together, or when their baby was born. Others might view the wedding of two who had long ago consummated their union to be somewhat "humorous . . . because it strikes a chord in human sensibilities as the *ritual* which somehow seems to be lagging behind the real contract." Burger argued that even out of expected order, a union publicly solidified before a community of witnesses was a necessary part of the social process. "What we don't realize," Burger wrote, referring to a couple wed after years spent together, "is that the ritual *is* the contract in this case, because it is the *acknowledgement before the community*." The personal nature of the celebration could and should be shared between a couple and also among their family and friends. Burger was direct in his advice: "[M]ake the most of all ceremonies, celebrations, and observations that come your way. See them as things in themselves. See them for their value to you—in allowing you and your loved ones to lead a fully *social* life. Create your own personal way of celebrating love and living."[36]

Rather than relying on the help of professionals, many new wedding brides and grooms found they could personalize their weddings by doing most of the planning themselves. If couples took advantage of the many available wedding services, their autonomy in the wedding planning could be jeopardized as "experts" planned the wedding based on the standard model. Hosting a wedding in a banquet hall or hiring a catering service removed both the couple and the guests from the celebration. One man, whose father-in-law offered the couple any kind of reception they desired, reported that he and his wife were uncomfortable with the idea of an elaborate reception. "We wanted people to remember the *wedding*, which we had taken such time to plan."[37]

Another one of Kirschenbaum and Stensrud's interviewees indicated that he enjoyed the many hours he dedicated to the planning of his wedding reception: "[A]fter we realized that the wedding would be very special, we decided it would be senseless not to carry that feeling to the reception, too. After all, it was *our* party. We wanted a hand in planning the details." Friends contributed food and liquor while the couple's parents and some other friends helped to prepare the food and clean up. The informality of the party made everyone comfortable, and when all was said and done, the groom concluded, "It was one hell of a good party, too!"[38] By focusing on the emotional rather than the material, couples aimed to enhance the meaning of their celebrations.

Couples broke from cultural, familial, or religious expectations as they endeavored to create a celebration that communicated future hopes, but they often aimed to infuse celebrations with elements of their past experience and influences. Rabbi Richard J. Israel advised many young couples who wished to intermarry across faiths. While he indicated that, as a leader in the Jewish faith, he wanted "very much to break up the impending marriage," he also recognized the likelihood that he would "not succeed."[39] While Israel would not participate in marriage ceremonies for those choosing to intermarry without conversion to the Jewish faith, he believed he had a responsibility to counsel such couples, and he encouraged other rabbis to do the same. He credited couples wishing to write their own weddings for their preparedness: "They have a view of marriage and its meaning. They have an image of the future they want for themselves and a notion of the kind of community with which they wish to be affiliated. I am willing to encourage them to devise a liturgy which will express these views in a public ceremony." Despite his preference for a more traditionally Jewish union and celebration, Israel appreciated the possibilities provided by couples' creations of alternative celebrations, and expressed his willingness to support such pairings. About his experiences working with couples to create personally significant celebrations, he wrote that the process met "a series of standards which are important to me; it fits the integrity of the couple and does not force them to lie at an important occasion of their lives. It forces them to think about their life commitments together in a serious way. It does not force me to 'rent out' the Jewish tradition."[40]

Similarly, ministers who presided over new or alternative weddings often emphasized the forethought and planning that went into the ceremony.[41] But this planning differed from the planning recommended by the many advice books couples had relied upon in the past. Men and women thought more about their relationships than the requisite ceremonial components or the suggested protocol of a white wedding. Most couples did not opt for a nontraditional wedding in order to shock or embarrass their families. Like Jones and Cummings, other new wedding celebrants made choices based on personal preference rather than social or familial expectations. Focusing on individual desire and the potential for personal fulfillment within marriage, new wedding brides and grooms were not anti-family, but instead embraced an altered idea of the family, one that encouraged each partner in a relationship to continue achieving individual growth and personal satisfaction.[42]

One member of Twin Oaks, a commune located in rural Virginia, recorded her surprise at the response provoked by her desire to host a wedding in 1975. While there were no rules against marriage, Linda Merion assumed it just was not done. She anticipated criticism for wanting to embark on a relationship she feared others would see as laced with "possessiveness, jealousy, dependency." As she recalled, "It was scary to announce our intentions. I wondered if people would be utterly offended, tell me that I was crazy, regressive, in general, a bad seed."[43] Rather than being censured, however, Merion was met with "open-minded" curiosity. She recalled that the spirit of the wedding affected everyone involved:

> I was overwhelmed by people's help and support in arranging the wedding. People cooked and cooked, picked flowers, sewed and embroidered, made beautiful cakes, churned ice cream, cleaned and cleaned the

house, the yard, everything. My parents, Daniel's family, and his older brother's family came and stayed with us, getting acquainted and helping with preparations. It was such a high time that folks whom I might have otherwise considered too different to get along were all working together, happy together. It was inspiring to see us all doing our best for this occasion. I was happily surprised at how well we got the whole thing together.[44]

Merion's initial visions of a wedding and marriage—and her trepidation regarding popular response—were shaped by the mainstream expectations of white wedding ideal and traditional marriage. She believed the wedding celebration reflected only one set of values. What she came to realize, however, was that she and her husband-to-be, along with their friends, could create a vision of a wedding—and, by association, a marriage—that fit with their lifestyle and beliefs.

Two officiants presided over the outdoor ceremony—Daniel's father and a local minister. Friends played Mozart and performed songs they had written for the occasion. Reverend Williams, the local minister, offered an official speech of welcome to the communal group, noting that they had proven themselves to be wonderful neighbors. Nearly 100 guests attended the celebration. As Merion noted, "It was so good to see ourselves as part of this whole society of simple rural folks, all joining together in this celebration—a ceremony recognized in so many lands for so many centuries as an expression of the love and the joy that we can all share and reflect."[45] The public nature of the celebration cemented the private relationship she shared with her husband. Being part of a network of committed, caring people made the wedding ceremony even more meaningful.

Beyond their commitment to individuality and personal consequence, couples' efforts to make marriage relevant to contemporary social circumstances and political beliefs inspired alteration of the wedding form. Khoren Arisian justified the need for his 1973 wedding guide, *The New Wedding: Creating Your Own Marriage Ceremony*, by emphasizing the importance of the new wedding and the reason for its creation: "As a permanent institution marriage is dignified and strengthened by ceremonial observance. Only in stagnant times does such observance become archaic, absurd, and worthy of satire. But in times of change, ceremonial observance becomes even more pertinent and vital as it expresses the dynamics of the day."[46] As Rockwell Stensrud speculated more than 30 years after *The Wedding Book* was published, "[C]ouples . . . rewrote their ceremonies to reflect more honestly their view of themselves and the changing world they inhabited."[47] As a site of such personal importance, the wedding provided the perfect location for expressing the cultural and political beliefs that were so important to the participants.

New wedding celebrants identified as part of a new generation and a new culture.[48] Because so many young couples believed that their relationships differed from the relationships of their parents and generations before them, they believed that their weddings should reflect this difference. Suspecting that their parents' generation had succumbed to societal pressure and entered into "compulsory marriages," many young brides and grooms imagined that they represented a new kind of couple and thus required a new kind of wedding. They entered into their unions with what they considered to be more realistic expectations about the difficulty of sustaining a marriage and the possibility that the marriage might not last forever.[49] While the pomp of the white wedding never lost its appeal entirely, enough brides and grooms found the practiced language and rehearsed components incompatible with their view of themselves and their relationship to reject the white wedding style altogether. Those celebrating with a new wedding strove to make sure that their weddings reflected their visions of married life and their place within the broader culture, or, increasingly, within the expanding counterculture.

As they endeavored to infuse their celebrations with countercultural views, alternative wedding celebrants blended 1960s political activism with the lifestyle focus of the early hippies. So-named by Theodore Roszak in his 1968 study, *The Making of a Counterculture*, the counterculture was "a vision that, to one degree or another, drew the attention and fascination of passing many." To Roszak, the counterculture was most notable for questioning the most rudimentary aspects of American life. In his reconsideration of the counterculture three decades after his initial study, he wrote that countercultural dissent produced "the most ambitious agenda for the reappraisal of cultural values that any society has ever produced. Everything was called into question: family, work, education, success, child rearing, male-female relations, sexuality. . . . The meaning of wealth, the meaning of love, the meaning of life—all became issues in need of examination"[50]

The politics of liberation increasingly focused on the idea of personal liberation. Young men and women believed in the necessity of implementing their personal, political beliefs into their daily lives. As countercultural ideals made their way into the American mainstream, more brides and grooms integrated characteristics of the counterculture into their weddings. While the counterculture may have been fading by the mid-1970s, ideas of the counterculture continued to influence American youth across the United States. As noted by sociologists Lester Kirkendall and Robert Whitehurst, hippies and flower children set a standard of behavior that influenced youth, even those who refused "to adopt their extremes of dress, and [did] not feel the intense need to rebel."[51] Instead, they found other ways of expressing their alignment with this alternative lifestyle. Demonstrating countercultural sensibility, couples infused their celebrations with specific values such as authenticity, honesty, and personal autonomy.[52]

New wedding participants expressed determination to make sure their ceremonies reflected their personal beliefs. Relying on the standard model, one that held no individual meaning, was akin to committing an act of dishonesty. One interviewee from Texas told Kirschenbaum and Stensrud that she and her fiancé "talked it over and agreed to make a few changes to our service. Nothing dramatic, you know, but enough to make us feel more honest about the whole thing."[53] Reverend A. Myrvin DeLapp of Philadelphia echoed this view: "Their great concern is for the honesty of the human relationship; the sense of personhood is to be honored and respected. They don't view marriage as simply entering into a contract, nor the wedding as a performance. They want their marriage to have the fullest possible meaning, validity and integrity."[54] A desire for honesty and authenticity inspired men and women to embrace an individualized approach to their weddings. This new approach allowed a familiar ceremony to be infused with new meaning.

Countercultural values also led to the introduction of new styles of wedding dress. As noted by Charles Reich in his evaluation of countercultural American youth, clothing held special significance. The embrace of informal garments composed of natural materials rejected the status associated with expensive fashions. A new wedding bride might opt against the pricey, traditional white wedding gown for a garment that was inexpensive, comfortable, and expressed her individuality. She was not just another bride in another big, white gown. Grooms likewise rejected the formality of a suit or tuxedo and instead chose comfortable garments, such as the corduroy pants, horse-bit belt, and free-flowing shirt worn by Carl Cummings at his daffodil wedding. The feeling and meaning of the wedding rather than materiality were the focus. But clothing could still play an important role in the couple's self-expression. As noted by Reich, "The new clothes express a shared set of attitudes and values. They express the new unity of youth, and the reality of the new consciousness. It is not an exclusive society; the smiles are for anyone who will smile back." For example, Roberta Price described having worn a "turn-of-the-century, intricately embroidered white lawn slip dress . . . found in a junk-antique shop in Buffalo" over a full nude bodysuit. David wore a "white fitted shirt with a deep V neck and dark blue velvet bell-bottoms" and "beads he bought at a reservation store near Cherokee, North Carolina, after his father's funeral."[55] The greater informality or individuality of new wedding attire, some believed, allowed the couple being wed and those witnessing the celebration to feel more relaxed during the celebration, and thus able to enjoy the wedding more.[56]

New weddings differed from those of the past in part because relationships before the wedding were so different. Couples rejected notions of 1950s propriety as they engaged—openly and unabashedly—in premarital sexual relationships and, in a dramatic break from long-accepted moral codes, premarital cohabitation. While sexual freedom may have suggested a steady round of bed-hopping to observers (and in some instances, this certainly was the case), many countercultural youth interpreted sexual freedom as an opportunity to design new codes of sexual morality rather than do away with morality altogether.[57] Reverend Cecil Williams of the Glide Memorial Church in San Francisco presided over many new weddings and often came to know the couples quite well. He noted of the brides and grooms he joined in marriage, "Almost all of them have already been living together, so they see their wedding as a celebration of what has already begun. They want to announce to the world with their friends that they are coming together in a new kind of meaningful commitment."[58] The wedding represented a confirmation of the relationship rather than the relationship's beginning. By hosting a wedding after already having lived together, couples demonstrated that they were choosing to wed rather than feeling that they must.[59]

Shirley Wise, once a regular in the Haight-Ashbury hippie scene, expressed a desire to marry once and only once. But she rejected the notion that what she desired was a "traditional" marriage. She stated, "The thing that isn't traditional is that I won't get married because I want to sleep with somebody. . . . But I don't feel that you've got to have permission from society in order to live with somebody."[60] Beyond commitment to the idea of sexual freedom, Wise also reflected the countercultural questioning of authority. Rejecting "traditional" values as false, new wedding brides and grooms viewed their alteration of the wedding ceremony as a protest against social expectations that neither appealed to nor made sense to their new lifestyle approach. Speaking in 1968, Wise publicly and unashamedly presented a view that continued to challenge accepted relationship norms but would have been nearly unthinkable a decade before.[61] The introduction and legalization of an effective birth control pill in 1960 and a changing social and sexual culture allowed for a new view of marriage and a new view of romantic relationships, more broadly.[62] Reinterpretations of the relationships between the sexes inevitably led to reinterpretations of the standard wedding form, and a feminist perspective influenced the course of many new weddings.

In some of the most popular chronicles of the new wedding, observers specifically credited the Women's Liberation Movement with the move away from the traditional wedding. A feminist perspective altered expectations for marriage and thus led to the modification of the wedding celebration.[63] In the late 1960s, many women of New Left became increasingly vocal critics of the inequality between the sexes, both within the movement and within American culture more broadly. Women's liberationists built upon the early successes of the National Organization for Women (NOW) while challenging NOW's mission. They hoped to change not only the way women participated in the existing society; they wanted to change society altogether. Activists demanded change within the marketplace and political arena, but they also strove to revolutionize personal relationships and domestic roles and expectations.[64]

The perceived relationship between the personal and the political expressed by new wedding brides and grooms demonstrated a direct link to the fight for women's liberation and the New Left more broadly. Most famously, women who identified as feminists opted to remove "obey" from their marriage vows. Many new wedding ministers supported this decision and changed other chauvinistic elements of the standard ceremony.[65] Claiming a desire for a more egalitarian partnership, men and women of feminist leanings found the standard white wedding incompatible with their personal relationships and public political beliefs.[66] One woman from Texas expressed very clearly a feminist perspective in her decisions to alter the standard wedding language and personalize it to fit her beliefs:

> For one thing, I never liked the idea of my father "giving me away" like I was a piece of merchandise or a prize farm animal. I also didn't like the part in the service where it says "to love, honor, and obey." Love and honor, yes. But obey—forget it! I may be getting picky but I also didn't like that bit, "I now pronounce you man and wife." To me that's like saying he's a person and I'm his possession. It's just as ridiculous as saying, "I now pronounce you woman and husband."[67]

While the politics of women's liberation initially may have appeared to be at odds with the celebration of a wedding, and as some members of the movement declared, at odds with marriage altogether, the belief that the personal was political allowed women to shape their weddings—personal but also public events—to express their political views. As women's liberationists declared the private domain the starting point of women's political oppression, the reclaiming of the wedding as a site of political relevance allowed feminists to celebrate a wedding without betraying their political principles.[68]

Feminist politics called for a union committed to equality and personal development. A focus on honesty and personal expression pervaded the motivations of many new wedding participants. Women reclaimed the marital relationship and family as the sites of personal politics as they rejected the call to embody the political ideal projected by advertisements, media, or government.[69] Feminists aimed to make their personal and individual lives sites of political activity as defined by themselves and on their own terms. One woman from New York demonstrated how a different style of ceremony reflected both a different relationship before marriage and a hope for a different kind of marital relationship. She recalled, "We made our wedding different from the usual because we wanted it to symbolize a life that would be different—one with more interaction, acceptance, and caring—more flexible roles."[70] This woman and her fiancé embraced the intersection of public and private provided by the wedding. The couple wanted to be sure the wedding provided an accurate public display of their private relationship and their political ideals.

Personal participation in the Women's Liberation Movement also influenced new wedding brides. A woman from Virginia who became increasingly politically active over the course of her relationship related how she and her fiancé came to an agreement regarding marital division of domestic tasks. "We made a loose contract of sorts," she said. "I wanted this not so much because I thought Peter would turn on me and shackle me down once we were married, but because I wanted my ideals and values made public, at the wedding. I didn't want anyone to be mistaken and think we were just another young couple doing the usual thing." Stressing the importance of individuality, this woman indicated her need for personal autonomy but also for recognition that her relationship was not just like every other relationship. And so, her wedding could not be just like any other wedding. Worried that she was presenting her fiancé as a detached observer, she noted:

> (I'm afraid this sounds too much like only I had these ideals. Peter agrees completely. He was the one who suggested the contract in the first place.) So our wedding vows were actually what we agreed to in the contract, which essentially declared our own separate identities and our equality as two people in a journey together in matrimony.[71]

This couple not only rejected the unequal division of wedding labor but also the prescriptive behavior they believed influenced so many married couples. Through their wedding, they refused pre-designed roles and communicated how their vision of married life differed from larger social and cultural expectations.

In the vision of a new wedding shaped by feminism and women's liberation, men, for the first time, became recognized as contributing participants in the wedding celebration. No longer was the father of the bride or the presiding minister the sole vocal male. Kirschenbaum and Stensrud included male new wedding participants' comments in their evaluation of the new wedding, and these men reflected the emphasis on egalitarianism and honesty within the marital relationship. One couple, Betsy and Alex, embodied the sharing of labor and the desire for expression so typical of new weddings. As the couple prepared to be married, they read through the Book of Common Prayer from 1549, 1560, and 1602. Determined to use the Elizabethan language, Alex remembered, "The heavy emphasis on obedience and duty was something neither Betsy nor I wanted in our wedding, so we had to choose with care." The couple combined elements of the past with a personal and modern philosophy of marriage to create a unique celebration.[72] The integration of feminist politics into the wedding ceremony allowed for personal expression and emotional intimacy and allowed that men, too, might join in the process of defining wedding goals. In a turn from literature that focused solely on the bride, often recommending how she might prepare her groom for the wedding day, new wedding texts spoke to both the bride and the groom. In an attempt to reflect the desire for emotional egalitarianism, these texts suggested that an equal division of wedding labor and decision-making would create a foundation for a marriage committed to the same values.[73]

On their vision of the egalitarianism in their relationship, one new wedding celebrant concluded, "The main thing is that we made these feelings public. . . . I think we got away from some of the deviousness that can easily happen in a marriage by trying to get as much as possible out in the open. To me, that's a lot of what love is."[74] By being open and honest—and in a public way—couples might avoid the pitfalls that led to the failure of so many marriages. With a growing divorce rate looming overhead, many young couples thought long and hard before deciding to move into a marital relationship.[75] The wedding allowed for an expression of their thoughtfulness. In the ceremony, they might declare publicly why they believed their marriage would survive and what steps they planned to take in order to ensure their relationship's survival.

Radical feminists staged various protests against the wedding, from guerilla theater performances and picketing at bridal fairs—bazaars of opportunity for wedding expenditure—to consciousness-raising sessions that questioned the very nature of the relationship between the sexes.[76] For women's liberationists, the white wedding as celebrated in its popular postwar form represented the many layers of women's oppression: patriarchal control of women and the family; socialized and racialized expectations of female beauty; targeting of women as conspicuous consumers; and the presumption that women gladly deferred to these expectations. Robin Morgan, a public face and well-known champion of the women's movement, recalled her own 1962 marriage to Kenneth Pitchford. Even before her feminist awakening, Morgan demonstrated nervousness about her impending marriage and the expected marital roles as she vowed to maintain her independence while fulfilling all of her husband's expectations. As a twenty-one-year-old bride, Morgan declared, "I will remain me."[77]

Morgan came to feminism in the late 1960s, several years after she married Pitchford, and afterwards became a vocal "'feminist' committed to a Women's Revolution." Thinking back to the unrealistic social expectations of her female adolescence and young adulthood, Morgan channeled her energy and anger into her political participation and feminist writing. She described these emotions in her introduction to *Sisterhood is Powerful*, the earliest collection of women's liberation literature, in a list of "Barbarous Rituals" endured by American women. Added to the collection as an anonymous contribution, Morgan later claimed the list in *Going Too Far: The Personal Chronicle of a Feminist*. Reprinting the piece because of the response it received upon its first publication, Morgan confessed her early fear of admitting to the anger and vulnerability she expressed in the article. Women identified with any and all parts of the list, glad to know they were not alone in their distaste for what they had assumed to be "natural" female behaviors. Inspired by her personal "memories, fears, dreaded expectations, and fury," Morgan included specific grievances against the standard white wedding on her list.[78] Among the "Barbarous Rituals" she described were:

- going the rounds of showers, shopping, money worries, invitation lists, licensee—when all you really want to do is live with the guy.
- quarreling with your fiancé over whether "and obey" should be in the marriage ceremony
- secretly being bitched because the ceremony says "man and wife"—not "husband and wife" or "man and woman." Resenting having to change your (actually, your father's) name.
- having been up since 6:00 A.M. on your wedding day seeing family and friends you don't even really like and being exhausted from standing just so and not creasing your gown and from the ceremony and reception and traveling and now being alone with this strange man who wants to "make love" when you don't know that you even like him and even if you did you desperately want to just sleep for fourteen hours, *or*
- *not* getting married, just living together in "free love," and finding out it's just the same as marriage anyway, and you're the one who pays for the "free."[79]

Morgan debunked the notion that a woman's wedding day—when celebrated as a white wedding—was the best day of her life. Social expectations might not fit with personal preference, but these expectations exerted tremendous influence on brides-to-be, most of whom had learned they should anticipate the wedding day as a woman's crowning glory. Morgan criticized not only the language of the wedding but also the pre-wedding rituals women were expected to embrace and skillfully deploy. Critiquing the division of wedding labor, Morgan questioned the necessity of what prescriptive literature would have termed "requirements" for wedding planning. Morgan protested the behaviors society expected a woman to adopt and enjoy as she prepared to be married, emphasizing how this vision often failed to consider the desires of the woman herself. Demonstrating that a woman's displeasure with the wedding process was not a singular experience, Morgan described practices with which others might identify and from which they might gain a sense of solidarity. And as other women came to their own wedding planning, those reading Morgan's list in the early 1970s might challenge the wedding socialization process and more vocally assert their displeasure with wedding language or expected wedding forms.

* * *

Alternative weddings caused much public contemplation. In 1970, Dorothy Le Sueur of the *Washington Post* speculated, "By the end of this decade, the traditional wedding dress may be a thing of the past along with the arbitrary 'obey' in conventional nuptial rites." Le Sueur was not the only one to notice the change. The white wedding appeared to be in serious danger. As the late 1960s ushered in the rise of new, alternative forms of wedding celebrations, and the 1970s saw unconventional wedding styles grow in popularity, observers raised questions about the sustainability of the wedding ceremony altogether. In their varied forms—the personal wedding, the hippie wedding, the new wedding—alternative celebrations represented the same trend toward re-imagining the traditional white wedding. Drawing attention to barefoot brides and grooms, ceremonies held on mountaintops, and unconventional requests sometimes asked of wedding guests, American media highlighted these new wedding forms. By all accounts, tradition was out. "Doing your own thing" was in.[80]

Concerns over the nature of the wedding celebration demonstrated just how important the ceremony had become in American life. In the politically charged sixties and seventies, a wedding communicated a great deal about the couple being married. New ideas about sex, gender, and marriage all made their way into the celebration and served as a reflection of the couple's values and views. Marriage and family played a central role in postwar understandings of the American nation, and personal relationships were bound up in the domestic component of the American battle to win the Cold War. Like the institution of marriage, the wedding represented core American values and ideals. It had become the quintessential starting point of American marriage, and adherence to the traditional model suggested an alignment with the values of the recent past.[81] Questions about what the white wedding should be and do had changed to become questions about whether a white wedding was the best form of celebration, or merely an outdated relic.

As baby boomers bred in "homeward bound" families grew to maturity, they questioned earlier interpretations of the ways in which the personal was also political. They found their personal lives could reflect their politics and persuasions rather than reflecting the vision encouraged by business, government, or media. New wedding participants, many of them politically active, adopted "the personal is political" as their mantra, and they went on to apply it to their relationships, homes, and families, in ways earlier generations never would have imagined. While each factor that moved couples away from the white wedding—individualism, countercultural values, and women's liberation—played a distinct role in influencing alternative wedding celebrations, the three components intertwined, almost seamlessly, to make new weddings representative of a specific time and place. As modern brides and grooms altered wedding traditions to fit contemporary beliefs, bystanders wondered what these alterations meant for the future of the American wedding and American marriage more broadly.

4

"Lots of Young People Today Are Doing This"

THE WHITE
WEDDING
REVIVED

In 1978, a young Barnard College graduate began the process of planning her wedding. As the bride-to-be—a working woman and vocal feminist—filled out the paperwork for her wedding license, she was surprised to find that there was no place on the form for her occupation. When she asked the clerk at City Hall where she should provide that information, the woman responded, "Oh, we don't ask the girls for their occupations." The bride insisted her profession be recorded, and the kindly clerk willingly obliged. "Well, we've never done that before," she said, "but . . . all right, sweetheart, what is it?" Twenty-six-year old Anna Quindlen—future columnist for the *New York Times* and *Newsweek*, novelist, and Pulitzer Prize winner—asked the woman to type in "newspaper reporting." "Well, isn't that exciting," the clerk proclaimed. She then asked, "Have you quit your job now that you're tying the knot?"[1] New weddings may have raised questions about the white wedding's staying power, but old ideas held strong.

Chronicling the months leading up to her wedding in the pages of *Ms.* magazine—the publication born of women's liberation—Anna Quindlen grappled with the inevitable tension faced by someone who was both a feminist and a woman raised in an American culture that venerated the white wedding. Like Robin Morgan before her, Quindlen recognized and admitted to the often ridiculous nature of the wedding process. Wryly reporting on the process of choosing a wedding dress, the bride-to-be concluded, "There is no serious way to shop for a wedding gown." But even as she noted the silliness of bridal consultants who had "only a first name with the word 'Miss' in front of it," and filled their days seeing one grown woman after another clad only in their undergarments, Quindlen also recognized that these women bore witness to the intimate, sometimes heartbreaking moments that only took place in anticipation of a wedding. "They hear daughters tell their mothers that they don't want to marry their fiancés," Quindlen wrote, "and they also hear mothers tell their daughters that the caterer's deposit is nonrefundable." Quindlen realized some American brides celebrated a white wedding for reasons other than expectations of connubial bliss— to experience the excitement of the day, to legitimate a pregnancy, to join the adult married world, to make their families proud. Even as she wrote of these women with a sense of melancholy, she was undeterred by the less romantic vision of the American wedding. Like the alternative wedding brides and grooms that had come before, Anna Quindlen and her fiancé, Gerald Krovatin, would have the wedding they wanted. But their desires were somewhat different than their recent predecessors: they would celebrate their marriage with a white wedding.[2]

Quindlen explicitly expressed her disinterest in the possibility of a new wedding celebration. In her *Ms.* article, she highlighted the wedding's cultural cachet and the ways it had affected her ideas about the ceremony. Pointing specifically to the influence of the Madame Alexander "bride doll," Quindlen was clear about the power of this childhood ideal: "[I]t shaped my adult life, emerging as the primary reason why I did not want to wear a sensible suit, a chaste column of crepe, or a Mexican dress for my wedding. I wanted to *be* a Madame Alexander doll." But if she knew exactly what she wanted, she was just as specific in realizing what she did not want: "monogrammed cocktail napkins, a new name, an umbrella with streamers on it, life insurance, a Merry Widow undergarment, and engraved stationary from Tiffany's."[3] Quindlen wanted the white wedding she wanted. Rather than following each suggested detail to a tee, she would pick and choose, making the wedding specific to herself and her husband-to-be. Admitting publicly and unabashedly to *Ms.* readers that she had dreamed of her wedding gown since girlhood, Quindlen proclaimed her desire to have it all: "What I wanted was to be the feminist I'd always been, the journalist I'd managed to become, and the—let's face it—vision of loveliness I'd always hoped for one shot at being."[4] Quindlen wanted to have her wedding cake and eat it, too.

Anna Quindlen's 1978 white wedding and her very public desire for such a wedding present something of a puzzle. The beginning of the 1970s witnessed the declaration of the white wedding's impending—but seemingly certain—fall from favor. The old-fashioned white wedding was to become a relic of the not-so-distant past. By all accounts, new weddings were the rage. Or so it seemed. The evolution of the wedding celebration was more complicated than a mere replacement of one style with another. Alternative wedding couples had shaped the wedding to fit their personal preference. Along the way, couples who desired a white wedding likewise recognized the opportunity to individualize the ceremony. Even the white wedding—assumed and alleged to be the traditional style—might be modernized. A couple could embrace the tone and spirit of the familiar white wedding, marry in the traditional ceremony, and still be thoroughly modern.[5]

Quindlen struggled with the desire to have a white wedding. "On a good day, I could almost see the whole scenario as an answer to the not-quite-cosmic question," she wrote. "Can a woman who is assumed to have clawed her way to the top waltz her way up the aisle and not be trashed? It was not unlike my old college quandary—can a bona fide feminist wear eye shadow?"[6] Ultimately, Quindlen believed she could celebrate a white wedding and still maintain her feminist credibility. She would not adopt her husband's name; she would continue working; and she flatly rejected a suggested prayer that would have had her promise that she would never forget the importance of her husband's work to his happiness and that she would sacrifice her life for her children. As she recalled the prayer, she noted, "That was when I first began to see the connection between marriage and drowning." But the recognition of that connection did not deter her. Like feminists of the late 1960s and early 1970s, Quindlen believed she could work with her husband—who supported each decision she made—to make a ceremony and a partnership that would reflect her political and personal values.[7] By challenging the expectations of what a white wedding might mean, Quindlen effectively legitimized the use of traditional wedding components beyond the interpretations formulated by new wedding brides and grooms. Quindlen and Krovatin found expression through the celebration of a new white wedding.

The modern version of the white wedding, Quindlen concluded, need not be in opposition to a bride or groom's personal and political values. Quindlen's wedding, from the outside, might appear traditional and conformist, but her *Ms.* article proved that the couple had worked tirelessly to create a perfect blend of wedding styles that reflected their personal desires. Having struggled to make the wedding representative of herself, her politics, and her relationship, the bride-to-be made sure that her old-fashioned wedding included modern ideals. But Quindlen did not invent this marriage of the old and the new. Many other couples similarly came to this realization, and well before the close of the 1970s. The white wedding, like the new wedding, could be shaped to reflect a couple's individual beliefs, be they liberal or conservative, socially radical or religious in practice. Quindlen merely followed—and through her article, called attention to—a trend that had been overshadowed by a widespread fascination with the new wedding. The white wedding lent itself to personalization and expression, and brides and grooms eagerly embraced the opportunity to share their views in a recognizable wedding form.

* * *

By the late 1960s, the white wedding had acquired a public reputation for garishness. Kitty Hanson's 1967 *For Richer, For Poorer* painted, at best, an unflattering picture of the American wedding. Looking specifically to the wedding industry, Hanson reported, "Working on the principle that the surest way to turn a luxury into a necessity is to endow it with status, the wedding merchants have been able, within the space of the past twenty years, to transform the wedding ceremony from a dignified ritual into a gaudy rite." Hanson indicted the business side of weddings, but she was equally unwilling to let brides, grooms, and their families off the hook. The wedding industry merely responded to the demand of an eager consumer market. As white weddings grew in size and scope, Hanson argued that they lost the personal meaning they had once possessed.[8] The perceived focus on material excess and the seemingly mindless following of a standardized form led, not surprisingly, to the young generation's critique and often full rejection of the white wedding. These young men and women, with their suspicion of affluence, distrust of authority, and desire for self-expression, inevitably looked to a different way of celebrating entry into marriage.

Because they were so different from the modern white wedding, hippie and alternative weddings of the early 1960s and early 1970s caught the eye of many social observers. Some of these weddings veered into the realm of the bizarre. Sometimes they were as marked by consumer expenditure as was the typical wedding. But they rarely were the unself-conscious spending sprees that critics believed the white wedding had become. Skewing public perception of the new wedding's popularity, media devoted coverage to the weddings that were the most sensational. Americans were treated to accounts of couples wed while skydiving or scuba-diving or, on dry land, but while entirely nude.[9] Even *Look*'s daffodil farm event might be seen as fairly tame in comparison. Like other elements of mainstream American life in these tumultuous years, the white wedding—no longer extraordinary in its excess—was overshadowed by the more colorful, unusual "hippie" or "alternative" weddings, embraced by the counterculture and its fellow travelers. Because new weddings were considered so unusual, they often received coverage that "typical" weddings did not. Thus, many people suspected that unconventional weddings were becoming the standard wedding form. Further, media coverage of the new wedding provided participants a platform from which they could communicate the rationales behind their decision to celebrate in an alternative way. White wedding brides and grooms still publicized their unions through wedding announcements in their local newspapers, but these announcements rarely provided information beyond the couple's wedding garments, the location of the ceremony, and the bride and groom's post-wedding plans.[10]

By defining new weddings as "honest" or "meaningful," celebrants as well as media, critics, and observers suggested that the white wedding was quite the opposite. If brides and grooms embraced the new wedding because it allowed them a chance at authenticity, it stood to reason they rejected the white wedding because it denied them that opportunity. Journalist Marcia Seligson, in her 1973 exposé of the wedding industry, *The Eternal Bliss Machine*, described middle-class youth's rejection of the white wedding as a "bloodless revolution" designed "not to rend the family fabric." Ultimately, the rejection of the white wedding reflected a "rebellion . . . against what the kids consider a dearth of values and values of the wrong kind. It is a rejection of plastic, of false emotion, of obsession with material things to validate who we are, of sterility, of hollow forms, of competitiveness, of white bread, of super-technology, of isolation."[11] If rejection of the white wedding demonstrated a rejection of artificiality and falsehood, then acceptance of the traditional wedding form indicated complicity with the conformity associated with the event. If an alternative wedding was cool, a white wedding was undeniably square.

Given this square stigma attached to the white wedding, one might question: Did anyone still marry in the white wedding style? Seligson asked and aimed to answer this question in *The Eternal Bliss Machine*. In her exploration of the American wedding, she identified the creation of the "new wedding," a style somewhere between the "white wedding"—the ceremonial form accepted as traditional—and the "hippie wedding"—the form assumed to be entirely outrageous. Seligson likely would have identified the Jones-Cummings ceremony as a prime example of this new celebration style. The new wedding allowed for identification with the beliefs of the counterculture, expression of the values of the 1960s social movements, and the opportunity to express the individualism that had become increasingly fundamental to young Americans raised in the decades following World War II.[12] But even as she identified the trend toward a new style of celebration, Seligson suggested that those worried about the white wedding's survival had a distorted understanding of both American youth and American weddings. She wrote:

> Woodstock makes headlines, as do campus demonstrations, marijuana busts, freaky outfits, Mick Jagger and the wedding on a Big Sur cliff where the bride and groom arrived on horseback—nude—and all the guests peeled off their jeans and tie-dyed shirts in a whooping tribal celebratory

dance. One makes vast assumptions based on *Time* magazine covers and seven o'clock news, but the question always remains: How many? How many kids are dropping out, dropping acid, dropping their drawers at their weddings? Many, many fewer, I believe, than we think.[13]

Seligson argued that declarations of the wedding's extinction were premature. She presented statistics to support her suspicion that the white wedding was still going strong: In 1971, 7 of 8 first-time brides married in a church or synagogue; 7 of 8 first-time brides received an engagement ring; 80 percent of all first time-weddings were formal as compared to 73 percent in 1967; 96 percent of marrying couples held a reception; 84.5 percent of first-time brides wore a formal gown; and the wedding industry continued to thrive as a $7 billion a year business.[14] The white wedding, despite reports of its impending doom, was doing just fine.

While alternative forms of wedding celebrations became more visible in the late sixties and seventies, the white wedding, as Seligson's statistics attested, continued to be a popular form of wedding celebration, just as it had been since the early postwar period.[15] Contrary to popular worries about the state of American marriage, many young people continued to marry, albeit often after they had dated for several years or, in some cases, lived together. Men and women, particularly of the younger generation but increasingly among the middle-class mainstream, were more likely to accept premarital sex. In 1960, only 30,000 American couples lived together without the benefit of wedlock; by 1970, the number had climbed to 286,000 couples. The unmarried no longer were universally viewed as deviant. Men and women thus could delay entry into marriage, if they so chose, without appearing sick or delinquent. Divorce rates increased, thanks in part to passage of no-fault divorce laws, but marriage rates held strong. And if marriage rates were somewhat lower than the previous two decades, they represented more a leveling off than a substantial decline.[16]

Even with the growing acceptance of various relationship models and early marriage seemingly the unhip choice, young brides and grooms dominated the wedding population. A demographic composed of couples who would need (and seek out) guidance and start marriage without any of the material comforts accrued during premarital cohabitation continued to exist. In 1971, men still married at an average age of 23.1 and women at 20.9. More brides married at 18 than any other age, while 47.8 percent of all brides were under 20.[17] Wedding literature such as *Bride's* magazine kept close watch on this portion of American youth. Research conducted by and for the magazine demonstrated the continued appeal of the white wedding even during its allegedly lean years. The periodical worked to convince businesses and advertisers that potential brides and grooms represented a dream consumer population—renewed annually and eager to spend.[18]

Estelle Ellis, long-time marketing guru and founder of Business Image, Inc., a firm dedicated "to helping business understand the impact of social change on business trends," advised *Bride's* as the publication faced the 1970s. As indicated by Ellis and her team's marketing proposals, social changes were not incompatible with the wedding. They only needed to be incorporated into the existing wedding process. Using sales numbers and marketing research as their evidence, Ellis's team maintained that many of the couples who opted to wed during their teens and early twenties cared little for the countercultural appeal of the new wedding. Likewise, Seligson rejected the notion of a marrying population composed solely of Big Sur brides and grooms. This view matched Ellis's evaluation, which eventually became the pitch adopted by *Bride's* magazine. An estimated 70 percent of the 1,192,000 brides-to-be of 1969 were bridal magazine readers, with *Bride's* reaching 90 percent of that population. In their 1969 study, Business Image, Inc. reported that these readers eagerly anticipated the time when they could celebrate in the "traditional" style and embrace their middle-class adult lives. As the marketing team for *Bride's* surmised, "The bride's market is traditional even though the girls who are getting married are not."[19]

Under Business Image, Inc., *Bride's* viewed youth of the late 1960s and 1970s in a generational context. In its plans for marketing to potential brides-to-be, the magazine insisted that the bride—and specifically the bride—might be a "non-conformist—typical of her generation," but she remained so only "*until* the moment she decides to get married. From then on she turns traditionalist in everything—from her choice of wedding dress to her dream of a honeymoon."[20] Arguing the existence of "more brides than ever before," *Bride's* justified expansion from six to eight issues a year, a move that would increase annual circulation to 1,840,000 copies. By 1975, Business Image, Inc. predicted, weddings would "overtake the all time World War II peak, rising to an unprecedented 2,300,000." Even if some brides opted for a simpler, "new wedding," the money spent by the bridal population in its entirety allowed *Bride's* to pitch contemporary brides and grooms as "more free-spending, more self-indulgent, more sophisticated and more affluent."[21] The existence of such a market demanded attention, and *Bride's* was eager to cash in.

While *Bride's* and related wedding media recognized the sustained appeal white weddings held for young men and women, white wedding brides and grooms often went unnoticed by non-wedding media. Observers assumed the alternative wedding population to be more exciting due to their departure from the expected American ideals.[22] Brides and grooms who chose a white wedding made what appeared to be an uninspired choice. The white wedding was the wedding of the past, of the previous generation. Thus, 1970s white wedding brides and grooms were hopelessly out of date, detached from the excitement and change of their generational counterparts. But as Richard Nixon, the leader of the Silent Majority he had so-named, prepared for his daughter Tricia's wedding, Americans learned that a white wedding could embody just as much meaning as the most alternative style of celebration.[23]

Look magazine, despite its June 1971 coverage of the "untraditional wedding," confirmed Seligson's and Ellis's observations of the white wedding's continued popularity. Just two weeks before its article on the new, natural wedding of Laura Jones and Carl Cummings, the magazine had published another, seemingly opposite cover story about President Nixon's daughter Tricia and her plans for a June White House wedding. The cover bore the caption "Father and the Bride: Close-up of a proud President and his firstborn" and, essentially, this was the image presented on *Look*'s cover—a beaming father and his pretty, clean-cut daughter. Posing on the White House porch, Nixon wore his usual suit and tie, and Tricia might have been a bride from 1961, so conservative were her pink and white shift, pearl studs, and the pink bow in her blonde hair. Plans for a wedding in the Rose Garden of the White House, attended by friends and associates of the Nixon family, seemed about as far as one could get from a "natural wedding" held on a daffodil farm in eastern Virginia. While June 1971 may have been "peak season for "marriage al fresco," Tricia Nixon opted for what appeared to be a traditional white wedding.[24]

Inside the issue, readers were invited to learn about the Nixon family dynamic. Fitting seamlessly into the familiar and pre-designed roles of father and mother of the bride, the President and Mrs. Nixon spoke like any parents would, about their pleasure in seeing Tricia grow and their hopes for her future happiness. Unlike the "new, natural wedding," where the couple's respective families were peripheral, the Nixons played an important role in Tricia's wedding. Mrs. Nixon expressed her delight in being asked her advice on the ceremony and other wedding particulars. Like Ellie Banks of *Father of the Bride*, Pat Nixon had celebrated her own marriage with a small wedding because, she noted, "that's what Dick and I wanted." Like both Mrs. Banks and Lady Bird Johnson, Pat Nixon's modest wedding shaped her desire that Tricia might have the wedding of her dreams. She willingly deferred to her daughter's wishes for the celebration and enjoyed her role as involved mother of the bride.[25]

The president's central role was underscored by the "Father and the Bride" headline of the *Look* article. Shown spending quality time with Tricia in *Look*'s spread, Richard Nixon appeared the ideal father. Taking time out from his presidential duties for an Oval Office chat with Tricia, playing outdoors with their beloved dogs, or strolling around the White House grounds, the president appeared to share an intimate, loving relationship with his daughter. Nixon indicated that the family would miss having Tricia with them in the White House, but looked forward to the impending nuptials. The president's comments dealt explicitly with his hopes for his daughter's life as a married woman. While preparing to participate in what routinely was described as a "traditional wedding," the president recognized a modern trait in his oldest daughter: "Tricia is independent and wants to be appreciated for what she is, not for what her father and mother are." More than anything, the president wished for Tricia and her husband-to-be, Edward Cox, "to be out of the glare of merciless publicity," hoping for the two "to lead their own lives, to make it on their own and to develop individual careers."[26] While the president's comments on the potential unpleasantness of the public eye reveal the specificity of a First Daughter's circumstances and suggest something about Nixon's own relationship with the press, his hopes for her future happiness might have been expressed by any pleased father and indicated the growing focus on individual achievement and personal fulfillment in American culture.

As she prepared for her historic wedding, Tricia expressed total delight with the wedding process. With a dress from famed designer Priscilla of Boston (the same Priscilla who designed Luci Johnson's 1966 White House gown), china patterns picked from Lenox, flatware from Lunt, and a wedding cake custom-made by White House Pastry Chef Heinz Bender, the wedding appeared entirely conventional, as predictable as it possibly could be.[27] She was not alone in choosing this style of wedding celebration. Local newspapers continued to be filled with announcements of weddings of small-town brides and grooms who adhered to the wedding ideal standardized during the early postwar period. Pre-wedding fetes, formal dress, religious ceremonies, catered receptions, gift registries, and post-wedding honeymoons continued to mark the majority of weddings across the nation.[28]

Tricia Nixon was exactly the kind of bride Business Images, Inc. imagined in its pitch to *Bride's*. A series of 1969–1970 trade advertisements traced the steps this idealized bride would take: The Proposal, The Engagement, The Shower, The Registry, The Trousseau, The Wedding, The Honeymoon, and The New Home. Tricia Nixon's wedding journey stopped at each requisite location. The trade advertisements proposed by Business Images, Inc. refused to concede the elimination of any part of the wedding industry as it had been conceived throughout the postwar years. Critique of extravagant weddings or extravagance in spending, more generally, failed to make a mark in the trade ads. Instead, the series of advertisements emphasized the steps to a wedding as "the biggest personal spending spree of a lifetime."[29]

None of the designated stops outlined by *Bride's* could be skipped. Even elements that might seem antiquated or out-of-date would have a place in the white wedding celebration of the fast-approaching 1970s. But these traditional components were marked by modern interpretation. On the establishment of the pre-wedding trousseau, "The Trousseau" copy read: "Never before did she have a better excuse for being self-indulgent. Never again will she have the liberty to concentrate so intensively on herself."

While critics of the white wedding would have found fault with the link between spending and personal fulfillment (and the notion that personal fulfillment must end with marriage), the recognition of the importance of the individual was central to countercultural values and beliefs. Additionally, the models in the advertisement hinted at a new aesthetic. The women were gathered in the bedroom of the bride-to-be. Her collection of goods and garments—all necessary for her impending marriage—were spread across the room. Young and fashionable, the women wore short dresses or mini-skirts. Though carefully styled, the bride and her friends enjoyed an air of informality that represented a sharp departure from the images of Luci Johnson and her band of bridesmaids. While not quite fully "natural" by standards of hip youth, the women's straight, shoulder-length hair was a clear contrast to Johnson and her friends' teased bouffant styles. The models' modern look seemed to confirm the continued relevance of the trousseau. Adding credibility to this notion, *Look*'s spread of Tricia Nixon included an image of Tricia and her mother "think[ing] trousseau."[30]

The emphasis placed upon "The Registry" replicated the pre-wedding importance of "The Trousseau." Having grown in popularity during the 1950s and 1960s, the registry, *Bride's* suggested, would remain an essential part of the wedding process. "With two million or more brides getting married each year, bridal registry business is booming," ad copy asserted. Noting a modern spin, the text read, "It's so big retailers are putting it on computer." This relatively new tradition had become a staple, and modern technology had improved the process. *Bride's*, perhaps unintentionally, captured another new element of the registering process that was influenced by the alternative celebration. The image accompanying the ad copy featured a saleswoman showing her customers fine silverware, china, and crystal. The customers: the bride *and* the groom-to-be. Copy suggested that the bride was the lead in the selection of which goods would make the registry, but the presence of the groom represented a marked departure from wedding registry selection of years past. Whereas brides of the 1950s and early 1960s typically shouldered the responsibility of registry selection, *Bride's* indicated that this responsibility might now be shared. A more egalitarian approach to the wedding planning represented a direct connection between alternative and traditional weddings.[31]

"The Trousseau," *Bride's* Magazine Trade Ads, 1969–1970. Courtesy Estelle Ellis Collection, Archives Center, National Museum of American History, Smithsonian Institute.

White weddings might have played to the traditional wedding style and pre-wedding routine popularized during the early postwar years, but they still offered the bride and groom an opportunity to express the modernity of their relationship or an alternative view of marriage. Given the variety of their experiences and political perspectives, the generation coming of age during the late 1960s and early 1970s cannot be considered monolithic. Despite their diversity, however, the political climate of the time period allowed for a fairly universal experience of personal realization. Questions of individual fulfillment and identity marked the generation's coming of age.[32] Men and women of the

"The Registry," *Bride's* Magazine Trade Ads, 1969–1970. Courtesy Estelle Ellis Collection, Archives Center, National Museum of American History, Smithsonian Institute.

baby boom, conservative, radical, or apolitical, experienced a sense of self-realization through their engagement with social and political issues in contemporary America. Personal expression played a role in multiple facets of their lives, including their wedding celebrations.[33] As Washington correspondent Helen Thomas reported on Tricia's wedding, she identified a connection between Tricia and other young women: "Like every bride," she noted, "she wants her wedding to be distinctive." Thomas suggested this impulse reached across the youth population, a link among the varied populations composing American youth.[34]

At age 25, Nixon was a more mature bride than 19-year-old Johnson had been, and was four years older even than the average bride of the time.[35] This maturity came through in her discussion of the wedding. Nixon believed her wedding offered a unique opportunity for expression and aimed to use the celebration as a time to communicate the views she and her fiancé, Ed Cox, shared about the nature of their relationship. "Ed and I wanted our wedding to be expressive of us," she explained. "So the service combines the things from different services that we think are important about marriage, with something we want to say to one another." Justifying their decision to personalize the wedding to fit their individual style, Tricia commented, "Lots of young people today are doing this."[36] And Nixon's plans did reflect an alternative to the recent First Family celebrations: her wedding differed from the pageantry of Luci Johnson's 1966 celebration at the National Shrine, Lynda Johnson's 1967 White House wedding, and her sister Julie Nixon's quiet 1968 New York City celebration. As if to add further credibility to Tricia's identification with a hipper kind of wedding, an article in *Business Week* remarked on Tricia's decision for an outdoor wedding, the first ever to take place in the Rose Garden of the White House, and declared this a clear break with tradition.[37] Likewise, *Look* noted that Tricia had "nixed the traditional bride-only engagement picture," opting instead to sit for a portrait with Ed. For Tricia, distinctiveness was in the details. The power of ceremonial interpretation popularized by the new wedding directly influenced the willingness to make these breaks, no matter how small or insignificant they might appear.

In many ways, Nixon's wedding reflected the enormous difference just a few years' time made during the late 1960s and early 1970s. Between 1966 and 1971, a more critical view of government and political leadership, a growing generation gap, and emergent critiques of marriage had dramatically changed the American social and cultural landscape. Nixon's wedding—still very clearly a white wedding—provoked less debate than Luci Johnson's celebration had among the American public due, in part, to this shift. With the rise of new weddings and the emergence of alternative relationship styles that pushed marriage from its pedestal, even a modified version of the white wedding seemed acceptable and, one might suggest, refreshingly "normal." And if Tricia challenged tradition by hosting a white wedding in the Rose Garden and being explicit in her desire for personal expression, these seemed fairly minimal challenges in comparison to media suggestions about the ways other young couples were celebrating.

Like new wedding celebrants, Tricia Nixon and Ed Cox believed that their wedding expressed their vision of themselves and their expectations of married life. Media implied that atypical or outrageous weddings represented a couple's views and values more than a white wedding, but Tricia Nixon suggested either style of wedding—traditional or alternative—might serve a similar purpose. Her wedding contained traditional white wedding elements, such as sustained familial participation, detailed pre-wedding planning, and standard wedding attire, but the wedding also deviated from the expected. While Tricia played the lead in media coverage of her wedding, she credited Cox for his participation, far more than Luci Johnson had Pat Nugent. Their white wedding clearly was connected to and influenced by both the alternative weddings of the time and an evolving American culture. Just as in the case of the Nixon-Cox wedding, where the ceremony spoke to the concerns of Tricia and her husband-to-be, young men and women across the nation might find the same personal significance in their own weddings, even as they looked incredibly similar to outsiders. And outsiders would find these weddings nearly identical. Marcia Seligson, who covered Tricia's wedding for *Life* magazine, recalled the wedding as a "standard WASP frolic. . . . [F]undamentally like all other weddings. Sweet, joyous, utterly predictable. Splendid, regal, elegant and absolutely inoffensive."[38]

Seligson's point mirrors the views new wedding celebrants held about the white wedding, but the easy dismissal of the white wedding celebration obscures both the broader shift in American views of private life and communal influence and the importance of the ceremony as imagined by its participants. Just five years prior, the public took great offense to decisions Luci Johnson and Patrick Nugent made for "personal" reasons. This was not the case for Tricia Nixon. Her "standard" celebration provided a refreshing contrast to the hippie weddings that had cropped up throughout the nation. Like the alternative wedding, the traditional wedding might be shaped to represent the values of the bride and groom. As personal motivation became more accepted across the population, individual expression remained a key component of the wedding's continued appeal.

Holidays and celebrations—even those celebrated at a national level—historically have allowed for personal interpretation or individual appropriation.[39] The wedding was no different. In 1970, Bill Weatherford, a 21-year-old life insurance salesman from Harris County, Texas, described his and his fiancée's rationale for getting married and celebrating that marriage with a traditional wedding: "We don't feel we could have a guilt-free marriage if we had lived together first. We would always have the feeling we did something wrong, and no marriage should start off that way." For Weatherford, the standard white wedding celebration was filled with meaning: it symbolized his and his wife-to-be's personal values and commitment to marriage as an institution. This couple's wedding, like new weddings, symbolized a transition in their relationship. For them, the transition focused on the new experience of living together, but only as husband and wife. And while this may have been viewed as an old-fashioned or uninspired interpretation of the celebration, it was still a personal preference the wedding allowed the couple to express.[40]

The white weddings may have looked familiar, and one wedding might seem identical to the next. But it is unfair to discount the personal significance attached to this wedding form. "Traditional" in the eyes of its proponents and "conformist" to its detractors, the white wedding spoke to millions of American youth who married in the familiar ceremony. As they celebrated in this way, brides and grooms believed they were sending a message about their views of love and their expectations for married life. Just because couples represented their views in ways that were quietly familiar did not mean that their ceremonies were without meaning. The new generation of white wedding brides and grooms did not see their choice of wedding as without statement—to follow tradition, particularly in the 1970s, *was* to make a statement.[41] While the cultural or political views of white wedding celebrants may have differed from those held by their alternative wedding contemporaries, brides and grooms of all politics and predilections shared a desire for a wedding that allowed personal expression.

Of course, even those who wed in the "traditional" style might embrace a more modern approach to married life or align with the values of countercultural youth. Priscilla Kidder, the grande dame of wedding dress and recognized expert on questions of etiquette, identified, at least in part, with the motivation inspiring new wedding celebrants.

Echoing Kitty Hanson's critique of the white wedding, Kidder suggested that parents should remember that the wedding was a day to celebrate the bride and the groom rather than a chance for parents to show off. Aligning with new wedding celebrants' desire to shape the wedding on their own terms, Kidder advocated that they control the guest list. She stated, "Let the two youngsters select the guests, and you'll have a much happier wedding." And while she continued to push for fairly traditional gowns, Priscilla used new wedding language as she advised parents not to frighten the bride by demanding tradition. Instead, Priscilla suggested that parents should "let her do her own thing." Further, recognizing the imperative for individuality, Priscilla insisted that a bride could wear a Priscilla of Boston frock and "still have their own very individual look for their own very special day."[42] No novice to the world of bridal marketing, Kidder responded to the demands of the young generation even as she aimed to shape their ideals in an effort to sustain and even expand her bridal empire during the years when all signs pointed to the traditional wedding's demise.

Kidder wisely embraced elements of the new, natural wedding in her advertising campaigns of the 1970s. Even in the fairly staid pages of *Bride's*—still advocating white wedding celebration styles—Kidder placed images of hand-drawn brides that closely resembled the style of sketching that might be found in underground publications or hip-inspired posters.[43] While pushing the long, white gown, Kidder and *Bride's* showed models strolling through quaint villages, standing along the seashore, or basking in the sunlight of an open field. Even in formal wear, the wedding could be uniquely designed to suit the couple's tastes. The text of her advertisements likewise revealed her willingness to adapt: "Priscilla believes in the look of TODAY—and offers wedding gown designs as suitable for a country church or meadow ceremony as for formal cathedral rites."[44]

And yet, Kidder revealed her business savvy as she pursued her own interests in playing to the new wedding style. A white gown, purchased by a renowned designer, still fit into Kidder's projected image of the wedding. She would make gowns for alternative wedding brides, but she still believed in the white wedding, albeit, as she claimed, for unselfish reasons. "Let's face it," she said, "If the bride gets married in a short dress in a justice of the peace's office, it seems too quick and easy and

teeny

MISS BETSY

CHICAGO (CLARENDON HILLS) ILL.—**JEROLD'S**   COLUMBUS. OHIO—**COLE OF COLUMBUS**   HARTFORD. CONN.—**BRIDAL PARTY PENTHOUSE**
NASHVILLE, TENN.—**RICH SCHWARTZ**   NEW HAVEN, CONN.—**HAROLD'S**   NEW YORK (BROOKLYN) N.Y.—**KLEINFELD'S**
ST. LOUIS, MO.—**HOUSE OF GIUSEPPE**   SUMMIT, N.J.—**LILLIAN O'GRADY**   WHITE PLAINS, N.Y.—**L. A. SCHULMAN**
'or write **PRISCILLA OF BOSTON**, 498 SEVENTH AVENUE, NEW YORK 10018

Priscilla Advertisement, 1970. Courtesy Priscilla of Boston Collection, Archives Center, National Museum of American History, Smithsonian Institute.

not too important. But if the bride and her family go to a lot of trouble arranging a big wedding—and if her father has paid a lot of money for it—she'll think twice about running home to Mother after the first tiff." Priscilla, "Queen of the Aisle," may have embraced elements from new and alternative weddings, but the importance she placed on wedding attire revealed her stance as a white wedding proponent.[45]

Couples aiming for a traditional wedding could blend elements of the new wedding with the standard white wedding. In its yearly bridal supplement, the *Boston Globe* recognized a possible 1970s move away from tradition. Calling the youth of 1970 the generation "that threw out the rule book," the article acknowledged the trend toward alternative weddings. Like Seligson, however, author Virginia Bohline was skeptical about the numbers of couples celebrating in the new style. "[F]or the most part," she wrote, "today's young romantics follow tradition on that day of days, their wedding day."[46] Whether a nervous attempt to inflate industry confidence or an accurate portrayal of the less publicized white wedding, Bohline's assessment was accurate: the white wedding was still going strong. Accounts on women's pages and bridal supplements in local periodicals across the United States reported similar findings. The current generation, unique by so many standards, might look to their wedding day as a time for greater formality and decorum. In fact, the growing informality of modern American life, some asserted, contributed to the desirability of wedding day formality.[47]

By using language that suggested uniqueness, individuality, or independence, manufacturers, advertisers, and periodicals appealed to a cultural sensibility among those who had not become full-fledged members or followers of the youth counterculture. The appeal of these countercultural staples proved just how pervasive they had become in American culture. Businesses demonstrated marketing savvy as they pitched contemporary bridal fashions that hinted just enough at difference but still adhered to the long, white wedding gown model. Brides and grooms could embrace a countercultural style without embracing the counterculture itself. They could have their white wedding with just a hint of the rebellion associated with the new wedding.[48] Or, they could push more modern styles to the side as they shaped their wedding to fit the standard white wedding model still considered by so many to be the appropriately traditional style of celebration.

* * *

The freedom and flexibility of alternative weddings appealed to many brides and grooms. But others, like Anna Quindlen, continued to privilege the traditional wedding and rejected the move away from the standard celebration. Tradition, in and of itself, was the draw. In June 1980, the *Chicago Tribune* compared weddings of 1970 to weddings of 1980:

"Matrimonial love fests in the park, popular a decade ago, are passé. Casual is out. Old-fashioned is in. Never mind the cost." Ignoring the sustained appeal of the white wedding, the article perpetuated a myth that tradition, at one point, had gone out of style. Stanley Horwich, a bridal consultant and president of the wedding planning agency Weddings, Inc., added his perspective to the *Tribune*'s findings. Mr. Horwich identified a trend in wedding planning, claiming, "Weddings are definitely coming back in style, and they're more traditional," he said, going on to note, "The brides are more involved in the planning now than they ever were, and they're looking to the elegance and formality of years ago."[49] A 1979 article in the *Los Angeles Times* found that Los Angeles area department stores, many of which had closed their bridal salons during the 1970s due to waning consumer interest, had been caught off guard by a growing demand for traditional, formal gowns.[50] By all accounts, men and women had abandoned the traditional white wedding during the 1970s. Kitty Hanson had predicted as much in 1967.[51] But Tricia Nixon and Ed Cox had celebrated with a white wedding. And they were not alone.

Men and women of Middle America never truly abandoned the white wedding. It was only after new and alternative weddings became more commonplace—and then less stylish as the 1970s continued—that observers pronounced the white wedding fashionable once again. By the late 1970s, style pages across the country declared the brides and grooms were embracing a return to tradition. The language of tradition's "return," however, masked what had been an on-going relationship. Publications like *Bride's* and *Modern Bride* remained newsstand staples. Publishers continued to produce "how-to" wedding guides, and brides continued to buy or borrow these books from their public libraries. When interviewed before Tricia Nixon's wedding, Priscilla Kidder declared the "business of traditional weddings" in "splendid health." "That princess image—being a bride—is even more prevalent among young girls now than it used to be," she said. "It's a security blanket for them."[52] The wedding and its association with tradition maintained appeal, in part, *because* of the transformative nature of late 1960s and early 1970s America. A sense of continuity with the past provided a sense of comfort in a rapidly changing cultural climate.[53] Even the more traditionally minded population made small but significant changes to the wedding. Like Tricia Nixon and Ed Cox, brides and grooms hosted traditional weddings but infused the celebrations with personal style. But to declare a "return to tradition" ignored the fact that many men and women had upheld the traditional wedding even when it failed to make headlines.

Coverage of unconventional weddings in the late 1960s and early 1970s led to dire predictions about the white wedding's longevity. Even Priscilla of Boston's Priscilla Kidder, having declared the wedding industry in "splendid health," admitted that change was upon her. When asked how she felt about "off-beat, way-out weddings," she responded: "They're doing their own thing and I don't condemn it." Even so, Priscilla refused to give up the element of tradition. Of these new brides and grooms, she noted, "[I]t's nothing new. People were having off-beat weddings in the old days. In history you read about brides walking up and down the street in wedding gowns. I don't mind the barefoot bride either. Most brides take their shoes off and dance after the wedding." A 1967 article from the *Boston Globe* was more certain about tradition's fate: "Tradition has been thrown to the winds by young brides."54

Despite recognition of new wedding styles and fears that tradition had been abandoned, the white wedding maintained its popularity during the 1970s, albeit outside fashionable urban hubs. According to a 1970 survey conducted by the Harris County clerk's office in Texas, most couples still married for "love, home, security" and disavowed "unconventional 'happenings' as replacements for formal church weddings." Nearly all marriages reportedly took place at one of Houston's 1,350 churches and synagogues. Bridal consultants in the area agreed that traditional weddings remained the most popular. Two Houston stores, home to busy bridal shops, reported that "no mini-bride dresses have been sold, and only one or two pants bridal outfits." Mary Ann Maxell, manager of the bridal shop at Foley's Department Store, noted the difference between a woman's everyday look and her desired bridal appearance. "Some of these brides drag in here looking scraggly with their long hair and boots," she said. "But for their wedding day, they want the most traditional dress."55

A 1973 article from a local Texas newspaper, the *Odessa American*, offered a fairly balanced view of wedding trends. Recognizing the appeal of the alternative wedding, the article maintained that most brides continued to feel the pull of the traditional white wedding. Citing the 2,300,000 marriages of 1972 and anticipating an added 190,000 celebrations in 1973, the article confidently stated, "Marriage is definitely not on the wane." Chronicling major events and movements of the previous decade and noting the political activism that characterized the generation, the article admitted that the couples of 1973 had matured. It was this maturity that would lead them to make wiser, more balanced decisions about marriage and commitment than had the generations before them. But the article was also clear that brides and grooms could celebrate in a traditional fashion even as they embraced a non-traditional approach to married life. A traditional wedding might be marked—just as a new wedding—by the influence of women's liberation, the recitation of self-written vows, and a sermon that reflected a couple's new expectations for married life.[56]

And yet those covering weddings in the later 1970s and early 1980s insisted on using phrases such as "return" or "renewed" when discussing tradition, thus ignoring what had more accurately been an uninterrupted run.[57] Of course, the traditions these observers referred to were typically the invented traditions of the early postwar era. The wedding industry had successfully created a sense of the white wedding as a time-honored tradition, in and of itself. Modern weddings of the late 1970s and 1980s incorporated tradition, but such traditions were hardly replicas of "traditions" of the 1950s. More accurately, most men and women followed the lead of brides and grooms of the more recent past. Couples selected wedding elements that fit personal preference and amended traditions as need be. As Carol Newman advised brides and grooms on how to have a wedding their way, she specifically addressed the role of tradition: "A tradition used in a wedding celebration can be lovely and important. But only if the particular tradition applies to you. Embracing traditions that are not a statement of yourselves is an act of insecurity, an unwillingness to define what is significant in your own lives."[58] Tradition had its place, but a couple's personal values and interests were primary.

Members of the wedding industry worked to discredit existing beliefs about the wedding's fall from grace. Barbara Tober, editor-in-chief of *Bride's* during the late 1970s, reported that people often asked, "Are people still getting married?" Not only were people getting married, they were marrying in unprecedented numbers. Since 1976, rates had climbed. Tober noted, "1979 chalked up the highest marriage rate in history . . . higher than the post World War II peak of 1946." The wedding's popularity was due more to a sustained evolution rather than a miraculous re-emergence. New and alternative weddings' influence extended beyond their celebrants. The freedom to add or omit elements and to make stylistic changes based upon personal interest helped to create an environment in which tradition was seen as a choice rather than a requirement.

Priscilla Kidder added her voice to those discussing the wedding's late 1970s return. Ever the salesperson, she admitted, "I've always known what my customers wanted, even when I didn't like it."[59] And yet, other statements suggested that Kidder was uncomfortable admitting that the white wedding had been or even ever appeared to be in danger. Despite her constant willingness to adapt to new demands, she said, "I see slight changes every few years, but basically the business has been the same for me for 40 years." Although sure of knowing what to expect of brides, Kidder was clear in recognizing generational differences. The wedding business may have been the same, but brides had changed. "When I started out if they didn't come in with their best underwear, they would apologize and say they were saving it for the wedding," Kidder recalled in 1979. "Today they come in without any underwear, and they don't apologize."[60] Changed notions of decorum affected young women's sense of propriety and view of their bodies, but failed to alter their desire for a beautiful wedding gown.

Many of the "girls" who came to Priscilla of Boston's shop asking for the most atypical ensembles, she recalled, regularly ended up with fairly typical gowns. As though referring specifically to Anna Quindlen, Priscilla Kidder noted, "A girl has dreamed all her life of being a bride." Revealing her true feelings for alternatives to tradition, Kidder seethed, "[A bride] doesn't want a sexy, stupid dress. She wants her gown to be a classic."[61] But while Kidder recognized the power of the establishment gown, she also noted the strength of contemporary trends. Suggesting that one could have the best of both worlds, she classified her gowns as "basically traditional" but "also fashionable."[62] Kidder spoke to any number of brides in her many interviews, demonstrating, perhaps unintentionally but likely with calculated business acumen, the coexistence of different wedding styles and bridal preferences.

More accurately, the alleged return to tradition signaled a newly chic iteration of the ceremony style identified as traditional. Elite observers, in particular, confirmed as much. Carol Troy of the *New York Times* succinctly described the path of the white wedding: "The formal wedding never really vanished but it did go out of style." Viewing the 1970s as the decade when couples to be wed were found "hopping a cab to City Hall or traipsing about a country meadow at dawn," the white wedding had regained momentum, even among the sophisticated set. And while reflecting a turn in fashion, views of 1970s weddings (having their origins in the tumultuous sixties) also reflected an increasingly monolithic view of recent American history. Popular memory of the 1960s and 1970s held that young people embraced the hip lifestyle en masse. In fact, a full adoption of this lifestyle was quite rare. Far fewer brides and grooms had celebrated their weddings by "traipsing about a country meadow at dawn" than suggested by Troy.[63]

For the modern bride and groom, a white wedding no longer reflected complicity with conformity or outdated models of marital relations. Instead, the decision to celebrate with a "traditional" white wedding might be a response to an aesthetic a couple found appealing. The white wedding might appear entirely traditional on the surface, but reflected a blend of tradition and modernity upon closer inspection. Wed in March 1979, Troy recalled of her own wedding day garb: "My wedding gown, by Monica Hickey for Bendel's was the stuff of childhood dreams . . . all those teeny, tiny buttons, that satin, that lace, that train! . . . Yet I couldn't resist adding a visual wink to all that bridal white—firehouse-red stockings."[64] The gown might place Troy within a community of traditional brides, but the stockings set her apart, confirming her individuality and even her irreverence on her wedding day. Writing for the sophisticated set of the *New York Times*, Troy indicated that a formal white wedding could, indeed, be traditional and cosmopolitan, formal and fun.

Drawing attention to Anna Quindlen's *Ms.* article, a report in the *Los Angeles Times* reported that Quindlen was just one "among a growing number of young, independent-minded women . . . once again opting for formal bridal gowns." Designer Holly Harp weighed in on this decision: "Most of us have this dream about our wedding day no matter how liberated we may be or what kind of life we anticipate."[65]

Harp's comment suggested that liberation and a white wedding were not mutually exclusive. Men and women touched by women's liberation and an American culture newly remade by alternative viewpoints could celebrate their union with a traditional wedding even as they aligned with modern views of life and love. To some extent, this vision reflected a sense that liberation had been achieved.[66] Weddings no longer had to serve a political function. Childhood dreams of a grand wedding, like those expressed by Quindlen and Troy, needed not be shelved in an act of deference to political values or lifestyle choices.

Many observers heralded the royal wedding of Prince Charles and Lady Diana Spencer as the moment of traditional revival. Describe as "the wedding of the century," the ceremony proceeded like something from a fairytale with Diana arriving at St. Paul's Cathedral in a horse-drawn carriage, wearing a wedding gown with a 25-foot train. But this extravagant event might better be regarded as an embodiment of renewed interest in tradition rather than an instigator of the trend. Charles and Diana's wedding served as a very public reminder of the white wedding's appeal. The royal wedding pushed the white wedding to the forefront once again. Certainly, the wedding was influential. As with Elizabeth Taylor or Luci Johnson, women flocked to bridal stores to obtain a duplicate of Diana's elaborate gown. But the wedding was responsible more for publicizing an ongoing trend that had never gone totally out of style.[67]

Even the typically saccharine world of wedding advice literature recognized that this "traditional" white wedding had experienced some alterations. George W. Knight advanced the typicality of the desire to have a unique wedding. He asked brides, "So you want something a little different in your wedding ceremony?" His answer:

> Welcome to the group! During the past few years more and more engaged couples have been searching for the same thing. The typical church wedding of today is likely to include such innovations as vows that were written by the bride and groom, prayers by members of the wedding party, a welcome to the wedding guests from the bride, hymn singing, and congregational responses by the wedding guests.[68]

Knight clearly referred to a white wedding rather than an alternative celebration. While recognizing the amended wedding, Knight still presumed the wedding would be held in a church—and would involve vows, guests, and song. The unabashed and self-conscious focus on the individuality of the couple being wed represented the real change in these new white weddings.

Elements of the wedding celebration remained similar to weddings of 30 years before. But the bride—and increasingly the groom, too—were very clear that they would make no apologies for a wedding focused on their interests, their relationship to one another, and their lives beyond the scope of their respective families. Weddings looked similar to the 1950s-style white wedding, and so a "return" to tradition was proclaimed. However, new white weddings incorporated elements of alternative celebrations as a couple's interests or politics determined the direction a wedding would take. A surface-level glance at weddings of the early 1980s suggested a return to tradition, but the visible traditions of formal dress, religious expression, and catered reception masked the continuing development of the wedding as a time of personal significance for the couple being wed. Emphasis on tradition veiled just how modern the wedding celebration had become. More accurately, brides and grooms reinterpreted tradition. As with changes in American relationships, families, and communities more broadly, the wedding reflected a growing focus on the individual and the emotional, on the tie between personal feelings and public performance.[69]

Representing a similar break from the typical wedding guide, a 1984 *Modern Bride* guide to wedding planning admitted that contemporary brides and grooms entered into marriage with a different set of experiences than had generations before: "Having once served as the official beginning of a marital relationship, weddings now often acknowledge a lifetime commitment that has already been made, never mind consummated." The editors of *Modern Bride* willingly admitted that the wedding's meaning was flexible. To fit the increasingly diverse population of brides and grooms, it had to be. The range of wedding options likewise had become flexible: "And while there is still, to be sure, a correct way to do things, the range of rightness has broadened considerably to accommodate a myriad of circumstances."[70] Recalling the etiquette-based system designed to aid brides-to-be during the early and mid-century United States, the guide indicated that there remained a system of "rightness." Couples of the 1980s, however, could be less fearful of violating the now expanded range of possible wedding decisions.

With information compiled by the editors of *Modern Bride*, the magazine's guide to wedding and marriage offered an interpretation of Americans' relationship to the wedding celebration. Stressing American individualism, the guide flattered brides and grooms' sense of self, and reinforced the idea that it was appropriate—even patriotic—to shape the wedding to a couple's personal preferences. "Our strong individualism and our common-sense adaptability challenged Old World social customs with new needs. Americans continue to seek the best of both worlds, the old and the new, with characteristic ingenuity. The result is a unique culture of our own . . . we will no longer accept institutions and mores that restrict, rather than reflect, our national character."[71] Crediting influences both old and new, the guide valorized American independence and individuality, both of the distant past and the current age. Rejecting individuality's association solely with the now-dated counterculture, *Modern Bride*'s guide for the modern bride suggested that the wedding celebrated characteristics as old as the nation but still relevant to contemporary circumstances.

Guides also recognized the dilemma faced by women like Anna Quindlen, whose feminism might seem an impediment to marriage and a wedding. *The Executive Bride* of 1985 attempted to quell career-driven women's insecurities as they prepared for their weddings. Using language that suggested understanding of and even sympathy toward anti-marriage views, the book's author Ellen Freudenheim perpetuated the mythic existence of a seemingly innate quality that led women to want a wedding. She leveled with the bride-to-be: "Even if you find it hard to picture yourself, a hard-driving professional woman, in something as traditional, as corny, as, yes, romantic as a wedding, you know you want one."[72] Planning a wedding might seem a daunting task, particularly for a woman who worked full time and had little or no interest in "doilies or flowers." But Freudenheim assured brides that planning a wedding was possible—in part because of the skills women had acquired in their careers and in part because they could rely on their grooms more than generations before them. Although this was no traditional bride, she could still have the traditional wedding of her dreams.

Freudenheim was clear in designating her target audience: "people whose mothers aren't likely to be intimately involved in the process, for women over twenty-five who never quite believed they would get around to this marriage business, and for future husbands, too, who may become more involved in wedding logistics than they ever expected." *The Executive Bride* was designed for the modern 1980s yuppie bride. She was prominently displayed on the book's cover, wearing the requisite corporate suit, complete with shoulder pads. However, the book used language that would have appealed to any alternative bride: "Your wedding is going to be one of the great events of your life, an emotional turning point, a rite of passage you'll never forget. . . . It's a time when your private relationship becomes a public declaration of love and partnership, a commitment full of hope and promise." And yet, *The Executive Bride* also advanced ideas espoused in the late 1940s and early 1950s. Freudenheim wrote of the wedding's appeal, "And you, the bride, are center stage. It's *your* day."[73] Like Kay Banks, 1980s brides might imagine the wedding as a day of their very own. Unlike Kay Banks, they need not see this wish squashed under the expectations of parents, community, or friends. This long-existing bridal wish now could be expressed as a demand thanks to the increased acceptance of individualism and personal fulfillment in modern American life. Weddings of the 1980s—and the brides and grooms who planned them—did return to tradition. But their weddings incorporated a series of modified traditions rather than a set of static rules and requirements produced by social experts of decades past.

As the white wedding enjoyed renewed visibility in the late 1970s and throughout the 1980s, it was not the same ceremony it had been in the early postwar years. The heralded "return to tradition" did not lead to the replication of the then-new white wedding style. Brides and grooms, and American culture as a whole, had adapted to the changes brought about by the social and political upheaval of the 1960s and 1970s. Understandings of marriage and the weddings that served as its starting point inevitably changed as well. The fact that observers used the language of tradition obscured the fact that the values and ideals—and sometimes even wedding practices—were as modern as they were traditional. Just like brides and grooms of the 1950s, new white wedding celebrants of the 1970s and 1980s could mask their challenges to the status quo—consciously or without intent—through their embrace of tradition.

* * *

Had the wedding been static and resistant to change, it may very well have become a relic of a past age. Those wishing to host a new wedding or an alternative wedding focused on making the wedding relevant to their relationship and their expectations of married life.[74] But even alternative weddings, meant to reject the falsehood of the American Dream couples had seen their parents so obsessed with achieving and their country so insistent on perpetuating, often borrowed heavily from the white wedding. They incorporated special dress, witnesses to the ceremony, a post-ceremony celebration, a sanctioning of the marriage, and presentation of gifts to celebrate that union. And, of course, when the ceremony was over, the couple was married. One American Dream was replaced with another.

"Nature's children have been rigging their own ceremonies on beaches and mountaintops for some time now," *Look* reported in its coverage of the Jones-Cummings wedding. The simplicity of the ceremony, the cool fashions, and the relaxed atmosphere might appeal to any number of readers. Hardly vagrant hippies or "street people," Laura Jones, Carl Cummings, and their wedding guests were attractive, educated young adults. While the natural wedding did not align with the standard white wedding, it did embrace elements of the American wedding and American consumerism, albeit in alternative ways. The couple wore designer costumes, and the article chronicled the gifts the bride and groom might look forward to receiving: "a handwoven wall hanging, ceramic pots, a fishing trip, a windowbox herb garden, membership in a group like the National Audubon Society or Zero Population Growth."[75] The new wedding intersected with mainstream American culture in a manner unlike the white wedding, but alternative celebrations were just that—alternative takes on a familiar model.

Media attention given the "new wedding" suggested that alternative weddings had overpowered the white wedding. This perception was, at its base, false. Throughout the 1960s and 1970s, the new wedding and white wedding coexisted. While the new wedding may not have revolutionized American weddings in the way contemporary observers anticipated, it did have a lasting and meaningful influence on the American celebration style. As she emphasized couples' ability to make the wedding a site of personal expression, Tricia Nixon revealed the changed world of wedding culture, and of American culture, more broadly. Even if personalization was obvious only to the bride and groom, it was obvious to them. This opportunity for expression was the alternative wedding's primary influence on the white wedding celebration style. The celebration survived because of couples' ability to combine the old and the new, the communal and the individual, the personal and the political.

The desire for a meaningful wedding celebration existed long before the youth of the late sixties and seventies embraced the notion. Demonstrating a clear link to the values of the counterculture and the even longer-standing tradition of American individualism, the widespread, unapologetic, emphatic focus on personal significance changed American wedding culture.[76] The attractiveness of personal expression and the desire for meaning expanded beyond the bounds of the counterculture, as men and women with any number of perspectives or persuasions imposed their individuality upon the wedding. The social and political revolutions that altered the wedding also had altered the very core of private life. While the American public may have recoiled from overt displays of political fervor as the 1970s continued, the politicization of private life allowed that a personal act, such as a wedding, served as a site of public demonstration.[77] The white wedding, which might have otherwise faded into obscurity with its seemingly old-fashioned notions of what a marriage should be and mean, was updated by couples through their own words and beliefs. Ideas of marriage changed, but the wedding remained a central starting point to the institution because it allowed for the representation of these changed ideals.

Ultimately the wedding as ritual succeeded because of the possibility of variation. Americans continued to draw upon a standard when they imagined the wedding, but moderations—slight or dramatic—were accepted fairly readily. Looking back on the embrace of the new wedding, Rockwell Stensrud concluded, "The value of that 60s–70s rebellion . . . is that many people felt freer to shape their ceremonies in more personal ways, and that freedom is now taken for granted today."[78] Modifications, whether in the form of self-written vows, unconventional wedding attire, or informal post-ceremony celebration, allowed the wedding to remain relevant in the face of social and political change.

The intangible that attracted men and women to the celebration was the ability to be both part of and apart from the masses. The ceremony provided a couple an opportunity to make a distinct statement but with the familiar language of love and commitment. Like other holidays and rituals, the wedding allowed participants to inscribe the celebration with personal significance, which ultimately strengthened its appeal.[79] New styles of celebration, through their challenge, actually reinvigorated the white wedding. New wedding celebrants proved that individuals could infuse their ceremonies with individual meaning. Those more likely to align with conservative values or mainstream culture likewise embraced this trend, and thereby helped to make what was old new once again.

Thus the wedding appealed to a diverse collection of brides and grooms who might fall anywhere on the spectrum of social and political life. Men and women of different classes and tastes projected their visions of themselves and their places within their communities onto their weddings. The flexibility of the ritual assured its enduring power. Even those who rejected the values of the counterculture embraced the wedding as an intersection of public and private, personal and political. The wedding provided a couple with a moment when the eyes of those they held most dear to them might understand how they viewed themselves and what they expected their married life to provide. Armed with this belief, any number of couples could justify any number of wedding styles. As the 1970s came to a close and the 1980s declared tradition newly chic, couples embraced a wedding ceremony that looked incredibly similar to the weddings of the 1950s. But even as the political element of personal expression was somewhat more muted than it had been in previous years, the politics of individualism shaped the new white wedding. This acceptance of individualism opened doors for new styles of celebration—and the celebration of new relationships—in the years to follow.

5

"It Matters Not Who We Love, Only That We Love"

SAME-SEX WEDDINGS

On October 10, 1987, nearly 7,000 people witnessed a wedding on the National Mall in Washington, DC. Men and women cheered and threw rice and confetti as family, friends, and community members took part in the largest mass wedding in American history. After the celebrants exchanged rings and were pronounced newlywed, guests released hundreds of balloons into the air. Brides and grooms, dressed in formal wedding attire, cried and embraced after an "emotional and festive" ceremony. Like so many brides and grooms, participants identified the wedding day as one of the happiest, most meaningful days of their lives.

But this was no ordinary wedding. And these were not typical brides and grooms. This wedding held special significance for its participants. Beyond the "mass" nature of the celebration, something else was unique. The newlyweds that fall Saturday paired off as brides and brides, grooms and grooms. "The Wedding," as it came to be known, marked the symbolic beginning of nearly 2,000 same-sex marriages. Rejecting the idea that a wedding—and by implication, a marriage— should have one male and one female participant, the grooms and their grooms, the brides and their brides presented a striking picture.

A wedding, a fairly conventional affair, became a site of radical protest. Layered in meaning, "The Wedding" celebrated the personal commitments of those being wed. At the same time, it was a direct political act that challenged the legal, religious, and social barriers against same-sex relationships.[1] Like couples before them, gay men and lesbians found they could use their weddings to make a statement about the world and the place of their relationship in it.

Designed to reflect an alternative approach to love and marriage, "The Wedding," part of the 1987 March on Washington for Gay and Lesbian Rights, rejected the narrow definition of marriage that limited the relationship to members of the opposite sex. "The Wedding" likewise rejected a narrow view of the standard wedding celebration. Dina Bachelor, metaphysical minister, hypnotherapist, and "Wedding" officiant, designed a new-age style ceremony. Bachelor recognized the uniqueness of the celebration and chose her words and actions carefully. Standing under a swaying arch of silver, white, and black balloons, Bachelor omitted any mention of the customary "honor and obey, till death do us part." Including observers in the celebration, she asked witnesses to join hands and encircle the celebrants. For participants, "The Wedding" was not about fitting into a pre-arranged style. Instead, it was about expanding the celebration to include various approaches to marriage and family. Like alternative wedding celebrants of the 1960s and 1970s, same-sex partners recognized the flexibility of the wedding and used the celebration to express their views about life and love. Bachelor likewise noted the celebration's significance and concluded the event by stating, "It matters not who we love, only that we love."[2]

Gay community leaders emphasized the political component of the celebration. Drawing on the activist view that the personal was political, the public pronouncement and celebration of a long-ridiculed personal lifestyle served as the ultimate political statement. Those present rejected the shame associated with their relationships and proved that many same-sex couples shared long-term, committed relationships. Courageously displaying their individual love and their membership in a community of likeminded gay men and lesbians, "Wedding" participants did not demand a social inclusion marked by assimilation or guarded emotions. Rather, they demanded full acceptance of their lifestyle and relationship choices. Reverend Troy Perry, a minister evicted from the

Pentecostal Church of God for his own homosexuality and founder of the Universal Fellowship of Metropolitan Community Churches, spoke to this desire for openness and acceptance as he rallied his congregants with a shout of "Out of the closets and into the chapels!"[3]

Hosting "The Wedding" in front of the Internal Revenue Service's building was a symbolic choice meant to protest the tax office's refusal to accept taxes jointly filed by same-sex couples. As activist Sue Hyde recalled, couples participated in "The Wedding" "both to protest discrimination against them and to celebrate their love and commitment to each other."[4] Challenging conventional views of family and marriage, groom and "Wedding" organizer Carey Junkin of Los Angeles echoed "The Wedding's" official slogan when he said, "Love makes a family, nothing else." Adding his own sentiment, he stated, "We won't go back."[5] Marriages celebrated that day held no legal standing, but that did not diminish the emotional impact of the event. The community of couples who wed accomplished their political objective by making their private relationships part of the political discourse. The very public, very political event demanded recognition of the legitimacy of the relationship between two brides or two grooms.

As for "The Wedding" participants (composed of more male than female couples, suggesting an ongoing discomfort with weddings and marriage among politically active feminists), they expressed warm praise for the celebration, as well as a sense of anger that any members of the gay or lesbian community would criticize their decision to wed. Dressed in suits, tuxedos, and wedding gowns, albeit with little regard for normative notions of gender, the celebrants saw the day as an important turning point in their lives and relationships. Despite their unorthodox appearances, many participants noted that they would have been comfortable with an even more "traditional" ceremony. The only registered disappointment pertained to the desire that the ceremony might have been more explicit in regard to monogamy or couples' exclusivity.[6] The mass "Wedding" was not intended to replicate heterosexual marital relationships or wedding celebrations, but the importance given the celebration and the desire for expression of personal preference—be it for a more or even less traditional form than the ceremony before the IRS—hinted at possible similarities between same-sex weddings and their opposite-sex counterparts.

Two brides at the 1987 March on Washington. Courtesy of the ONE National Gay & Lesbian Archives, Los Angeles, California.

While "The Wedding" looked unlike the individual white weddings celebrated by heterosexual couples, the event incorporated familiar elements of the wedding ceremony. Most participants wore some sort of special dress; an authority figured presided over the celebration; and guests bore witness to the event. The relationships may have seemed atypical or strange in the eyes of the mainstream observer, but there could be no question as to what had transpired that October day. The familiarity of the wedding served as a valuable political tool even as it fulfilled the personal desires of same-sex couples who wished to share their lives together. For a population who had the option—admittedly the very unpleasant option—of invisibility, the choice to make public the intimacies of private life was a political statement in and of itself.[7]

Same-sex weddings transcended the "difference vs. accommodation" debates often raised in subcultural groups and hotly contested within the queer community.[8] In the years following the celebration of "The

Wedding," gay men and lesbians expressed a blend of intentions and motivations with their celebrations. The flexibility of the wedding, continually tested by the heterosexual marrying population in the decades since World War II, likewise served the personal as well as the political objectives of queer couples. Moving from the mass to the individual, weddings legitimated and celebrated relationships that had long been deemed wrong or strange and had thus been cloaked in secrecy. Such celebrations allowed men and women to celebrate their private lives in a public style and with the sanction of chosen and accepting family and community members. By publicly celebrating their relationships, queers challenged a political system that refused to recognize their right to wed.

Like the weddings of those before them, the white weddings hosted by same-sex couples in the 1990s and in the early years of the new century seemingly adhered to a standardized form of celebration. The similarity between opposite-sex and same-sex events, of course, was noticeable in the continued reliance on a wedding industry and adherence to wedding norms: formal dress, recitation of vows, and elaborate receptions. On the surface, this suggested a kind of queer accommodation to the standard form. Even though a gay couple might purchase a cake topper that featured two grooms, the couple still purchased a cake topper. The prerequisites of a wedding had tremendous staying power. But same-sex couples shaped their weddings in ways specific to their relationships and cultural identifications. Ceremonial alteration and amendment, whether slight or pronounced, reflected the beliefs and desires of same-sex couples.[9]

Queer couples, like other brides and grooms, negotiated tensions created by family, cost, and the overall wedding planning procedure. Unlike heterosexual couples, same-sex brides and grooms challenged existing authority in the very act of celebrating a wedding. Couples celebrated the communities from which they came, to which they currently belonged, and those they created, if only for their weddings. They exerted individual authority over their ceremonies not only in their selection of music, dress, and wedding style, but also in their very direct rejection of a legal system that denied them access to the rights and privileges of marriage. They publicly celebrated relationships long denied public recognition. Weddings could be and could say whatever the celebrating couples wished. As various states began to recognize same-sex marriages, acceptance of same-sex unions extended even beyond the queer community. Weddings both affirmed the political victory achieved by those who had long advocated on behalf of equal rights and marked the triumph of personalization in American wedding culture.

* * *

Throughout American history, same-sex relationships often were shrouded in secrecy.[10] Homosexuals created a subculture in which their desires and lifestyles were accepted, but mainstream American culture marked homosexuality as deviant. Like their straight counterparts, gay men and women moved beyond the confines of their small towns and local communities due to the mobilization required by World War II. The homosocial nature of military life and the concentration of military populations in coastal urban centers allowed for sexual experimentation among members of the same sex. Men and women embraced the freedom to pursue non-normative sexual desires. The years following the war, however, were marked by a commitment to the policing of the queer behavior identified during the war years and punished by the undesirable "blue discharge." Cold War insecurities demanded strict adherence to normative gender roles. Those who rejected the ideal of the nuclear family and American way of life were circumspect. Beyond communists, McCarthy-era witch hunts identified homosexuals as security threats and systematically removed queers from their positions within government and the military.[11]

Given the potential for arrest and public exposure, most gay men and lesbians kept their homosexuality a secret.[12] But while police efforts quieted queer activism, the gay subculture was not silenced. The sizable homosexual population exposed by World War II–era mobilization and the confirmation of widespread homosexual experience among American men, reported by Alfred Kinsey's *Sexual Behavior in the Human Male*, proved the existence of a queer community.[13] Gay men and women were not alone in their feelings of difference. And while communities could be entered only through knowledge of certain codes and behaviors, men and women found each other, despite the antagonism of law enforcement. Early efforts by organizations such as the Mattachine Society (founded in 1950) and the Daughters of Bilitis (founded in 1955) protested inequalities faced by gay men and lesbians as they aimed to present a "respectable" homosexual community to the American public, a community defined by more than sexual behavior.[14]

Given the need for secrecy, sexual acts, especially between two men, could be fairly fleeting experiences. Cruising was a normal element of gay men's lives. Those who viewed homosexuality as a sickness or perversion believed that homosexuals thrived on such promiscuity.[15] But quick meetings and aversion to monogamy did not mark all queer relationships. *ONE*, the publication founded by members of the Mattachine Society, addressed the relationship between gay men and marriage as the 1950s came to a close.[16] While an April 1959 article recognized the appeal of marriage's "stability" and "the taking of vows which are to ensure that two persons will be loyal," author Hermann Stoessel also pointed to the potential collapse of heterosexual marriage. By necessity, queers had had to create alternative relationships, and Stoessel believed this might serve the gay community well. The heterosexual seemed increasingly inclined to strive for elements found in the ideal gay life such as "freedom, variety and experience."[17]

On the other hand, some queer couples embraced what they called the "homophile married life." A December 1959 piece by Jim Egan asked the question, "Homosexual Marriage: Fact or Fancy?" Ultimately, he declared committed relationships—or marriages—fact. Egan and his partner of 11 years knew many committed couples who had been together "for from one to two to over forty years." To his knowledge, nearly all the relationships were monogamous. Egan recognized the emotional as well as the financial benefits of these pairings: "All these relationships . . . bring love, companionship and meaning to the participants' lives" while also serving as "stepping-stones to material benefits that would otherwise most likely never have been realized." Like all marriages, the homosexual marriage required work to succeed. Love, trust, and respect created strong and lasting relationships, as did the need for self-acceptance, often challenging for homosexual couples given the negative public view of homosexuality.[18]

A 1963 issue pressed the issue even further. Randy Lloyd published an article entitled "Let's Push for Homophile Marriage." Lloyd critiqued a March 1963 *Harper's* article on "New York's Middle-Class Homosexuals" for its failure to address the experience of married queers. In Lloyd's eyes, the homophile married life was "much more preferable, ethically superior, enjoyable, exciting, less-responsibility-ridden (contrary to a lot of propaganda from the single set), and just plain more fun." In a style not unlike women's magazines of the time, Lloyd provided a list of tried and true tips for those interested in a marital relationship: "How To Succeed in Getting Married By Trying." Using advice taken from happily married friends, Lloyd directed readers to stay optimistic, remain physically fit, befriend members of the homophile married set, and preserve some sexual energy even while enjoying single life.

Lloyd suggested that readers should not allow expected family response to deter their quest for a happy marriage. "Don't worry in advance what your heterosexual mother, father, sisters, brothers, or neighbors 'will say' about your homophile marriage. You'll be surprised at how heterosexuals' attitudes change to respect when faced with what they've been told is impossible from homosexuals—a show of guts. The chances are they will never 'say' anything."[19] Lloyd did not call for total openness or a demand for acceptance, but he promoted a relationship beyond the closet. Given the predominant views on homosexuality, it would be too much for families to discuss the existence of a homophile marriage or, even more outrageous, to celebrate the marriage. However, given the respectable—and brave—nature of the relationship, they should, Lloyd asserted, be willing to accept it.

Expecting that some queers would critique homosexual desire to marry, Lloyd rejected the notion that marriage was an institution only for heterosexuals. Instead, Lloyd viewed marriage as a relationship style open to anyone desirous of and willing to participate in it. He wrote, "Marriage is not more a strictly heterosexual social custom than are the social customs of birthday celebrations, funerals, house-warmings, or, for that matter, sleeping, eating, and the like. I participate in those, not because they are heterosexual or homosexual things, but because I am a human being." Lloyd was one half of a marital pair not because he wished to replicate heterosexual life, but because he "discovered that it is by far the most enjoyable way of life for me." He continued by writing, "And I think that's also the reason heterosexual men and women marry, though some people twist things around to make it appear they are merely following convention."[20]

While it is impossible to know the actual number of committed gay and lesbian couples during the 1950s and 1960s, queer marriages existed in the immediate postwar decades and in the years before the official start to Gay Liberation. While "marriage" may have been announced upon cohabitation rather than celebration (although some sympathetic clergy would officiate over gay unions), the commitment to the relationship matched the commitment of heterosexual married couples.[21] A primary difference was the need for discretion—or outright secrecy—in public and in dealings with family, neighbors, employers, and friends. Gay men and women might have had a community with whom they could be themselves and celebrate their relationships, but the public recognition and open communal celebration afforded a marriage between a man and a woman were absent.

Inspired by the movements of the 1960s, many young homosexual activists rejected the need for secrecy. They refused to believe society's negative view of homosexuality, and they looked critically at what they interpreted as the self-censure and attempted mainstreaming of 1950s-era homophile organizations.[22] Participating in protests inspired by the civil rights movement and Women's Liberation, activists promoted equal treatment under law and advocated on behalf of a united gay rights movement. The transitional event was the June 27, 1969 confrontation between New York City police and the patrons at the Stonewall Inn, located on Christopher Street in Greenwich Village. Bar patrons refused arrest in a dramatic fashion, torching the bar and drawing a crowd of approximately 2,000 supporters. By July, men and women in New York created a Gay Liberation Front, advocating for gay rights in a style similar to the radical edge of other 1960s movements. Activists rejected assimilation and celebrated gay difference.[23] Gay rights activism grew in strength, and gays and lesbians attained greater visibility.

By the 1960s and 1970s, mainstream periodicals such as *Harper's*, *Life*, and the *New York Times* published stories on emerging gay ghettos and increasingly visible gay life.[24] Even as marriage was not a particular goal of the GLF, gay couples made the news. In 1971, *Look* magazine chronicled the monogamous relationship of Mike McConnell and Jack Baker. McConnell, a librarian, and Baker, a law student at the University of Minnesota, believed their relationship mirrored romantic relationships enjoyed by their heterosexual friends. Having lived together since 1967, the two argued that their relationship was "just like being married."[25] Baker directly linked his responsibilities as a citizen with the rights and protections of citizenship: "If I'm going to pay taxes, I want the same benefits." In 1970, the two attempted to register for a marriage license at City Hall but their request was rejected. When Baker challenged the rejection, the Minnesota Supreme Court ruled, "In commonsense and in a constitutional sense, there is a clear distinction between a marital restriction based merely upon race and one based upon the fundamental difference in sex." The state would not recognize their union.[26]

Beyond their desire for equal civil rights, Baker and McConnell looked to the religious realm for sanction of their relationship. Baker, a lifelong Catholic, and McConnell, a Southern Baptist, regularly attended the University of Minnesota's Newman Center Chapel. One Sunday, as the priest sermonized about the "openness of Christ in accepting people," Baker pressed him to consider how homosexuals fit into this openness. Baker asked, "Do you feel that if two people give themselves in love to each other and want to grow together with mutual understanding, that Jesus would be open to such a union if the people were of the same sex?" The young priest, speaking on his own and without adherence to official doctrine, agreed that Jesus would bless such a relationship. Social and cultural acceptance of same-sex relationships seemed to be expanding.[27]

Baker and McConnell were in the minority as they publicly pushed for the right to marry. Many homosexuals rejected marriage and monogamy. Some, having been one half of a heterosexual marriage, negatively associated the institution with their closeted lives. Marriage was not an initial goal of the gay rights movement, and many activists of the 1970s and early 1980s offered explicit critique of the institution or ignored the subject. Others seemed content to create their own versions of marriage, untouched by state sanction and unmarked by public recognition or celebration beyond their closest friends.[28]

Mary Mendola, a writer "married" to another woman, conducted an investigation in the late 1970s to determine just how many same-sex couples existed. The resulting publication, *The Mendola Report*, while hardly scientific, proved that gay men and lesbians resided together as married couples throughout the United States. Using only an informal network of gay and lesbian contacts, Mendola found 1,500 potential couples to survey and received an astonishing 27 percent return on her distribution. Of her return sample, 67 percent of respondents described themselves as permanently committed or "married."[29]

Many couples interviewed by Mendola emphasized the similarity between homosexual and straight marriages. One interviewee commented, "I don't think there's that much difference between gay and straight marriages . . . Not only do the same type of problems come up, but the *reasons* for those problems are even the same. I don't see any differences. Faith and hope and love and understanding are priorities in any relationship—gay or straight." His partner emphasized one important distinction: "The big difference between gay and straight marriages is the legal aspect. Our home is in both our names, and, should one of us die, no will is going to guarantee that a family won't create problems. . . . There is no getting around it: legal marriage protects you." As Mendola wrote, "Lesbian and homosexual couples have no 'legal step' to legitimate, make public, or solidify their relationships. The step, it seems, is taken privately when two gay people make a commitment to each other."[30] For many, the private step was enough. Those who desired public or legal recognition were on their own, particularly since most national and local organizations devoted to gay rights saw marriage as a "hopeless cause" or had other goals.[31]

In the years following *The Mendola Report*, the necessity of a legally recognized union became increasingly important to many queer couples. Marriage was a community goal that grew out of lived experience. The impact of the AIDS virus coupled with the experiences of child-rearing and parental rights brought on by the "lesbian baby boom" made many couples painfully aware of the limitations of their legally unrecognized partnerships. AIDS revealed the tenuous nature of rights and recognition won in the gay liberation struggle as partners and friends were denied access to their ailing loved ones. Couples whose relationships were acknowledged and accepted by their friends and communities faced public institutions such as hospitals and state agencies that refused to recognize their relationships. Mothers and fathers faced similar struggles as they battled with courts to attain legal guardianship for each parent in a same-sex relationship. No matter how accepted a gay or lesbian couple might be by their families or friends, legal inequality severely limited their rights. A relationship that included a commitment of "until death do us part" held a certain immediate appeal for many same-sex couples of the 1980s as the AIDS epidemic spread; by 1988, just seven years after initial diagnoses, 82,000 people had been diagnosed and 46,000 had died. To have full protection in their personal relationships, couples required political recognition. As men and women came to grips with the limitations of their partnerships, grassroots activists looked to marriage as a strategy for attaining equal rights.[32]

Weddings became a political instrument in efforts to attain legally recognized same-sex marriage. The 1987 Wedding was the first but certainly not the last mass wedding used as a tool of protest. The symbolic power of "The Wedding" inspired mass weddings during the 1993 March on Washington for Lesbian, Gay, and Bi Equal Rights and Liberation and the 2000 Millennium March on Washington. Troy Perry was present for both events. In 1993, he communicated the importance of the right to same-sex marriage as he proclaimed,

> We stand before our nation and our friends because we wish to proclaim our right to love one another. . . . We stand here knowing of the lies and untruths that have been told about us by some in the larger community. But we stand here pure of heart and unafraid in proclaiming that our concern and care for one another is as rich as that in any culture or community.[33]

A letter to the editor published in a Syracuse newspaper communicated the significance of the wedding for one couple involved: "[T]wo of my closest friends attended the march, which also included a symbolic mass marriage. While not legally binding anywhere . . . they, along with thousands of other couples in love, joined hands and exchanged vows. It was one of the happiest moments of their 12-year relationship."[34] Like celebrants in the late 1960s and 1970s, queer activists recognized the power to be found in the language of weddings. Political objectives intertwined with personal celebrations.

Even as same-sex couples were denied the right of legally recognized marriage, the wedding still had immense symbolic power. As queer novelist Christopher Bram suggested, "[S]ymbols are very interesting, not least because we are free to choose or reject them."[35] Celebrations grew beyond the scope of protest as couples realized they could use their weddings to express any number of views. Same-sex weddings were not marked only by political activism, although that aspect of such celebrations will remain until full legal recognition of same-sex unions. On days when no march was held, when no protest was planned, men and women increasingly chose to celebrate their relationships with white weddings and variations of the white wedding form. The same-sex wedding, while not always intentionally linked to political protest, grew in popularity during the 1990s and first decade of the 2000s. The appeal of personal expression, which had been so attractive to heterosexual couples, likewise attracted gay men and lesbians. Like celebrants before them, same-sex couples responded to the power of ritual and to the possibility of shaping that ritual to reflect their relationships, their communities, and the world around them.[36] Before long, a same-sex wedding phenomenon was born. And with its focus on love and commitment, the wedding proved a valuable tool for those advocating on behalf of marriage equality.

* * *

In 1992, Tess Ayers and Paul Brown set out to write a how-to manual for gay men and women wishing to marry. *The Essential Guide to Lesbian and Gay Weddings* offered queer couples a new kind of wedding guide, one designed specifically for same-sex unions. Ayers and Brown self-consciously recognized the possibilities available to lesbian brides and gay grooms. "How fortunate you are," they wrote, "that there are no rules, no scripts, no long lists of 'Have to's' that your mothers will wave under your noses. It's *your* wedding ceremony, and anytime you choose to draw on established traditions, you will be doing so with an acute awareness of why you're doing it, not just because 'that's what you do in a wedding.'" Books of etiquette and wedding guides had long negotiated the necessity of wedding tradition. In many ways, Ayers and Brown's text followed the standard wedding guide format. They recognized wedding celebrants' personal authority in selecting which traditions to use and which to discard. They explicitly noted the flexibility of the celebration. And so, while they provided a fairly conventional wedding guide, complete with lists and suggested deadlines, Brown and Ayers affirmed their readers when they wrote: "We think anything's okay, as long as it's what *you* want to do."[37]

When Ayers and Brown began compiling *The Essential Guide to Lesbian and Gay Weddings*, their goal was to help same-sex couples figure out how to find friendly vendors or, if necessary, negotiate with vendors who were less than thrilled with the prospect of outfitting a queer wedding.[38] Ayers, with Brown's help, had planned a 1992 wedding to her partner of ten years, and the two had found the available straight advice literature lacking. As the book went to print in 1994, they noted, "there is a veritable stampede of same-sex weddings taking place."[39] By the time of the 1999 revision, the relationship between gay weddings, the wedding industry, and American media had changed even more dramatically. Movies and primetime network television shows featured same-sex couples tying the knot, often in the still standard white wedding style. Starting in August 2002, the *New York Times* included same-sex celebrations in its wedding announcements. Newspapers around the country followed suit.[40]

Business became one of the staunchest supporters of same-sex weddings. The wedding industry, while encouraging the wedding as a spending free-for-all, long supported transition within the celebration. Savvy entrepreneurs responded to and even pushed for a flexible wedding style. The power of old traditions and the presence of newly created traditions expanded just how many people the industry could reach and just how many goods and services businesses could provide. Same-sex couples might plan a different kind of wedding, or look for inspiration from different sources, but undoubtedly they would need professional services along the way. And profits were not relegated only to those in the business of weddings. Even non-wedding-related products promoted same-sex weddings or commitment ceremonies and enjoyed financial return. For example, in 2004, Absolut Vodka ran a guide to gay commitment ceremonies in *The Advocate* and *Out*.[41] Rather than writing off experimental brides and grooms as a lost cause, marketers realized they could reach those with an alternative vision of the wedding.

While some professionals may have supported queer weddings in political solidarity, others were more interested in the bottom line. Same-sex couples offered a newly expanded market for wedding professionals. As of 2000, the U.S. Census estimated that approximately 1.2 million adults identified themselves as part of a same-sex couple household. The actual number might have been much higher, given the potential reluctance of some same-sex couples to identify as such on the Census. A 1999 estimate put the number far higher: anywhere between 1.6 million and 6 million couples. A 2004 study by the Congressional Budget Office suggested that the number of likely-to-wed couples, were same-sex marriage to be legalized, could reach as many as 600,000.[42] This was music to a wedding professional's ears. Rather than selling one dress, shops welcoming lesbian clientele might sell two dresses per wedding. Wedding industry businesses and vendors eagerly promoted same-sex weddings through queer-specific advertising and participation in Gay Wedding Expos. "A Commitment to Love," the first noted gay and lesbian wedding fair, took place in Chicago in February 1995. This fledgling event drew 1,000 people. Two thousand prospective brides and grooms attended the first Los Angeles Gay and Lesbian Wedding Expo in 2003. The next year, the L.A. Expo welcomed 4,000 brides and grooms-to-be and selected 42 vendors from a pool of 100 applicants. Replicating straight bridal fairs, these events offered gay and lesbian couples selections from a variety of queer-friendly photographers, caterers, disc jockeys, and wedding locations.[43]

Wedding Planning and Management: Consultancy for Diverse Clients, a 2007 publication designed to aid those involved in the business of wedding planning, spoke directly to the issue of same-sex weddings. Detailing the gay marriage debate, the text suggested that planners needed to "determine if this is a niche market you would like to pursue." Emphasizing the bottom line, authors Maggie Daniels and Carry Loveless noted that most wedding planners generally "are not in the business of turning away clients." They reminded their audience that "same-sex ceremonies and receptions tend to be as extravagant and planning intensive as those of heterosexual couples."[44] Cindy Sproul of Rainbow-WeddingNetwork.com, a website for same-sex wedding celebrants, noted that couples in states that refused to recognize gay marriage still spent nearly $17,000. In states where civil unions were recognized, the average budget was slightly higher, at $23,000–25,000. Lower estimates still put projected spending output near the $10,000 marker.[45] While these figures were less than the projected average spent by opposite-sex couples, which before the economic bust of 2008 inched ever closer to $30,000, the market still promised a boom to industry professionals.[46] Daniels and Loveless indicated that shunning same-sex business was not an acceptable option. If a professional felt uncomfortable taking on gay or lesbian clientele, he or she should be prepared, at the very least, to recommend a local consultant who would welcome the business of same-sex wedding celebrants.[47]

As same-sex weddings became increasingly visible during the 1990s and into the twenty-first century, they took a variety of shapes and forms. Ayers and Brown noted, time and again, the uniqueness of the queer wedding. When it came to gay weddings, they explained, there were no "true traditions." Brides and their brides, grooms and their grooms celebrated in whatever style they saw fit. Couples interviewed for *The Essential Guide to Lesbian and Gay Weddings* reflected numerous wedding possibilities. Ayers and Brown reported that weddings were "interpreted differently by each couple, for reasons sometimes having to do with their cultural, religious, or ethnic background, and sometimes not. Some did their weddings just like their parents had done; other made it up as they went along. But they all approached their weddings with pride and a sense of humor." The wedding could be as queer as the couple desired. It could reflect favorite memories from the drag ball or "little girl dreams." Few wedding guides admitted to the tradition-making possibility held by brides and grooms. *The Essential Guide to Lesbian and Gay Weddings* told same-sex couples that they stood as pioneers in same-sex wedding celebrations. Someday there would be tradition for same-sex wedding celebrants to follow, and as Ayers and Brown told their readers, "you're making it right now." They wrote, "[Y]ou get to create your own symbols that are new and appropriate—symbols that reflect your own personal realities, as well as the reality of you as a couple."[48]

The lived experience of a wedding, however, extended beyond marketplace interactions and "personal realities." Couples had to consider the reactions of those around them. They existed within a broader community of potentially unsupportive coworkers, neighbors, and even family and friends. The queer wedding of a daughter had different implications than the queer wedding of a fictional character on television. Further, most same-sex couples lived in a world where legal marriage was still out of reach. The prospect of a wedding could be somewhat overwhelming. But as queer brides and grooms learned, celebration of gay weddings provided a means of reaching those around them.

The creation of the wedding celebration as a reflection of a couple's "personal realities" had been a goal since the immediate postwar years. As with heterosexual wedding celebrations, motivations behind gay and lesbian weddings led couples in any number of directions. Most couples hoped to blend a sense of community or belonging with the same kind of individuality or personal expression desired by their opposite-sex peers. The familiarity of the ceremony made it a perfect location for bringing together the often disparate groups to which queer couples belonged. Same-sex couples designed their weddings to honor the community and the relationships that had been important to them on their journey to the courthouse, the altar, or the botanical garden. Depending on the couple's preference or experiences, these relationships could be those of fictive or biological kin. The guest list might be composed of a fairly traditional, easily recognizable community, or it might be one of the couple's invention. At the same time, these weddings demanded the couple's rightful place as members of the national body politic as they expressed desired inclusion among the majority of citizens whose right to lawful marriage was guaranteed. They celebrated couples' styles and beliefs and insisted upon the legitimacy, recognition, and acceptance of same-sex unions.[49] Public and private, personal and political blended together in a single celebration.

Evan Wolfson, an attorney formerly on staff at Lambda Legal, a national organization devoted to achieving civil rights for gays, lesbians, bisexuals, and the transgender population, argued that marriage was an important goal if only for its recognizability. "One of the main protections that comes with marriage is the word marriage," Wolfson argued, "which brings clarity and security that is simply not replaceable by any other word or by a sheaf of documents."[50] Likewise, the wedding provided a common starting point for marriage, a location familiar both to homosexuals and heterosexuals. While couples of the 1950s used their weddings to mark their separation from their respective extended families, same-sex couples often used their weddings to strengthen familial ties or to explain their relationships. For many same-sex couples, the wedding was a site of education for perplexed or even outright resistant family members. Just as Wolfson noted the importance of the familiarity of marital language, the familiarity of the wedding communicated an important message to those attending same-sex marriage celebrations.

While the message might be the "just like us" notion so abhorrent to radical queers, it might also serve as the push toward communal and familial acceptance so desired by many gay men and lesbians. On the other hand, the wedding could be used to express an alternative view of family and community. Same-sex couples used the ceremony to either or sometimes both ends. Queer wedding celebrants took the wedding— a celebration typically viewed as a conservative component of American culture—and made it radical.

Meg Stone, whose plans to wed Karen Malme were chronicled in the *Boston Globe*, recognized the political power of marriage and weddings when the Massachusetts Supreme Judicial Court declared same-sex marriage legal in 2004. The decision received intense public attention as state officials debated whether the ruling would stick, if provision of civil unions would satisfy the court, or if the state constitution should be amended to ban same-sex marriage. Beyond the world of media and state government, the debate led to a new kind of political consciousness among Stone and Malme's friends and families. Stone noted, "Family friends I've known since childhood are asking me about gay rights for the first time ever. They express more anger about discrimination and antigay attitudes because those beliefs threaten my marriage. People who love me but never understood my life choices understand marriage." The language of marriage and the familiarity of the institution created a new kind of political dialog for Stone and her loved ones. Stone was explicit in her desire for a wedding to celebrate the marriage her family and friends so strongly supported. "Creating a ritual to affirm what our relationship means to us is important," she wrote, "as is sharing that ritual with all the people we love." By using the wedding to communicate the "warmth, ease, and partnership" between them, Stone and Malme aimed to demonstrate that their relationship—one that might at first appear atypical or unusual to some observers—was still a loving relationship people could understand.[51]

In 2002, the Bravo television network broadcast a reality special entitled *Gay Weddings*. Following four same-sex couples as they prepared for their wedding days, the six-episode series chronicled the ups and downs of the wedding planning process. *Gay Weddings* featured events very clearly influenced by the commercialized nature of modern American weddings. The economic standing of each couple marked the style of celebration, from the Hollywood power couple who wed in an elaborate celebration arranged by a fashionable event planner to the Latina and African American lesbian couple married in a friend's backyard. But while the weddings of those chronicled on the *Gay Weddings* series were seemingly far removed from the revolutionary efforts of those participating in a mass wedding on the National Mall, the featured weddings indicated the possibilities of queer wedding celebrations. Couples aimed to make their weddings expressive of their relationships, even as they saw the wedding as a tool to aid their families in coming to terms with their relationships.[52]

In many ways, the featured couples blended focus on themselves with a greater focus on their friends and families. For one couple, Scott and Harley, the wedding provided the perfect opportunity for Scott's traditional New England family to see just what his relationship to Harley was all about. By attending the wedding, they could see that Scott and Harley took their relationship "very seriously." During a destination wedding in Puerto Vallarta, Mexico, Scott's parents Barbara and Paul attended a rehearsal dinner with a drag queen ensemble for entertainment and participated in a specially arranged beach wedding. As Barbara and Paul witnessed the relationship between the two men, they became increasingly supportive. While they may not have rejected their initial view that the relationship was "not normal," they did admit to finding the ceremony the most "emotionally moving" they had ever attended and noted that the two men were lucky to have friends so unique and caring.[53] In their interview, post-production, the two men agreed that the best part of their wedding was the time they spent with their friends and family in Mexico. Having these disparate communities together validated and confirmed the two men's decision to wed.[54]

For many same-sex couples, their weddings communicated the serious nature of the relationship they shared. The Human Rights Campaign, the largest national lesbian, gay, bisexual, and transgender civil rights organization in the United States, offered advice for same-sex couples hoping to wed and featured testimonials from those who already had. The HRC fielded questions about same-sex wedding etiquette and provided answers from Tess Ayers, *Essential Guide to Lesbian and Gay Weddings* author. In 2001, "Walt" wrote to Ayers and expressed his desire to hold a commitment ceremony with his partner, in part "to proclaim our commitment to each other in front of our family and friends." Unfortunately, some members of Walt's family were not supportive of his relationship. His query: how to have them at the ceremony and make them part of the event? Ayers suggested that having a ceremony would "help family members to finally come to terms with the fact that this is not a phase you're going through. If you take your ceremony and commitment seriously, they might just follow." At the same time, however, Ayers advised "including" family members only selectively. Rather than asking a resistant brother to serve as best man, Walt might consider integrating family members into the receiving line, or seating them in a reserved location. In short, hesitant family members might be more comfortable with "things that might be done at a more traditional wedding." Ayers confidently and optimistically noted, "We've heard many stories of skeptical family members being transformed by the occasion when they see the love and support of your chosen family."[55]

Gay men and lesbians often faced more explicit challenges to their relationships and weddings than did their straight counterparts, making familial support and participation all the more important. *Gay Weddings* spoke to the very real possibility of familial rejection or insensitivity. Dale and Eve faced a hurtful reality when Dale's parents and siblings wavered on whether to attend their celebration—an unthinkable thing for Dale to have done when her brother and sister hosted their respective weddings. Dan and Gregg likewise experienced familial rejection. Despite sending an email that reminded Dan, "no one loves you as much as your mother," his mother opted not to attend his 2002 wedding to Gregg. In spite of a close relationship between the two, Dan's mother could not come to terms with his relationship with another man. In his vows, Dan thanked Gregg for allowing him to make his family "paramount" even when it "hurt" or "saddened" him. Their officiant recognized that there were people, who "for one reason or another" chose not to celebrate with them at their wedding, but emphasized that the partnership between the two men meant that they would never be alone.[56]

Ayers and Brown advised gay men and lesbians to invite even those who rejected their relationships. They suggested that a wedding—and even a wedding invitation—made a statement. While a brother might refuse to recognize a celebrant's partner, Brown and Ayers argued that receipt of a wedding invitation would communicate that "your committed relationship is not something you're ashamed of." They hoped that queer pride and confidence and the attempted inclusion of resistant relatives would make a difference. "Maybe, just maybe," they optimistically wrote, "this will help him to understand. And if he doesn't 'get it' right away, your act may help him over the coming years, to view your relationship with more legitimacy."[57]

As legal theorist Barbara J. Cox reminisced about her own commitment ceremony, she considered what it had meant for her partner, herself, and those around them. The celebration was meant to honor the relationship Cox shared with her partner, but family and friends also played a key role. She wrote, "When my partner and I decided to have a commitment ceremony, we did so to express the love and caring that we feel for one another, to celebrate that love with our friends and family, and to express that love openly and with pride." Cox rejected the view that she was merely "part of a mindless flock accepting a dehumanizing ceremony." Instead, she embraced the opportunity the wedding provided to share an alternative relationship style with others.

Throughout the process of planning for and then celebrating her union, friends, family, coworkers, and members of the surrounding community witnessed a committed relationship that did not fit with mainstream views. Cox announced her marriage to her students, who then presented her with a silver frame, engraved, "Barb and Peg, Our Wedding." A colleague told Cox of an important family discussion inspired by the fact that she would be attending a lesbian wedding. Cox celebrated the awareness stimulated by her ceremony and believed it to be "profoundly transformative." She surmised that the commitment ceremony

> affected our families, our friends, and even the clerks in the jewelry store where we explained we were looking for wedding rings for the both of us. Or on the two hundred people who received my mother's annual Xeroxed Christmas letter with a paragraph describing the ceremony. Or the clerk in the store who engraved the frame for my students. Or the young children who learned that same-sex marriage exists.[58]

Beyond educating others about same-sex relationships, the wedding also provided the opportunity to demonstrate a commitment to an alternative vision of community or, as Ayers called it, a "chosen family."[59] When Meg Stone reflected on her relationships with her chosen family and family of origin, she considered the importance of one family to the other: "Having a chosen family of people who understand me because they are like me makes it easier for me to love the family I came from." Her marriage to Karen Malme seemed to her an embodiment of this blend. Through her marriage to "Mal," Stone believed she was "joining tradition with nontradition, where I came from with who I am."[60] As Ayers and Brown might suggest, Stone was creating her own tradition, one that might someday be a hallmark of same-sex wedding style.

In an even more revolutionary possibility, the wedding allowed for the creation of a new community, even if only for the duration of the celebration. Mike and Duane, married in San Francisco in the early 1990s, celebrated the diversity of their guests: young and old, gay and straight, male and female, family and friends.[61] For Cathryn and Connie, lesbians married in October 1994, the guest population of their wedding reflected the couple's vision of an ideal, inclusive community. Nearly 125 people attended the wedding in the couple's backyard. Witnesses ranged in age from four to eighty years old, and reflected a diversity of races and sexual orientations. The women took pride in the composition of their wedding public. They celebrated the freedom they felt in having a lesbian wedding, the possibility that they might "make up [their] own script."[62]

Anne Campbell likewise celebrated the diversity of her wedding party. Grandmothers met friends from the leather bar—and this was the point. As Campbell recalled her wedding reception, she noted,

> I am quite certain we had the most motley crew of wedding guests ever assembled. Aside from our out-of-town guests, we welcomed: co-workers and their spouses from my big Silicon Valley employer; Drew's co-workers from Damron, the queer travel guide company; parishioners and clergy from my predominantly gay and lesbian Episcopal parish; and assorted other gay, straight, leather-inclined, and Goth friends and hangers-on.

Campbell recalled friends who responded to the wedding in a casual manner, and "even with a little disdain, as if we were undertaking something strangely old-fashioned and unnecessary."[63] While the decision to wed might be seen as a conservative choice, the celebration hosted by Campbell and her female-to-male transsexual husband Drew offered a radical alternative to the predictable wedding audience. The celebrants made a conventional celebration unconventional. Rather than assimilation, the wedding ceremony reflected a different view of ideal family and community relationships. Even queer theorist Michael Warner, a virulent critic of same-sex marriage as a political goal, concedes, "Ceremonies can do many laudable things, especially in making concrete the social worlds that queers make for themselves." Campbell's post-wedding reception not only made concrete her own queer social world, but also created a unique blend of queer and straight communities.[64]

Ultimately, many same-sex couples believed their relationships existed within a context of other social relationships. This was not a novel viewpoint, as alternative weddings of the 1960s and 1970s often emphasized a similar sentiment, but this sentiment moved away from the focus on the marital relationship as the primary or most important relationship a couple shared. Even as same-sex weddings celebrated the link between two men or two women, the mutual and respective relationships the couples shared with others retained their honored status. As Peter, married July 1, 1994, to Paul, noted, "A relationship cannot be sustained by two people alone."[65] While critiques from the queer community suggested that marriage placed one relationship above others, same-sex couples used their wedding celebrations to celebrate other intimate relationships, thereby challenging the supremacy of the marital relationship.[66] Couples achieved a form of independence in their weddings, but it was not independence in isolation.

Many same-sex couples emphasized the importance of community witness to their unions. As one couple on the Bravo television special *Gay Weddings* noted, their wedding was even more about family and friends because it was not recognized by law.[67] As counselor Douglas C. Haldeman finished his survey of several case studies of same-sex weddings, he concluded, "Relationships could not be fully honored without the public declaration of marital vows, so that the community would have the direct experience of the couples' commitment."[68] For same-sex couples, the need to prove the legitimacy or the seriousness of their relationships may have seemed a pressing issue, particularly given continuing stereotypes of the fleeting and fickle nature of queer relationships, especially among gay men.[69] Thus the wedding held a strong symbolic importance. For Cathryn, married in 1994, the fact that her marriage to Connie held no legal standing meant that the relationship was that much more heartfelt. She noted, "The marriage is more important because I get no benefits. I didn't do it for any social gain. I did it because I would stake my life on my love for her."[70] Cathryn's point is well taken, but there is social gain in a marriage, even without legal benefits. A wedding demonstrates a commitment between two people, and the witnesses who observe that commitment inevitably view that couple in a new way.

The social meanings of marriage and a wedding were not lost on gay men and lesbians. As Amie Evans recalled her childhood, she remembered playing "marriage" on rainy days. As an adolescent she had created a "Wedding Planner" scrapbook to hold pictures of potential dresses and flowers and "important notes on topics such as appetizers, cake toppers, invitations, table-setting arrangements, and reception etiquette." As she grew older and identified as a lesbian, it seemed that marriage was no longer a possibility. Thus marriage lost its appeal, and it became easier to feel disdain for the institution as a whole. The wedding, however, remained in the back of her mind. When friends started celebrating commitment ceremonies in the 1990s, they paled in comparison to the weddings Evans had imagined as a girl. While she felt joy for her friends, she felt no envy: these were not the marriages—or the weddings—she had envisioned. With the 2004 Massachusetts Supreme Judicial Court decision to allow same-sex marriage, Evans re-evaluated her view of marriage and the purpose of a wedding. She remembered her girlhood views and realized she had known even then:

> Marriage is a formal, institutional stamp of approval on love. Not crush love or lust, but a contract issued before friends and family, before government and god (if you believe), that two individuals are united as one. . . . By marrying, we publicly declare intention to our motivations and actions. The intent is a truly adult one and universally understood.[71]

Part of the power of the institution and part of the power of the celebration is created by the fact that the commitment demands witness.

Evans renewed her belief in the power of marriage and saw the public, performative nature of the wedding ceremony as crucially important to the intensified commitment. The legal arrangements that might be made outside the bonds of marriage were no substitution. As she wrote, "[T]he power of the affirmation that the ceremony bestows on the two individuals and their immediate family (whether blood or constructed) cannot be reconstructed without the public ceremony and the social acknowledgement a legal marriage bestows on the couple's position and psyche."[72] Those bearing witness to the ceremony again were key. Evans indicated the power of the same-sex couple to construct their own vision of family or community. Certainly this power sometimes stemmed from a painful necessity of biological family rejection or reticence to embrace a queer son or daughter. But the opportunity to shape notions of family and community, to bring light to the importance of previously unacknowledged or traditionally ignored relationships, made the same-sex wedding distinct—and offered the possibility of queering relationship practices even among the mainstream.[73]

Some queers found it hard to come to terms with marriage as a goal for the queer community. Many queers preferred to embrace the difference of the queer community's more open and flexible social structure. Marriage legitimized the structural inequality of heterosexual coupling and marked an effort to assimilate to what many regarded as flawed mainstream notions of love and morality. It elevated and celebrated one relationship style over all others. Best friends, ex-lovers, siblings, and long-lasting networks of community support became secondary.[74] The restrictions against queer participation in the institution demanded protest, but the history of marriage and the idea that other issues (healthcare, housing, education) should have taken precedence among activist queers made marriage, for some, a dubious goal. S. Bear Bergman, an artist and educator from Northampton, Massachusetts, admitted to feeling "ambivalent" about marriage—largely for want of a better word. However, Bergman was very clear on another matter: "I am not ambivalent about . . . weddings." Like Amie Evans, Bergman believed a wedding marked a powerful milestone in a couple's relationship to each other, especially when witnessed by friends and family. Bergman wrote,

> [S]omething about the process of getting up in front of our families (those parts of them that chose to attend), and our friends and saying out loud and for sure and with tears streaming down our faces and in

front of everyone that we were committed to each other, come what may, made something bloom in my soul. It made me look at Nicole with new eyes, marveling every time that this brilliant, beautiful woman had chosen to throw in her lot with me, and had been sure enough to say so in public where people could see.

The public nature of the event prompted a feeling of closeness and sanctity, not only between Bergman and Nicole, but also with the rest of the wedding participants: "[T]he raw, perfect energy of 75 people joyously affirming our choice to commit ourselves to one another nearly broke me up with how huge and vibrantly powerful it was; continues to surprise me with the ways in which it resonates between us, dimmer but undissipated. I felt . . . joined. And it was wonderful."[75] Even if Bergman's goal was not about the political necessity of marriage, it was a political act in the way it challenged existing views of marriage and family.

For others, however, same-sex unions were directly inspired by a couple's political values. Following San Francisco Mayor Gavin Newsome's February 2004 decision to issue marriage licenses to same-sex couples, a rush of more than 4,000 gay and lesbian couples lined up to receive their licenses. Many of those couples continued to express reservations about the connection between marriage and its provided benefits. They balked at the elevation of one relationship over others. Karen, a lesbian who decided to marry, did so with an explicitly political purpose: as long as rights were denied, she noted, "inequalities can only ferment and seep through our system of justice," and "equality can't happen." Her marriage stemmed from a decision to fight such inequalities. Another woman embraced the opportunity to marry despite having already hosted a commitment ceremony. About her marriage she stated, "I'm not doing this for the sanction of the state, but because it has made it clearer that this is about second-class citizenship."[76]

Same-sex wedding celebrations often reflected direct political purpose. In this way, they continued the tradition of highlighting the personal interests and views of the brides or the grooms. Some observers have noted the relationship between the experience of hosting a wedding and the experience of coming out. As an individual experience, "coming out" signified a new level of liberation during the 1960s and 1970s.

Ideas of authenticity, individuality, and personal honesty informed the process, just as these qualities had informed countercultural views more broadly. If private lives, relationships, and sexual behaviors were the source of gays' and lesbians' oppression, then public display of the homosexual's private life constituted a political act. As a clear embodiment of the movement's "personal as political" mantra, coming out had political and cultural significance. As noted by one lesbian interviewed for the 1978 queer documentary *Word is Out*, "[Coming out] is the only way to turn the society around in terms of its values." The shared experience of personal revelation helped build a movement among homosexuals as they prepared to push for their rights in the 1970s. Just as the individuality and independence spread beyond the counterculture to influence mainstream views, the queer population likewise adopted the values that celebrated self-awareness and fulfillment.[77]

Ayers and Brown's discussion of wedding planning in *The Essential Guide to Lesbian and Gay Weddings* mirrored Barbara Cox's observation that a queer wedding could touch a host of communities in a very positive way. Ayers and Brown suggest that in a "straight straight straight straight world," a same-sex couple preparing to wed goes through a process of "coming out over and over again." Beyond family and friends, queer couples announced their intentions to florists, department store registries, and any number of other wedding-related services. Ayers and Brown saw the wedding as explicitly political, if only because it was a non-legal, atypical kind of celebration. Beyond the wedding, they likewise saw the political possibility for couples as they went about their wedding planning, even if it was only in shattering stereotypes by being "polite, 'normal' queers." While some couples interviewed for the *Essential Guide* had experienced discrimination, a larger number indicated that they had been treated fairly, like any other customer. Rob recalled his interaction with a local printer, a man he suspected might be uncomfortable with the prospect of working on behalf of a gay wedding. He remembered saying to the printer, "this is an unorthodox, alternative-lifestyle wedding. Will you handle something like that?" The conversation continued as Rob tiptoed around the issue until finally the printer said, "Yeah, you're gay and you're getting married. So what?"[78]

"Coming out" provided a sense of personal freedom. Modern gay weddings had a similar cultural impact and offered another kind of liberation.[79] As one man married in October 1996 noted, his wedding was "the biggest outing I've ever been through."[80] But if coming out was a personal experience, albeit one shared by members of the queer community, same-sex weddings were communal experiences, shared by a more diverse community composed of both queers and heterosexuals. Novelist David McConnell, despite viewing marriage as "weird" and "unreal," also noted the appeal of "the public aspect of marriage" for many queers: "It's a bigger, better coming-out opportunity."[81] Same-sex weddings publicly celebrated private relationships deemed shameful and immoral during the majority of twentieth-century American life. To some degree, even heterosexuals were outed in the process of witnessing a same-sex wedding. Their attendance symbolized support and recognition. They, too, became part of the political process of the wedding. Through their presence, family and friends affirmed queer marital relationships.

Even if queer opponents deemed marriage conservative, the fact remained that the image of two men or two women reciting vows before an officiant was still, for many people, a very radical sight. Barbara Cox raised this point as she wrote, "I find it difficult to see how two lesbians, standing together openly and proudly, can be seen as accepting" the institution of marriage.[82] Same-sex wedding celebrations challenged the idea of the "typical" bride or groom. By association these weddings raised questions over who might lay claim to the title of "married couple" and what constituted a family. For Rabbi Julie Greenburgh, explicit discussion of the queerness of the couple being wed was essential. She said:

> As a clergyperson I think it is important to say the words *gay* and *lesbian* from the pulpit during a ceremony. Because it is a very powerful contradiction to people's shame and fear and sense that gays and lesbians don't "deserve" to have the same privileges of society and of long-term relationships. So I think it's important to stand up there in my robes and to say that we're celebrating the creation of a new lesbian or gay family.[83]

For Cox, her commitment ceremony was a very political experience. As she noted, "Some of the most politically 'out' moments I have ever had happened during those months of preparing for and having that ceremony." In particular, Cox noted the way that her ceremony demanded an explicit explanation of her sexuality for younger members of her family.

She returned to the feminist slogan of the 1960s and 1970s, as she noted, "As feminists we used to say that 'the personal is political.'" In Cox's eyes, her wedding was a concrete embodiment of this view. She believed in the power of the wedding to highlight the interconnectedness of two spheres previously thought to be mutually exclusive. For those who challenged her vision, she posed a question: "Have we lost that vision of how we can understand and change the world?" In Cox and her partner's experiences, the wedding provided a site for both understanding and changing the world in which they lived.[84]

In an important way, same-sex weddings offered a challenge to the dominant view of marriage and weddings. Despite his critique of same-sex marriage, Michael Warner has recognized the value of these celebrations: "They call attention to the nonuniversality of the institution. They force reactions in settings where scripts are not yet written. They turn banal privacy into public-sphere scenes."[85] Seeing the wedding as a moment of "banal privacy" ignores the power the celebration has held throughout the twentieth century and well into the twenty-first. Many couples saw their celebrations turned to "public-sphere scenes." Same-sex weddings did so in an especially explicit way. As gay men and lesbians celebrated their weddings, they challenged long-standing public and political views. They offered a public critique of the American legal system and offered an alternative to what were seen as mainstream social values. In their public nature, as Warner suggested, they responded to the policies that deemed these unions outside the bounds of legality.

Personal values and beliefs—even beyond the explicitly political—made their way into same-sex celebrations. These values ranged from the desire for a specifically "queer" event to a celebration that reflected the religious values of the couple being wed. Mike Rubin and Duane Thomas's early 1990s wedding in San Francisco was designed as a "theme wedding." When asked why, Duane exclaimed, 'Because we're *queer!*'" Combining a country-western theme with Jewish liturgical elements, the wedding reflected very specifically the couple being wed.[86] Other queer couples embraced the difference of their friends and the queer lifestyle as a whole. Leslea Newman and her wife Mary Grace "Flash" Newman Vazquez recited their vows before a wedding body composed of loved ones "who all wore their finest: everything from combat boots, cutoff shorts, and nose rings, to high heels, velvet gowns, and diamonds. And those were just the boys. The girls wore their best Birkenstocks, draw-string pants, and T-shirts with slogans on them, like, 'But Man, she *is* Mr. Right . . .'" Wed under a chuppah, accompanied by their "Best Butch" and "Dyke of Honor," the two recited their vows and stomped a wine glass before being declared, "Butch and Bride."[87] The couple took the familiar elements of the celebration and adapted them in a way that made sense to their relationship and their chosen wedding community.

For religiously affiliated queer couples, religious devotion was a nec-essary component of their ceremonies. The power of ritual attracted many same-sex couples. The possibility of creative liturgy—one that found a place in worship for those long denied recognition—held a par-ticular attraction.[88] Growing openness among religious denominations provided queer couples with a location for sanctioned spirituality and displays of personalized beliefs. Same-sex religious celebrations empha-sized not only the couple's relationship to God but also their view of a religious code that intricately linked issues of social justice to worship. Peter and David, two ministers of the United Church of Christ (UCC), followed the standard UCC ceremony but incorporated their own vows. Within these vows the two men invited participants to promise their support of the relationship. Rather than focusing on the couple alone, the wedding elicited the support of guests and made their promise fun-damental to the celebration. For some queers the church offered sup-port lacking in other relationships. Peter and David recounted a lesbian couple whose parents refused to support their union. In the creation of an alternative community—one marked by religious belonging—the women wed before their "surrogate" mothers of their parish.[89]

The commitment to social justice or community was integrated into religious wedding liturgy just as it was emphasized in secular ceremo-nies. For Grant and John's 1996 wedding, the female Unitarian minister blessed the couple:

> The ceremony in which we are now participating is a bold, even a revolu-tionary act. We pray that men who love men will one day be free to cel-ebrate their love openly, in every aspect of their lives. In the meantime, we can express the joy and approval we feel for Grant and John as they give public recognition to the love they feel for each other and the com-mitment they freely make to one another today.

The minister then asked those assembled to affirm the couple by joining together in pronouncing, "We do!"[90] Similarly, Eileen Brennan and Carmen Rodriguez arranged their wedding service so that "the congregation was asked not only to swear to uphold and support the marriage in the years to come, a common feature of Protestant weddings, but also to rise and vow to oppose homophobia wherever it might be encountered."[91] These ceremonies demonstrated the values of the couple by blending politics with personal views of faith. For those for whom legally recognized marriage remained elusive, the spiritual blessing of a union held tremendous value.

The creation of a beloved wedding community, the pronouncement of clear political goals, and the infusion of personal style and beliefs marked queer weddings of the late twentieth and early twenty-first centuries. Before legal recognition of same-sex unions, these weddings exposed publicly a civic inequality based upon sexual orientation. Weddings demanded public recognition of same-sex relationships while providing those being wed with a sense of personal triumph. For many queers, hosting a wedding before family and friends was an experience they believed they would never know. As same-sex marriage gained legal recognition, queer weddings celebrated not only personal commitment but political triumph as well.

* * *

Edwin Brent Jones and Edward Lee Reynolds, two middle-aged men who blogged under the title "Guy Dads," used their blog as a site to celebrate their families, their life together as a gay couple, their social activism, and, in 2005, their gay wedding. Over three months, the men shared the wedding planning process with their readers. Meticulously selecting their wedding location, music, flowers, and attire, Jones and Reynolds overlooked no wedding necessity. Representing their commitment to their Jewish faith, their wedding took place in a synagogue, led by a rabbi with whom they had participated in premarital counseling. Representing their love of theater, each table at the reception was thematically decorated by a musical or play. The two men shared every detail with readers, from the text of the wedding program received by guests to the reception dinner menu to a full wedding schedule with program notes.

For the most part, Jones and Reynolds experienced a wedding process that was a dream come true. Children from first marriages walked each man down the aisle. Other committed gay couples served as attendants. Nearly 200 friends and family participated in their celebration. A six-piece band performed show tunes, classic rock, and hits of Motown. The two men requested that guests abstain from the purchase of gifts and instead donate to charities or non-profits, among them the Human Rights Campaign.[92] In their wedding program, the men made public their views of the wedding. They wrote:

> While we follow the footsteps of many Jewish couples before us, we also know that ours is a less-trodden path as a same sex couple. Today we want to commit publicly our bond and love in the company of you, our friends and family, who have supported us in so many ways these past three years. We also want to affirm the ground-breaking stand Reform Judaism has taken that same sex unions are holy and valid. Finally, we want to proclaim by our and your presence that we all stand together in the belief that loving couples and families are of many sorts in America. Further, we today defy any so-called morality group to define for us what they see as the "only" way for marriage to occur. May the time be not too distant that our state and federal governments understand and act to assure the fundamental right to marry for all Americans.[93]

Jones and Reynolds's wedding had all the elements of a white wedding. It demonstrated just how far same-sex wedding celebrants had come as they enjoyed the love and support of those most dear to them. Through their attention to various details and their willingness to share their vision of what the wedding meant to them, they followed the postwar wedding tradition—gay and straight—of personalizing the celebration to express their relationship.

After the wedding, the two men sent their wedding announcement to several local newspapers in the San Francisco Bay Area. While they were away on their honeymoon, *The J* (a Jewish news weekly in Northern California) published a response to their announcement. The writer, a resident of Lodi, California, accused *The J* of heading down a "road to insanity." Seeing the men's marriage as an "effort to destroy the traditional family," the writer described the announcement and the accompanying image (a picture of the two men embracing on their wedding day) as "pornographic." Before Jones or Reynolds could respond, *The J* published four letters in support of the men's marriage, two from friends who had attended the wedding and two from people Jones and Reynolds did not know. A subsequent letter to *The J* critiqued the publication for even publishing the initial letter. When the editor publicly retorted that gay marriage was illegal in California, not to mention banned by traditional Jewish law, more letters supporting Jones and Reynolds (and same-sex unions more broadly) poured in. Ultimately, under a barrage of protest letters, the editor of *The J* apologized for offending the GLBT community and wished Jones and Reynolds "*mozel tov* and a happy life together."[94]

Jones and Reynolds experienced and embraced the politicization of the wedding. First, they used the language of the wedding to challenge anyone who considered their union unnatural or unholy. Then they spread word of their marriage to a wide audience, some of whom rejected their relationship and many more who publicly supported their union. Finally, when the California Supreme Court passed a June 2008 ruling to recognize same-sex marriage legally, Jones and Reynolds wed again. Wishing to marry legally before the decision of Proposition 8, in which California voters overturned the state court's decision and limited marriage to participants of the opposite sex, the two men used their second wedding "to affirm that what we want in the right to marry is all about LOVE and EQUALITY." Combining their second wedding with an event to raise funds to defeat Prop 8, the men wed again, this time joined by two lesbian couples who likewise had previously celebrated weddings. Initially the event was to be a fairly quick one, but as the number of guests grew, the couples "contemplated how important it was for everyone there to feel the love and to experience a 'real' wedding in order to feel how 'right' it was to be able to occur legally."[95] From there they increased the scope of the ceremony. The political component remained, but the couples also understood that the personal element of the wedding made it an important symbolic site where others could begin to understand the nature and necessity of legally recognizing same-sex relationships. The two men once again used the wedding celebration to demonstrate their commitment to one another, their faith, and equal rights and protection under the law.

While Californians ultimately voted to overturn same-sex marriage by supporting Proposition 8 in the November 2008 state elections, same-sex unions have grown in visibility. Even as the majority of states currently prohibit same-sex marriage, the issue has garnered more support throughout the nation. Even in California, challenges to Proposition 8 are ongoing and a February 2012 poll indicated that more Californians supported same-sex marriage than opposed it. Catholics, Latinos, and older voters—once thought to be among the staunchest defenders of "traditional" marriage—had begun to change their views.[96] In 2011, New York joined Connecticut, Iowa, Massachusetts, New Hampshire, Vermont, and Washington, DC in legalizing same-sex marriage. In May 2012, President Barack Obama, whose views on same-sex marriage had been "evolving" over the life of his presidency, came out in public support of the cause.

New York residents Kristen Ruff (left) and Amanda Bruton (right) on their wedding day, November 4, 2011. Photo by Erin McGrath. Courtesy Erin H Photography.

As Anna Quindlen, the young bride who saw so much meaning in her own wedding, speculated in 2008, the surest way to come to support gay marriage was to know a gay person. "Neighbors, friends and family members who have come out and made the political personal—and lovable" she wrote, were responsible for the increasingly changed minds of the American public. Quindlen alluded to the power of the wedding as a crystallizing moment for those thinking about gay marriage: "If two women in white want to join hands in front of their families and friends and vow to love and honor one another until they die, the only reasonable response to that is happy tears, awed admiration and societal approval. And—this part is just personal opinion—one of those big honking KitchenAid mixers with the dough hook."[97] Edwin Jones and Edward Reynolds and the couples before and after them advocated on behalf of civic equity through the public attention they called to their relationships. The wedding was fundamental to that effort as it transcended the personal experience of private life and expressed a public call for political rights.

Conclusion

On April 29, 2011, Prince William of Wales married Catherine Middleton. Before approximately 1,900 congregants, the wedding took place in Westminster Abbey, site of every royal coronation since 1066. Guests ranged from members of the British Royal Family to international superstars Elton John and David Beckham. The Prince wore a scarlet Irish Guards colonel's uniform, while Middleton emerged from the queen's 1977 Rolls Royce Phantom VI in a "lacy, long-sleeved, sweetheart-neckline gown with lace overlay" designed by Sarah Burton, creative director of the British label Alexander McQueen. The ceremony inside the church was broadcast worldwide. Those watching at home heard the opening words of the Abbey's Dean, John Hall, and the exact language of the vows, provided by Archbishop of Canterbury, Rowan Williams. Highlighting that even in this most traditional of traditional celebrations the couple represented some measure of modernity, the Lord Bishop of London, Richard Chartres's marriage address alluded to the need for acceptance and at least some measure of independence in marriage as he advised the couple that marriage can "transform" a couple but warned against the impulse to "reform each other." Gracious at beginning and end, Prince William and Middleton responded warmly to the throngs of well-wishers waiting outside the Abbey and Buckingham Palace, indulging the crowd by sharing a second kiss after their first kiss on the Palace balcony failed to meet the approval of the multitude. By all accounts, the Prince and his bride were, without question, living a modern day "fairy tale."[1]

The Royal Wedding drew international attention, and Americans, with their well-documented love of weddings, pageantry, and excess, seemed to be among the most enthusiastic onlookers. Media coverage certainly suggested as much. American viewers could follow coverage of the ceremony through any number of broadcasters: BBC America, MSNBC, WE, TLC, ABC, CBS, CNN, E!, Fox News, NBC, Univision, Fox, Reelz, and HLN. Before the ceremony, multiple stations aired a replay of the 1981 wedding of William's parents, Charles and Diana. Viewers were presented Oscar-style "red-carpet shots" of guests. After the ceremony, various television stations offered everything from recaps of the celebration to considerations of "the significance of the marriage and the future of the British monarchy" to a program called "Fashion Police Royal Wedding."[2]

In the weeks leading up to the wedding, tabloids, entertainment media, and mainstream news sources covered the pre-wedding preparation and chronicled Americans' plans to join in the celebration. Some Americans traveled to London to enjoy the festivities firsthand. Thousands of men and women joined together in the pre-dawn hours at Disney World, dressed in their best "princess or prince attire," to celebrate William and Kate's union.[3] Others planned novel celebrations closer to home. For example, Kassie Courson of Macomb, Illinois hosted a royal wedding party at her home. Guests were told to arrive no later than 3 a.m., and the hostess established a clear dress code: hats required, heels suggested, tiaras accepted. Courson's husband, Ron, acted as the butler and served scones, Earl Grey tea, and clotted cream from Devonshire on china bearing William's and Kate's likenesses. Columbus, Ohio resident, Anita Cullen, and her daughter had watched Charles and Diana wed in 1981, and she recalled that her daughter "always remembered how special the day was." For Will and Kate's wedding, she planned a similar celebration with her granddaughter, hoping to create equally fond memories.[4]

When *Today* co-host Meredith Vieira was asked to explain Americans' fascination with the royal wedding, she pointed to two factors. Understanding, to some extent, the uniqueness of Will and Kate's celebrity and the pressures it must entail, Americans, she believed, wished the best for this "young, charming, seemingly normal couple." Additionally, Vieira pointed to Americans' fascination with and admiration for the late Princess Diana, killed in a 1997 car crash. Vieira noted, "You can't help thinking about Princess Diana and those pictures of her with William as a little boy and wishing him the best with the second love of his life."[5] Blending celebrity, sentimentality, tradition, modernity, and romance, the royal wedding seemingly found a rapt stateside audience.

And yet, even with the saturation of royal wedding mania, there was another, far less positive, response to the event. When Conan O'Brien interviewed British actor Paul Bettany in May 2011, Bettany communicated a view of the wedding that was far from the romantic picture contrived by weddingphiles. Noting that the media had been discussing the royal wedding "ad nauseam," a clearly baffled O'Brien turned to Bettany as "a Brit" to explain its appeal. Bettany, as drolly as humanly possible, declared it a "great British tradition" when "the poor people of my country scrape together thirty-six million dollars to pay for two already massively rich children's wedding." He concluded, "I don't really get it."[6] He was not alone. O'Brien's audience applauded wildly. Those on Facebook and Twitter shared a link for Americans who wondered what the hype was all about: http://whyamericansshouldcareabouttheroyalwedding.com/. Upon visiting the site, unsuspecting, inquiring minds learned, "They shouldn't."[7]

It was not only the late night humorists and social media critics who failed to be impressed by the royal wedding. Across the broader spectrum of the population, Americans shared this ambivalence toward the event. As it informed readers about their many opportunities for royal nuptial viewing and the immediate "retrospectives" to follow, the *New York Times* likewise published the findings of a *New York Times/ CBS News* poll that indicated that "only 28 percent of Americans [were] either somewhat or very closely following" news about the royal wedding.[8] Another article, which noted that the royal wedding drew "a yawn" from the American public, further specified that only 6 percent of Americans followed the wedding "very closely."[9] In reality, the media onslaught reflected a supply that far exceeded the actual demand.

This media blitz continued with another 2011 event, which *Good Morning America* deemed "America's Royal Wedding": that of reality star Kim Kardashian and professional basketball player Kris Humphries. Married August 20, 2011, Kardashian and Humphries celebrated with a wedding estimated to have cost $6 million (and that after substantial discounts received for promoting suppliers on television and through social media). *People* magazine paid $1.5 million for wedding photographs and exclusive access. An October 2011 behind-the-scenes special aired over the course of two evenings on *E!* drew an estimated 10.5 million viewers. Critics, stumped at the nature of Kardashian's appeal, expressed disgust with the excess of and publicity afforded the celebration. When Kardashian and Humphries filed for divorce just 72 days after the wedding, Kardashian faced criticism that she had embarked upon the union as a means of enhancing her celebrity and fattening her wallet. By all accounts, Kardashian confirmed wedding critics' fears and exemplified the worst of wedding culture: she was a bride who had devoted more time to her wedding than to her preparation for marriage. Even worse, she had potentially done so purposefully.[10]

Rather than highlighting continued interest in extravagant wedding styles, Americans' varying degrees of interest in and varied responses to the royal wedding and the Kardashian event suggested that Americans' relationship to the wedding was more complicated than media coverage indicated. Even among their admirers, the weddings represented some measure of fantasy, romance, or decadence—not to mention voyeurism—more than they reflected "how to" models for wedding planning.[11] Ultimately, even with the attention afforded them, neither the royal wedding nor the Kardashian wedding accurately represented current American wedding culture, and not only because of the celebrity of the celebrants. As a public figure, albeit one of a slightly different sort of celebrity, Jenna Bush celebrated her 2008 wedding in a manner far more representative of contemporary American wedding trends than either of the 2011 "Royal Weddings."

Demonstrating the continued focus on individualism and personalization, while emphasizing simple, natural style, the celebration of former President George W. Bush's daughter Jenna Bush to Harry Hager reflected many budding trends of modern American wedding culture. With relatively limited fanfare, especially given Bush's then-position as First Daughter, Bush and Hager wed on the Bush family's 1600-acre ranch in Crawford, Texas. They were feted by approximately 200 guests, comprised of family and close friends. Playing to the Bush family's Texas roots, the couple was accompanied by a maid of honor, a best man, and an extensive "house party" of attendants. Taking inspiration from the landscape, the women dressed in "seven different styles of knee-length dresses in seven different colors that match the palette of Texas wildflowers—blues, greens, lavenders and pinky reds."[12] Bush further achieved her desire for an "organic and natural" style through the choice to hold the ceremony outdoors, before a cross constructed of Texas limestone.[13] By hosting the celebration at the ranch, Bush and Hager could revisit the site of their wedding for years to come. In the aftermath of the wedding, *USA Today* reported, "Jenna's outdoor wedding at the ranch reflected her family's penchant for privacy and her preference for the casual over grandiose."[14]

In contrast to Luci Johnson's 1966 wedding, which saturated American media, and Tricia Nixon's wedding, which likewise drew national attention, Jenna Bush's wedding received comparatively limited coverage. Beyond reflecting the Bush family's "penchant for privacy," the Bush-Hager wedding demonstrated the clear evolution of the postwar American wedding—and of postwar American culture as a whole. The contest between public and private, communal or individual had, to some degree, been resolved. A couple's personal preference was privileged above all else, and they could choose their intended wedding community and the levels to which this community shared in their celebration. Those beyond that chosen community understood a couple's authority and accepted their decisions, and even if they critiqued decisions made, they were less likely to be outraged at calls for privacy than in years past.

Bush's electing to have the wedding outside Washington, DC negated the possibility of the wedding serving as both family and state occasion. Indeed, as Doug Wead, former aide to President George H. W. Bush speculated, "If they'd have gone on TV, the wedding would have been shown all over the world and Jenna Bush would have been an international celebrity." With the president's impending transition back to private life (and, one could assume, his low approval ratings at the time), such celebrity was deemed undesirable.[15] These decisions were widely accepted. Unlike Johnson's wedding, there was no sustained anger or backlash at Bush's desire to maintain this level of privacy and limit the details shared with the American people. Instead, such a decision was accepted as natural, or, even more, as Jenna Bush's personal prerogative. While this could be attributed to the more critical view of the presidency and First Family that developed from the 1970s onward, or the widespread possibility of another celebrity wedding on which to focus, one could argue that the public recognized Bush's wedding day authority, independent of her father's office. Jenna Bush's comparatively advanced age of 26 and greater independence from her family at the time of her wedding established her authority as distinct from that of her father (despite her parents' clear involvement in and financial support of the wedding). Even as marriage remained (and remains) an institution heavily regulated by the state and subject to some measure of communal control, American couples more firmly established the wedding as the private concern of the individual couple being wed. Jenna Bush and Harry Hager's wedding and the response it received reflected the wedding culture of the twenty-first century and indicated how much had changed—socially, culturally, and politically—since the weddings of Luci Johnson and Tricia Nixon.

Although they celebrated a "home" wedding, both Bush and Hager came from politically powerful and affluent families. As such, their wedding was hardly one in which budgetary concerns reigned in decision-making. While Bush declared her desire that the wedding be "low key," the celebration embodied the now-familiar shape of a "wedding weekend," in which guests are expected to travel sometimes substantial distances and devote two or three days to the wedding celebration. The night before the wedding, the groom's family hosted a rehearsal dinner for nearly 100 guests. The day of the wedding, they invited guests to a pre-wedding barbeque luncheon. In the days leading up to the wedding, the president assumed the tried and true father-of-the-bride routine when he told Anne Curry he had little say in determining the shape of the celebration. When asked what jobs wife Laura or Jenna gave the president, he responded, "They're letting me spend money."[16] And spend he did. The reception took place in several outdoor tents where guests enjoyed a sit-down, catered dinner and danced to a live band. Jenna Bush wore a dress created by famed designer Oscar de la Renta. When interviewed for a feature in *Vogue*, de la Renta assured readers that Bush was "totally, totally unspoiled" and that her gown was "in no manner a grand dress. There is zero pretense."[17] But as anyone who knows anything about weddings or wedding fashion knows, simple style, devoid of "pretense," generally does not come cheap. While the Bush-Hager wedding may have been organic and natural and representative of the couple's style and beliefs, it was still, without question, an elaborate and expensive affair.

Some couples of the late 2000s and early 2010s, to be sure, continued to embrace the elaborate, the excessive, and the over-the-top celebration style. And, as demonstrated by the Bush-Hager union, even "simple" weddings could be marked by great expense. But another trend marked contemporary wedding styles. Those outside elite circles, particularly in the aftermath of the economic collapse of 2008, adopted and influenced the trend toward the simple, the natural, and the organic. Indeed, many celebrants of "simple" celebrations were motivated not only by a desire for personal significance but also by a desire for thrift, environmental responsibility, and a sense of independence from the wedding marketplace. While wedding celebrants of the early 2000s seemingly competed to see who could host the most excessive, the most expensive, the most outrageous event, many weddings of the decade's end and second decade's beginning embodied a more simplistic, measured, and, as repeated by many couples, *sane* approach to celebration.

The expansion of wedding media influenced this trend directly. Rather than relying solely on bridal magazines, prescriptive literature, and the advice of industry "experts," brides and grooms found a host of alternative wedding options through online guides, the blogosphere, and sites of social media. Those familiar with and adamantly opposed to the power of the "Wedding-Industrial Complex," the term popularized by sociologist Chrys Ingraham in her 1999 critique of the commercial culture of American weddings, found an online community of other like-minded brides and grooms, committed to personal, meaningful, responsible, and affordable wedding celebrations. Even sites contributing to the mainstream, marketplace-infused wedding, such as The Knot, offered brides (and for this site, pretty singularly, *brides*) advice about alternative approaches to the wedding celebration through topics such as "Budget Weddings" and "DIY (do-it-yourself) Wedding Ideas." The Knot likewise offered opportunities for brides of particular persuasions to engage with other brides who shared their styles, goals, or strategies. Such networks offered celebrants an affirmation of their choices. Even when a bride and groom might reject expected wedding norms, online communities affirmed their selected alternatives.[18]

Beyond "official" wedding websites, the emergent world of social media influenced the shape of modern American weddings. In recent years, photo albums on Facebook served as inspiration to brides and grooms in their planning phases. Beyond the weddings they attended, men and women looked to the weddings of friends of friends (of friends) for ideas and inspiration as they planned their own celebrations. Those looking to stick to a budget relied on Twitter contacts for information about affordable wedding vendors.[19] Additionally, in March 2010, Yale alum Paul Sciarra and Ben Silbermann, along with former Facebook employee and web designer Evan Sharp, launched a new website: Pinterest. Acting as an online site where users could create and organize thematically arranged virtual catalogs or scrapbooks related to any number of topics, products, or interests, Pinterest immediately struck a chord with those planning weddings. Pinners had access to the ideas and inspirations of those within their network of friends, families, and colleagues, but each pinner also had access to networks beyond his or her contacts. In addition to directing users toward wedding vendors or designers, the site featured projects—wedding and otherwise—that users undertook themselves.[20]

As indicated by The Knot's addition of DIY Wedding Ideas to its categories of wedding advice and the "pinning" of DIY-inspired wedding projects, the DIY trend of recent years shaped not only home repair but also wedding celebrations. Since September 2007, Sherry (nee Treitler) and John Petersik, authors of the blog YoungHouseLove have tracked not only their home DIY projects on their site, but reported in detail on their 2007 DIY backyard wedding, which came in at just under $4,000. From the beginning of their wedding planning, they followed the inspiration "to keep things personal and meaningful." While their dedication to DIY required work and commitment, in the end, they achieved their goal. From save-the-dates to invitations to officiant to music to menu, the couple relied on their own (often recently acquired) know-how and the assistance of family and friends to make their wedding day a success. When they could not create something themselves, bargain-hunting and recycling allowed them to maintain their focus on an affordable and individualized décor. Involving friends and family in the process made the wedding planning intimate, enjoyable, and pleasantly memorable rather than stressful or anxiety-inducing.[21]

Even more ambitious was the author of 2000dollarwedding.com who aimed to celebrate her nuptials—as her blog title suggested—at a cost of less than two thousand dollars. Beyond their budgetary concerns, Sara Cotner and her fiancé, Matt Bradford, desired a wedding that afforded them a sense of autonomy and independence from the marketing and media onslaught of the wedding industry. In a summary of their wedding planning, from start to finish, they noted, "We didn't want to obsess about surface details or let the wedding overshadow our relationship. We wanted our wedding to be sincere, authentic, and memorable—a wedding focused on community and connection, not my wedding dress. We were convinced that we could make it work in a budget-minded, hand-crafted, eco-friendly way." Desiring a celebration that would leave them unstressed and able to spend time with the people who meant the most to them, the couple limited the guest list and asked guests to contribute to the wedding. Cotner recalled advice she received from an email sent by The Knot: it suggested that brides and grooms should involve guests in the wedding by creating a detailed ceremony program. Rather than following this advice to the letter, Cotner and Bradford took the suggestion of involving guests literally: they asked "friends and family to serve as the photographers, caterers, hair stylists, DJs, bartenders, officiant . . . , florist, traffic directors, and videographers." Instead of feeling put out at their contributions, guests were more invested and connected to the wedding because they took part in making it happen.[22] While staying within a limited budget was work, Cotner and Bradford deemed it worthwhile work, which brought them closer to each other and to their wedding guests. They assumed authority over their wedding rather than capitulating to the wedding-industrial complex, and as a result, their wedding was more personally meaningful and fiscally responsible.

Meg Keene, author of the blog turned book, *The Practical Wedding: Creative Ideas for Planning a Beautiful, Affordable, and Meaningful*

LEFT Photo strip from John and Sherry Petersik's 2007 DIY Wedding. CENTER Back-yard decorations for John and Sherry Petersik's 2007 DIY Wedding. RIGHT John and Sherry Petersik at their 2007 DIY Wedding.
Courtesy John and Sherry Petersik, younghouselove.com.

Celebration, echoed many of these points. Inspired to blog after the first few weeks of her own wedding planning had her feeling stressed and overwhelmed, Keene eventually found that her blog had created a community of like-minded women (called "Team Practical") who wished to approach their weddings (and, eventually, their marriages) with a sense of balance and control and were thrilled to find others who felt the same way. While aimed at readers planning any number of wedding styles, Keene's book consistently reflected the ideas of balance and control, assuming those to be universal desires among wedding celebrants. Recognizing that the decision to host a wedding automatically aligned a couple with "tradition," Keene likewise noted a couple's power to shape that tradition to fit their beliefs, their style, and their relationship. She noted, "Weddings provide a wonderful opportunity to sit down and discuss with our partners who we are and what we believe." As for concerns over proper etiquette, Keene observed, "if you're being kind and thoughtful, you're probably doing just fine."[23]

Keene weighed in—not uncritically—on the DIY trend. Noting that those choosing to embrace DIY projects did so for any number of goals, she encouraged readers to determine their motivation, whether it be to save money, keep the hands busy and the mind calm, or as a source of enjoyment. Where she urged caution: embracing DIY as a better, more authentic, truer option to store-bought or professionally crafted. Doing so could leave a person not only miserable but disappointed. Trends, she seemed to suggest, should be followed based on a desire to do so rather than due to a sense of obligation. With that warning issued, and assuming some measure of DIY remained an important wedding goal to readers, Keene echoed the sentiments expressed on younghouselove.com and 2000dollarbride.com. Rather than Do-It-Yourself, she encouraged a reorientation toward Do-It-Together. Replacing the isolation of wedding planning with a more community-based effort could, she suggested, relieve stress, strengthen bonds, and invest the wedding day with even greater meaning.[24]

Keene also offered an explicit critique of the wedding industry and the expectations the industry has left in its wake. Beyond the challenges of scheduling a wedding and deciding upon venues and guests and caterers, she noted, was the challenge of actually getting married. Merging families, negotiating conflicts with friends, and conceptualizing issues of faith presented their own challenges, longer-lasting and, many would argue, more important than the logistics of the wedding itself. Keene related her own experiences in facing these challenges as well as facing public expectations of her as "the bride." In so doing, she tackled the "Bridezilla Myth" head on and asserted that the wedding was an important event that women should be "allowed to care about." She wrote, "as a woman in charge of planning a large event, you might get accused of being controlling. You might get called a bridezilla. And that is not your issue. That's the issue of the person who feels at liberty to call you something really offensive."[25]

Keene and other "practical" celebrants like Treitler, Petersik, Cotner, and Bradford willingly engaged with and negotiated the world of wedding industry and expectations. But as other men and women joined the critique of American wedding culture—and marriage, more broadly—there were those who chose to skip the institution and the celebration entirely as they moved forward with their relationships. The best means of expressing their views was to reject marriage and host no wedding at all. No longer beholden to the social, sexual, or financial strictures that had pushed couples of the past toward early marriage, many contemporary couples delayed entry into marriage while others comprised a newly dubbed community of committed unmarrieds (CUs).[26] Cohabitation rates have risen since the 1970s as couples have moved in together as a cost-saving measure or as a natural progression of their relationship. While it is the minority of cohabitating couples who live together as an explicit alternative to marriage rather than a prelude, there are those Americans for whom marriage and, by association, the wedding have little appeal.[27] In many ways, the decisions not to marry or not to have a wedding (when these are decisions consciously made and not shaped by legal or financial limitations) demonstrated personal values and beliefs as much as a wedding. Those who rejected the celebration contributed their view of the event as conformist, exclusive, sexist, or overtly and emptily consumerist. In 2009, California resident Raymond McCauley indicated that his motivations for rejecting marriage were "political, in solidarity with gays who can't legally wed in most states, and personal—he and his partner both got divorced in their 20s." They believed allocations of time, energy, and capital were better spent elsewhere. Charles Backman of New Hampshire noted, "I saved $50,000 on a wedding, money I can use to help pay for the kids' college." Some, like Jaclyn Gellar, who chronicled her exploration of wedding culture in 2001's *Here Comes the Bride*, rejected the privileging of one relationship over all others and viewed social pressures to wed as insufficient motivation to do so.[28] In their ambivalence to or direct rejection of marriage and the wedding, these couples contributed to the ongoing negotiations and interpretations about individual authority, communal expectations, and these concepts' relationship to and influence on private life and romantic pairings.

* * *

In a sharp contrast to those who lambasted American wedding celebrations as excessive and their participants as mindless followers, at least one strain of contemporary wedding culture has demonstrated the celebration and its celebrants' thoughtfulness and care. While marriage rates have declined (in 1960, two-thirds of 20-somethings were married as compared to 26 percent in 2008), those choosing to wed still overwhelmingly choose to do so with some sort of celebration. Rather than the start of independent life, marriage has become the culmination, the finishing touch. As noted by sociologist and chronicler of modern American marriage trends Andrew Cherlin, "Getting married is a way to show family and friends that you have a successful personal life." As such, it makes perfect sense that those choosing to wed have a vested interest in representing the views and values that have shaped their lives and their decision to enter into a marital union.[29]

Even as understandings of marriage may have changed, wedding styles of recent years represent a fascinating blend of the modern and the traditional. The reliance on virtual communities and the massive networks they include has expanded the reach of wedding trends—and the possibility that trends might combine in unexpected ways as couples look to personalize their wedding celebrations. The continued focus on the desires and identities of the couple and the wedding as a site of personal expression reflect the triumph of the modern focus on the individual in American life. And yet, to some extent, celebrations of recent years offer a return to weddings of the late nineteenth and early twentieth centuries. In a nation where men and women often begin their courtships with partners far from either's point of origin, and where weddings take place hundreds and thousands miles from either's hometown, a desire for community and connection continues to mark wedding celebrations. Many contemporary couples have very specific views of themselves, their wedding, and the world in which they live. They are often unwilling to compromise on those views and are eager to share them with those they hold dear. These communities are not homogenous and bear little resemblance to traditional tight-knit communities marked by religion, ethnicity, or geography, but they are communities nonetheless. The desire to make one community from many—even just once—and the care with which many brides and grooms approach this goal demonstrates just how thoughtful couples are when it comes to their weddings. American weddings may be trending toward simpler celebration styles, but they are marked simultaneously by complex desires to unite disparate groups, provide honest and heartfelt expression, and contribute to an ongoing dialog about marriage and its many possible meanings.

NOTES

INTRODUCTION

1. *Bride Wars*. Directed by Gary Winnick. DVD. 2009. Twentieth Century Fox, 2009.
2. Manohla Dargis, "Two Weddings and a Furor," *New York Times*, Jan. 9, 2009, http://movies.nytimes.com/2009/01/09/movies/09brid.html?scp=2&sq=brid e+wars&st=nyt; Reyhan Hermanci, "Movie Review: 'Bride Wars,'" *San Francisco Chronicle*, Jan. 9, 2009, http://www.sfgate.com/cgi-bin/article.cgi?file=/ c/a/2009/01/09/DDRH1557PT.DTL; Lou Loumenick, "'Bride Wars' a Silly Chick Flick," *New York Post*, Jan. 9, 2009, http://www.nypost.com/p/entertainment/ movies/item_8jUVe3V4WsKvRap6RGGaBL#.ThxlirIPPas.email; Michael Phillips, "'Bride Wars' Stars Kate Hudson, Anne Hathaway," *Chicago Tribune*, Jan. 8, 2009, http://www.chicagotribune.com/entertainment/movies/chi-bridewars-review-0109_jan09,0,4416509.story; Peter Rainier, "Review 'Bride Wars,'" *Christian Science Monitor*, Jan. 17, 2009, http://www.csmonitor.com/The-Culture/Movies/2009/0117/p25s02-almo.html; Elizabeth Weitzman, "Review: Kate Hudson and Anne Hathaway's 'Bride Wars' is a 'Time-Waster,'" *New York Daily News*, Jan. 8, 2009, http://articles.nydailynews.com/2009-01-08/entertain-ment/17914815_1_matthew-mcconaughey-weddings-kate-hudson; Stephanie Zacharek, "Bride Wars," *Salon*, Jan. 9, 2009, http://www.salon.com/entertain-ment/movies/review/2009/01/09/bride_wars/index.html.
3. "2009 Domestic Grosses," Box Office Mojo, http://boxofficemojo.com/yearly/ chart/?p=.htm&yr=2009.
4. Cele C. Otnes and Elizabeth H. Pleck, *Cinderella Dreams: The Allure of the Lavish Wedding* (Berkeley: University of California Press, 2003), 3; Sandy Schreier, *Hollywood Gets Married* (New York: Clarkson Potter, 2002). In comparison to *Bride Wars*, *Runaway Bride* was a massive hit, earning $152,257,509, ninth overall among films of 1999. See "1999 Domestic Grosses," Box Office Mojo, http:// boxofficemojo.com/yearly/chart/?yr=1999&p=.htm.
5. Judy Berman, "When a Bridezilla's Family Attacks," *Salon*, March 10, 2010, http://www.salon.com/life/broadsheet/2010/03/10/bridezilla_video; Abby Ellin,

"It's Botox for You, Dear Bridesmaids," *New York Times*, July 24, 2008, http://
www.nytimes.com/2008/07/24/fashion/24skin.html?ex=1217649600&en=895f6
105b0665ba3&ei=5070&emc=eta1; Aislinn Simpson, "Bridesmaids may have to
sign weight contracts," *The Telegraph*, Feb. 8, 2008, http://www.telegraph.co.uk/
news/uknews/1577490/Bridesmaids-may-have-to-sign-weight-contracts.html;
"Pre-nups for Bridesmaids: Gain Weight and You're Out," *Los Angeles Times*,
Feb. 8, 2008, http://latimesblogs.latimes.com/alltherage/2008/02/pre-nups-for-
br.html.; Rebecca Mead, *One Perfect Day: The Selling of the American Wedding*
(New York: Penguin Press, 2007), 1–3.

6. Lea Goldman and Tatiana Serafin, "The 20 Most Expensive Celebrity Weddings," Forbes.com, July 12, 2007, http://www.forbes.com/2007/07/12/celebrity-
media-weddings-biz-media-cz_lg_ts_0712celebweddings.html; Pamela Paul,
The Starter Marriage and the Future of Matrimony (New York: Random House,
2003), 62–72, 191–95; Grace Wong, "Ka-ching: Wedding Price Tag Near $30K,"
April 29, 2005, CNN, http://money.cnn.com/2005/05/20/pf/weddings/. In
reality, divorce rates vary based on the age of the married couple, whether they
cohabitated before marriage, and on the number of previous marriages. See
Belinda Luscombe, "Are Marriage Statistics Divorced from Reality?" *Time*, May
24, 2010, http://www.time.com/time/magazine/article/0,9171,1989124,00.html?a
rtId=1989124?contType=article?chn=us.

7. Jaclyn Gellar, *Here Comes the Bride: Women, Weddings, and the Marriage
Mystique* (New York: Falls Walls Eight Windows, 2001); Chrys Ingraham,
White Weddings: Romancing Heterosexuality in Popular Culture (New York:
Routledge, 1999); Mead, *One Perfect Day*. For an affirmative review of Mead's
book, see Meghan O'Rourke, "Selling 'I Do': Wedded to Consumption," *Wash-
ington Post*, May 6, 2007, http://www.washingtonpost.com/wp-dyn/content/
article/2007/05/04/AR2007050402551.html?referrer=emailarticle. For "alterna-
tive" views, see Jill Corral and Lisa Miya-Jervis, eds., *Young Wives' Tales: New
Adventures in Love and Partnership* (Seattle, WA: Seal Press, 2001); Colleen
Curran, ed., *Altared: Bridezillas, Bewilderment, Big Love, Breakups, and What
Women Really Think about Contemporary Weddings* (New York: Vintage, 2007);
Kamy Wicoff, *I Do But I Don't: Why the Way We Marry Matters* (Cambridge,
MA: Da Capo Press, 2006).

8. As Warren I. Susman considered the cultural history of early twentieth century
America, he posed a question to those who looked to critique what he called the
"culture of abundance": "If the culture of abundance has become manipulative,
coercive, vulgar, and intolerable in all the ways these critics have it, why did
this happen? Did it have to follow? Were there alternatives? Only a historical
view—a vision of that culture as it developed and changed over time and in
interaction with the traditional culture itself—can provide hope of getting at
these crucial issues." In the same way, the culture and history of the wedding
demands exploration as much as it warrants critique. Warren I. Susman, *Culture
as History: The Transformation of American Society in the Twentieth Century*

(New York: Pantheon Books, 1984), xxix–xxx. On the standard expectation of American wedding ritual, see Pamela Rae Frese, "Holy Matrimony: A Symbolic Analysis of the American Wedding Ritual" (PhD diss., University of Virginia, 1982); Wendy Leeds-Hurwitz, *Wedding as Text: Communicating Cultural Identities through Ritual* (Mahwah, NJ: Lawrence Erlbaum Associates, 2002). On the history of the wedding, see Vicki Howard, *Brides, Inc.: American Weddings and the Business of Tradition* (Philadelphia: University of Pennsylvania Press, 2006); Katherine Jellison, *It's Our Day: America's Love Affair with the White Wedding, 1945–2005* (Lawrence: University Press of Kansas, 2008); Otnes and Pleck, *Cinderella Dreams*; Barbara Penner, "'A Vision of Love and Luxury': The Commercialization of Nineteenth-Century American Weddings," *Winterthur Portfolio* 39 (Spring 2004): 1–20.

9. Howard, *Brides, Inc.*, 1–5; Stephen Nissenbaum, *The Battle for Christmas: A Cultural History of America's Most Cherished Holiday* (New York: Vintage, 1997); Elizabeth Pleck, *Celebrating the Family: Ethnicity, Consumer Culture, and Family Rituals* (Cambridge, MA: Harvard University Press, 2000); Leigh Eric Schmidt, *Consumer Rites: The Buying & Selling of American Holidays* (Princeton: Princeton University Press, 1995).

10. On Americans' shaping and negotiation of celebrations' meanings, see David Glassberg, *American Historical Pageantry: The Uses of Tradition in the Early 20th Century* (Chapel Hill: University of North Carolina Press, 1990), 1, 124–26, 136; Ellen Litwicki, *America's Public Holidays, 1865–1920* (Washington, DC: Smithsonian Institution Press, 2000).

11. Karen M. Dunak, "Ceremony and Citizenship: African American Weddings, 1945–60," *Gender & History* 21 (Aug. 2009): 402–24.

12. Robert Bellah et al., *Habits of the Heart: Individualism and Commitment in American Life* (Berkeley: University of California Press, 1985), 89; Karen Lystra, *Searching the Heart: Women, Men, and Romantic Love in Nineteenth-Century America* (New York: Oxford University Press, 1989), 29–30, 225–29.

13. Bellah et al., *Habits of the Heart*; John R. Gillis, *A World of their Own Making: Myth, Ritual, and the Quest for Family Values* (New York: Basic Books, 1996); Henry Glassie, "Tradition," *Journal of American Folklore* 108 (Autumn 1995): 369–95; Leeds-Hurwitz, *Wedding as Text*; John Modell, *Into One's Own: From Youth to Adulthood in the United States, 1920–1975* (Berkeley: University of California Press, 1989), 8–19, 66, 267–91.

14. Cultural demonstrations of citizenship marked American life even in the prewar years. See Susman, *Culture as History*, xxii–xxiii. On the privatization of American citizenship in the years since World War II, see Susan A. Brewer, *Why America Fights: Patriotism and War Propaganda from the Philippines to Iraq* (New York: Oxford University Press, 2009), 4–9, 178–89, 277–80; Lizabeth Cohen, *A Consumers' Republic: The Politics of Mass Consumption in Postwar America* (New York: Knopf, 2003); Elaine Tyler May, *Homeward Bound: American Families in the Cold War Era* (1988; New York: Basic Books, 1999), xx–xxii.

15. Nancy Cott, *Public Vows: A History of Marriage and the Nation* (Cambridge, MA: Harvard University Press, 2000); Rebecca L. Davis, *More Perfect Unions: The American Search for Marital Bliss* (Cambridge, MA: Harvard University Press, 2010).

16. Peter Clecak, *America's Quest for the Ideal Self: Dissent and Fulfillment in the 60s and 70s* (New York: Oxford University Press, 1985); Daniel Yankelovich, *New Rules: Searching for Self-Fulfillment in a World Turned Upside Down* (New York: Random House, 1981).

17. For more on the shaping of culture, see Ann Swidler, "Culture in Action: Symbols and Strategies," *American Sociological Review* 51 (April 1986): 273–86.

18. Judy Kutulas, "'That's the Way I've Always Heard It Should Be': Baby Boomers, 1970s Singer-Songwriters, and Romantic Relationships," *Journal of American History* 97 (Dec. 2010): 682–702.

CHAPTER 1

1. Edward Streeter, *Father of the Bride* (New York: Simon & Schuster, 1948), 108.

2. *Father of the Bride.* Directed by Vicente Minnelli. 1950. DVD. Warner Home Video, 2003. Rachel Devlin, *Relative Intimacy: Fathers, Adolescent Daughters, and Postwar American Culture* (Chapel Hill: University of North Carolina Press, 2005), 109; Otnes and Pleck, *Cinderella Dreams*, 172–74.

3. Streeter, *Father of the Bride*, 66; Otnes and Pleck, *Cinderella Dreams*, 122.

4. Gillis, *World of Their Own Making*, 140–42.

5. Streeter, *Father of the Bride*, 37. Three months was a fairly standard period for engagement, as indicated by various wedding guides. See Marguerite Bentley (Mrs. Logan Bentley), *Wedding Etiquette Complete* (Philadelphia: John C. Winston, 1947), 60.

6. Streeter, *Father of the Bride*, 80.

7. Ibid., 180–81.

8. On Taylor's dress and the New Look style, see Lois W. Banner, *American Beauty* (New York: Knopf, 1983) 278, 285; Susan M. Hartmann, *The Home Front and Beyond: American Women in the 1940s* (Boston: Twayne, 1982), 203–4; Karal Ann Marling, *As Seen on TV: The Visual Culture of Everyday Life in the 1950s* (Cambridge, MA: Harvard University Press, 1994), 9–19; Otnes and Pleck, *Cinderella Dreams*, 173–74.

9. Streeter, *Father of the Bride*, 143–52.

10. Gillis, *World of Their Own Making*, 140–42; Pleck, *Celebrating the Family*, 217. Christen Diary 1941, 10, Folder: Inez Christen, Diaries, 1940–1944, Box 1, Inez Christen Papers (Iowa Women's Archives).

11. Mrs. Banks's remembrance occurs only in the film. See Otnes and Pleck, *Cinderella Dreams*, 43.

12. Howard, *Brides, Inc.*, 2–3; Katherine Jellison, "From the Farmhouse Parlor to the Pink Barn: The Commercialization of Weddings in the Rural Midwest," *Iowa Heritage Illustrated* 77 (Summer 1996): 50–65; Barbara Penner, "A Vision

of Love and Luxury," 5; Otnes and Pleck, *Cinderella Dreams*, 43–44; Pleck, *Celebrating the Family*, 207–32, esp. 207–13; Ellen Rothman, *Hands and Hearts: A History of Courtship in America* (Cambridge, MA: Harvard University Press, 1987), 80, 168–72, 274–77.

13. Frances Smith Foster, ed., *Love and Marriage in Early African America* (Lebanon, NH: University Press of New England, 2008), 133, 145–46, 157–58; Howard, *Brides, Inc.*, 1–2, 10–29; Jellison, "From the Farmhouse Parlor to the Pink Barn," 52–53; Stephen Kern, *The Culture of Love: Victorians to Moderns* (Cambridge, MA: Harvard University Press, 1992), 314; Linda Otto Lipsett, *To Love and to Cherish: Brides Remembered* (San Francisco: Quilt Digest Press, 1989); Barbara Norfleet, *Wedding* (New York: Simon & Schuster, 1979); Pleck, *Celebrating the Family*, 207–21, 224–32, Rothman, *Hands and Hearts*, 276; Gail F. Stern, ed., *Something Old, Something New: Ethnic Weddings in America* (Philadelphia: Balch Institute for Ethnic Studies, 1987).

14. Essie Hill Simmons to Minerva Houser, April 12, 1982, 17, "Voices of American Homemakers," Vol. 1 of 5, National Extension Homemakers Council Oral History Project (Sophia Smith Archives).

15. Ibid. See Jellison, "From the Farmhouse Parlor to the Pink Barn," 52–53.

16. Pleck, *Celebrating the Family*, 209.

17. On the role of family in immigrant life, see John Bodnar, *The Transplanted: A History of Immigrants in Urban America* (Bloomington: Indiana University Press, 1985), 84; Pleck, *Celebrating the Family*, 224, 227. On Lake County, Indiana's Romanian-American population, see Mary Leuca, *Romanian Americans in Lake County, Indiana: An Ethnic Heritage Curriculum Project* (West Lafayette, IN: Purdue University, 1978). Emilia Apolzan to Mary Leuca, Sept. 11, 1976, 12, Collection #012, Romanian Americans in Lake County, Indiana, CSHM accession #03-04-1 (Center for the Study of History and Memory). Elizabeth Drag interview by Rev. George C. Muresan, July 8, 1977, 9, Collection #012, Romanian Americans in Lake County, Indiana, CSHM accession #03-31-1, ibid. See also Stern, *Something Old, Something New*, 17–18.

18. Howard, *Brides, Inc.*, 1–4. Howard applies Eric Hobsbawm's idea of the "invention of tradition" to the white wedding. Eric Hobsbawn, "Introduction: Inventing Traditions," in Eric Hobsbawm and Terence Ranger, eds., *The Invention of Tradition* (Cambridge: Cambridge University Press, 1983), 1–14.

19. "Fashions 'Destination Matrimony,'" ed. Martha Stout, *Good Housekeeping* (March 1944): 45; Alexandra S. Potts, "How to Get Married," *Colliers* 115 (1945): 66.

20. June Lundy Boyd, *Memoirs of a Middle Child* (Burr Oak Farm Press, 2002), 36–38, Folder: Boyd, June Lundy 857, June Lundy Boyd Papers (Iowa Women's Archives). On other wartime weddings, see Eleanor McGovern, *Uphill: A Personal Story* (Boston: Houghton Mifflin, 1974), 59–63; Dorothy J. Place, "The War Years, 1938–1945: The Story of How World War II Shaped My Life," Folder: Place, Dorothy J. 547, Dorothy J. Place Papers (Iowa Women's Archives);

Kathryn Wycoff, 8, "Voices of American Homemakers," Vol. 2 of 5, National Extension Homemakers Council Oral History Project (Sophia Smith Archives).

21. Peggy Pascoe, *What Comes Naturally: Miscegenation Law and the Making of Race in America* (New York: Oxford University Press, 2009), 1–2.

22. Barbara G. Friedman, *From the Battlefront to the Bridal Suite: Media Coverage of British War Brides, 1942–1946* (Columbia: University of Missouri Press, 2007), 2, 25–28; Steven Mintz and Helen Kellogg, *Domestic Revolutions: A Social History of American Family Life* (New York: Free Press, 1988), 153–54; Judy Barrett Litoff, David C. Smith, Barbara Wooddall Taylor, and Charles E. Smith, *Miss You: The World War II Letters of Barbara Wooddall Taylor and Charles E. Taylor* (Athens: University of Georgia Press, 1990), 3–16; Marilyn Yalom, *A History of the Wife* (New York: HarperCollins, 2001), 320.

23. Brett Harvey, *The Fifties: A Woman's Oral History* (New York: HarperPerennial, 1994), 71; Modell, *Into One's Own*, 176.

24. Swidler, "Culture in Action," 279.

25. On the adjustments required of the Depression era and the expectations of what married life might provide, see Mary C. McComb, *Great Depression and the Middle Class: Experts, Collegiate Youth, and Business Ideology, 1929–1941* (New York: Routledge, 2006), 1–4, 113–23. On the transformations of postwar America, see Beth Bailey, *Sex in the Heartland* (Cambridge, MA: Harvard University Press, 1999), 5–7, 15–18; Gary Gerstle, *American Crucible: Race and Nation in the Twentieth Century* (Princeton: Princeton University Press, 2001), 227–35; Thomas E. Williams, "Rural America in an Urban Age, 1945–1960," in *Reshaping America: Society and Institutions*, ed. Robert H. Bremmer and Gary W. Reichard (Columbus: Ohio State University Press, 1982), 147–51. For a contemporary account on the influence of urbanization and mobility, see Francis E. Merrill, *Courtship and Marriage: A Study in Social Relationships* (New York: William Sloane Associates, 1949), 13–16.

26. Roswell H. Johnson, Helen Randolph, and Erma Pixley, *Looking to Marriage* (1943; New York: Allyn and Bacon, 1945), 58–59. Of course a "real community" was marked by youth, whiteness, and middle-class status. See Beth Bailey, *From Front Porch to Back Seat: Courtship in Twentieth Century America* (Baltimore: Johns Hopkins University Press, 1988), 7–12; Cohen, *Consumers' Republic*, 11, 119–26, 141–43, 194–200; Andrew Hurley, *Diners, Bowling Alleys, and Trailer Parks: Chasing the American Dream in Postwar Consumer Culture* (New York: Basic Books, 2002), 213–16; Kenneth T. Jackson, *Crabgrass Frontier: The Suburbanization of the United States* (New York: Oxford University Press, 1985), 231–45; Marling, *As Seen on TV*, 250–58; May, *Homeward Bound*, xviii–xxii, 10–22, 143–62; Lynn Spigel, *Welcome to the Dreamhouse: Popular Media and Postwar Suburbs* (Durham: Duke University Press, 2001), 31–34.

27. Stephanie Coontz, *The Social Origins of Private Life: A History of American Families, 1600–1900* (New York: Verso, 1988), 1–2, 13; Cott, *Public Vows*, 185–91; Hartmann, *Home Front and Beyond*; Marilyn E. Hegarty, *Victory Girls*,

Khaki-Wackies, and Patriotutes: The Regulation of Female Sexuality during World War II (New York: New York University Press, 2007), 158–63; May, *Homeward Bound*, 49–79; Meghan K. Winchell, *Good Girls, Good Food, Good Fun: The Story of USO Hostesses during World War II* (Chapel Hill: University of North Carolina Press, 2008), 4–11, 106–12.

28. Hartmann, *Homefront and Beyond*, 25–26, 169, 210–14; May, *Homeward Bound*, 10–29, 43, 49–79, 81–84, 89–90, 100–118; Rebecca Jo Plant, *Mom: The Transformation of Motherhood in Modern America* (Chicago: University of Chicago Press, 2010), 105–8; Judith E. Smith, *Visions of Belonging: Family Stories, Popular Culture, and Postwar Democracy, 1940–1960* (New York: Columbia University Press, 2004), 33–37; Jessica Weiss, *To Have and To Hold: Marriage, the Baby Boom, and Social Change* (Chicago: University of Chicago Press, 2001), 21.

29. *The Best Years of Our Lives.* Directed by William Wyler. DVD. 1946. MGM, 2000.

30. May, *Homeward Bound*, xviii–xxi; Smith, *Visions of Belonging*, 36–37, 242–83. For the variety of postwar experiences among American women, see Joanne Meyerowitz, ed., *Not June Cleaver: Women and Gender in Postwar America, 1945–1960* (Philadelphia: Temple University Press, 1994).

31. Stephanie Coontz, *Marriage, A History: From Obedience to Intimacy or How Love Conquered Marriage* (New York: Viking, 2005), 224, 229–31; Barbara Ehrenreich, *The Hearts of Men: American Dreams and the Flight from Commitment* (New York: Anchor Books, 1983), 14–28.

32. E. E. LeMasters, *Modern Courtship and Marriage* (New York: Macmillan, 1957) 35; Morris Fishbein and Ruby Jo Reeves Kennedy, eds., *Modern Marriage and Family Living* (New York: Oxford University Press, 1957), 41.

33. Coontz, *Marriage, A History*, 224, 229; Virginia Venable Kidd, "Happily Ever After and Other Relationship Styles: Rhetorical Visions of Interpersonal Relations in Popular Magazines, 1951–1972," (PhD diss., University of Minnesota, 1974), 50; May, *Homeward Bound*, 163–66; Mintz and Kellogg, *Domestic Revolutions*, 180; Weiss, *To Have and To Hold*, 115–39.

34. Friedman, *From the Battlefront to the Bridal Suite*, 2, 25–28; Jellison, "From the Farmhouse Parlor to the Pink Barn," 57. On trends toward individualism in mate selection and distance from extended families, see also Ernest W. Burgess and Paul Wallin, *Engagement and Marriage* (Chicago: J.B. Lippincott, 1953), vi, vii, 12–15; Lester A. Kirkendall, "Too Young to Marry?" Public Affairs Pamphlet, no. 236, 1956, in *Teen Love, Teen Marriage*, ed. Jules Saltman (New York: Grosset & Dunlap, 1966), 82.

35. Howard, *Brides, Inc.*, 71, 79–97; Jellison, "From the Farmhouse Parlor to the Pink Barn," 56; Otnes and Pleck, *Cinderella Dreams*, 42; Pleck, *Celebrating the Family*, 216.

36. May, *Homeward Bound*, 20–22.

37. John Morton Blum, *V Was for Victory: Politics and American Culture during World War II* (New York: Harcourt Brace, 1976), 9–10, 90–105; Cohen,

Consumers' Republic, 112–65; Harvey, *Fifties*, 70; Hurley, *Diners, Bowling Alleys, and Trailer Parks*, 7–12; Mark H. Leff, "The Politics of Sacrifice on the American Homefront in World War II," *Journal of American History* 77 (March 1991): 1313–18; May, *Homeward Bound*, 142–51.

38. Cohen, *Consumers' Republic*, 112–13, 118–21; Coontz, *Marriage, a History*, 224; Howard, *Brides, Inc.*, 31, 93–95, 208; Modell, *Into One's Own*, 120, 212; Pleck, *Celebrating the Family*, 4. For a contemporary view of postwar prosperity, see David Potter, *People of Plenty: Economic Abundance and the American Character* (1958; Chicago: University of Chicago Press, 1954), 75–110; 166–210.

39. Rothman, *Hands and Hearts*, 276.

40. Modell, *Into One's Own*, 66.

41. On the broader tensions between individualism and conformity, see Wilfred M. McClay, *The Masterless: Self and Society in Modern America* (Chapel Hill: University of North Carolina Press, 1994), 226–68.

42. Bailey, *Sex in the Heartland*, 45–47.

43. Glassie, "Tradition," 369–95, 405–9.

44. Hobsbawn, "Introduction: Inventing Traditions," 1–14; Howard, *Brides, Inc.*, 3–5, 38–43, 55–57, 71, 89–97, 98, 107–09, 115–21, 141. The celebration of the traditional wedding fits with Michael G. Kammen's idea about a need for "an authentic or meaningful sense of continuity." See Michael G. Kammen, *The Mystic Chords of Memory: The Transformation of Tradition in American Culture* (New York: Knopf, 1991), 533, 532–39.

45. Marjorie Binford Woods, *Your Wedding: How to Plan and Enjoy It* (1942; Indianapolis: Bobbs-Merrill Company, Inc., 1949), np.

46. Kammen, *Mystic Chords of Memory*, 10.

47. Margaret Scully, "She Makes a Career of Making Weddings a Success," *Chicago Tribune*, March 29, 1950, A1.

48. Bentley, *Wedding Etiquette Complete*, 232.

49. Streeter, *Father of the Bride*, 184.

50. Howard, *Brides, Inc.*; Glassie, "Tradition," 395–412, esp. 405.

51. Wini Breines, *Young, White, and Miserable: Growing Up Female in the Fifties* (Boston: Beacon Press, 1992), 30, 34; Stephanie Coontz, *The Way We Never Were: American Families and the Nostalgia Trap* (New York: Basic Books, 1992), 25–29, 66–67.

52. Swidler, "Culture in Action," 278.

53. On postwar abundance and upward mobility, see Alan Brinkley, "The Illusion of Unity in Cold War Culture," in Peter J. Kuznick and James Gilbert, eds., *Rethinking Cold War Culture*, (Washington, DC: Smithsonian Institution Press, 2001), 63–69; Cohen, *Consumers' Republic*; Robert M. Collins, *More: The Politics of Economic Growth in Postwar America* (New York: Oxford University Press, 2000), 14–16, 40–42; Hurley, *Diners, Bowling Alleys, and Trailer Parks*; Shelley Nickles, "More is Better: Mass Consumption, Gender, and Class Identity in Postwar America," *American Quarterly* 54 (Dec. 2002): 581–622.

54. Bailey, *From Front Porch to Back Seat*, 43–47; Breines, *Young, White, and Miserable*, 50; Coontz, *Marriage, A History*, 225.

55. Coontz, *Marriage, a History*, 234; Bella DePaulo, *Singled Out: How Singles Are Stereotyped, Stigmatized, and Ignored, and Still Living Happily Ever After* (New York: St. Martin's Press, 2006), 11–12; Ehrenreich, *Hearts of Men*,17; May, *Homeward Bound*; Modell, *Into One's Own*, 6; Weiss, *To Have and To Hold*, 17–18. For contemporary discussions of maturity, see John E. Crawford and Luther E. Woodward, *Better Ways of Growing Up: Psychology and Mental Health for Youth* (Philadelphia: Muhlenberg Press, 1948), 216–19, 232–34; "Old Enough for Marriage? Test is Emotional Maturity," *Washington Post*, Dec. 2, 1951, S4; Wellington G. Pierce, *Youth Comes of Age* (New York: McGraw-Hill, 1948), 267–70; William S. Sadler, *Courtship and Love* (New York: Macmillan, 1953), 29, 112; John Sirjamaki, "American Culture and Family Life," in Morris Fishbein and Ruby Jo Reeves Kennedy, eds., *Modern Marriage and Family Living* (New York: Oxford University Press, 1957), 41; Hannah M. Stone and Abraham Stone, *A Marriage Manual: A Practical Guidebook to Sex and Marriage* (1935; New York: Simon & Schuster, 1953), 4–5, 258.

56. William Graebner, *Coming of Age in Buffalo: Youth and Authority in Postwar America* (Philadelphia: Temple University Press, 1993), 107.

57. Ada Hart Arlitt, "The Wedding and Honeymoon," in Morris Fishbein and Ruby Jo Reeves Kennedy, eds., *Modern Marriage and Family Living* (New York: Oxford University Press, 1957), 177.

58. Journal 1953–4, Folder 24, Box 3, Alice Gorton Hart Papers, 1948–1988 (Sophia Smith Archives). See also Crawford and Woodward, *Better Ways of Growing Up*, 216.

59. Coontz, *Marriage, A History*, 227; Benita Eisler, *Private Lives: Men and Women of the Fifties* (Danbury, CT: Franklin Watts Publishing, 1986), 124–26, 182–83; Weiss, *For Better or Worse*, 17–31.

60. Howard, *Brides, Inc.*, 3–4; Jellison, *It's Our Day*, 17–18.

61. Kirkendall, "Too Young to Marry?" 78. See also Elizabeth S. Force, *Your Family: Today and Tomorrow* (New York: Harcourt, Brace, 1955), 84; Merrill, *Courtship and Marriage*, 4, 7–9; Pierce, *Youth Comes of Age*, 279. See also Jellison, *It's Our Day*, 16–25; Otnes and Pleck, *Cinderella Dreams*, 50, 117, 167, 172–74.

62. *Father of the Bride.*

63. Kirkendall, "Too Young to Marry?" 78.

64. Harvey, *Fifties*, 61.

65. Letter, Gretchen to Alice Gorton, June 26, 1954, Folder 24, Box 3, Alice Gorton Hart Papers, 1948–1988 (Sophia Smith Archives).

66. "Senior Co-eds Turn to Plans for Weddings," *Chicago Tribune*, June 12, 1956, B8.

67. Journal 1953–4, Folder 24, Box 3, Alice Gorton Hart Papers, 1948–1988 (Sophia Smith Archives).

68. May, *Homeward Bound*, 68–72.

69. David Boroff, "Jewish Teenage Culture," *Annals of the American Academy of Political and Social Science* 338 (Nov. 1961): 87–88.

70. Templecrone Scrapbook, 1957–1961, Templecrone Scrapbooks, box 3, Record Sub-Group 20, Record Group 22 C (University of Missouri Archives).

71. David Boroff, *Campus U.S.A.: Portraits of American Colleges in Action* (New York: Harper & Brothers Publishers, 1958), 92–93.

72. Templecrone Scrapbook, 1957–1961, Templecrone Scrapbooks, box 3, Record Sub-Group 20, Record Group 22 C (University of Missouri Archives).

73. Boroff, *Campus U.S.A.*, 89–92, 100; Kitty Hanson, *For Richer, For Poorer* (New York: Abelard-Schuman, 1967), 21–27; Otnes and Pleck, *Cinderella Dreams*, 122.

74. May, *Homeward Bound*, 21; Nancy A. Walker, *Shaping Our Mothers' World: American Women's Magazines* (Jackson: University Press of Mississippi, 2000), 145–88.

75. Bailey, *From Front Porch to Back Seat*, 48–56; John D'Emilio and Estelle B. Freedman, *Intimate Matters: A History of Sexuality in America* (1988; Chicago: University of Chicago Press, 1997), 261; Eisler, *Private Lives*, 107–11; Modell, *Into One's Own*, 233–43; Rothman, *Hands and Hearts*, 303–5. On contemporary discussions of and responses to going steady, see Evelyn Duvall, "Courtship and Engagement," in Morris Fishbein and Ruby Jo Reeves Kennedy, eds., *Modern Marriage and Family Living* (New York: Oxford University Press, 1957), 145; LeMasters, *Modern Courtship and Marriage*, 121–27; Edith G. Neisser, *When Children Start Dating* (Chicago: Science Research Associates, 1951), 31–32; Sadler, *Courtship and Love*, 22–23, 27. On the distinctiveness of youth culture, see Graebner, *Coming of Age in Buffalo*, 52–85; Grace Palladino, *Teenagers: An American History* (New York: Basic Books, 1996), 97–102, 107–15.

76. Judy Barrett Litoff and David C. Smith, eds., *Since You Went Away: World War II Letters from American Women on the Home Front* (New York: Oxford University Press, 1991), 30.

77. Elizabeth Stewart Weston, ed., *Good Housekeeping's Complete Wedding Guide* (Garden City, NY: Hanover House Books, 1957), 109.

78. Walker, *Shaping Our Mothers' World*, 21, 31–65.

79. "Mother Isn't Best Authority on Weddings," *Washington Post*, January 21, 1950, B4.

80. "From bachelor girl to bride . . . ," *Ebony*, June 1947, 7, 22.

81. Margaret Baker, *Wedding Customs and Folklore* (1972; Vancouver: David & Charles, 1977), 40–42; Rothman, *Hands and Hearts*, 76–77, 166–68. Paula Rothenberg recalled her working-class friend, Susy Grabowski, showing her hope chest. As a teenager in the 1950s, Rothenberg had never known anyone with a hope chest before; the upper-middle-class girls she knew "simply looked forward to inheriting the key to their mothers' safe-deposit boxes or registering at Tiffany's." Paula Rothenberg, *Invisible Privilege: A Memoir about Race, Class, and Gender* (Lawrence: University Press of Kansas, 2000), 60–61.

82. Eleanor Eyestone Trummel, "Bound Volume: Growing Up Eleanor: My Life and Times," 119 in Folder: Eleanor Trummel, "Growing Up Eleanor: My Life and Times," memoir 2002 [published 2000], box 1, Eleanor Trummel Papers (Iowa Women's Archives).

83. Ibid.

84. On changes in gift-giving, see Penner, "A Vision of Love and Luxury," 6. Howard, *Brides, Inc.*, 15–18; Pleck, *Celebrating the Family*, 212–13; Weiss, *To Have and to Hold*, 23–26.

85. "Bride's Presents Make a Proud Display," *Life* 23 July 14, 1947, 92–93; "Present for the Bride," *Mademoiselle* 40 (1955): 182–83; Bettina Loomis, "Tips on Wedding Gifts for the Guest and the Bride," *Good Housekeeping* 142 (1956): 34–35, 226; "Ten to One, She'll Not Get Ten of These," *American Home* 40 (Sept. 1949): 134; Dorothy Wasbburn, "The Bride of Today Fits Her Plans to Modern Living," *Chicago Tribune*, March 7, 1955, B11.

86. Scrapbook, folder: Myrtle Keppy, Scrapbook, 1944–51, box 3, Myrtle Keppy Papers (Iowa Women's Archive). Sometimes this dependence weighed heavily on shower attendees. For advice on how to manage a multiplicity of showers, see Lucia Carter, "Are You Getting Soaked by June Bridal Showers?" *Chicago Tribune*, June 9, 1957, E5. See also Beth Montemurro, *Something Old, Something Bold: Bridal Showers and Bachelorette Parties* (New Brunswick: Rutgers University Press, 2006), 20–32; Otnes and Pleck, *Cinderella Dreams*, 72–74.

87. Weiss, *To Have and To Hold*, 54–56; Weston, ed., *Good Housekeeping's Complete Wedding Guide*, 34.

88. Breines, *Young, White, and Miserable*, 30, 34, 37–38; Coontz, *Marriage, A History*, 224, 229, 233; Harvey, *Fifties*, 71.

89. Vicki Howard identified Chicago's Marshall Fields as the first North American department store to offer a gift registry in 1924. Cele Otnes and Elizabeth Pleck argued that the first registry was created at China Hall in Rochester, Minnesota in 1901. The authors agree, however, that by the postwar period, brides could find a pre-designed registry at any number of stores. Howard, *Bride's Inc.*, 2, 116–20; Otnes and Pleck, *Cinderella Dreams*, 75–76.

90. "Modern Brides Shun Fancy Linen Sheets; They Prefer Plain Cotton and Twin Beds," *New York Times*, April 10, 1954, 18.

91. See Ruth MacKay, "Today's Daughter Marries Young," *Chicago Tribune*, June 27, 1954, E1; "Wedding Gift Notes: Work-Savers for Brides," *New York Times*, May 28, 1955, 9.

92. Mead, *One Perfect Day*, 116.

93. Betty Harper Fussell, *My Kitchen Wars* (New York: North Point Press, 1999), 69.

94. Arlitt, "Wedding and Honeymoon," 177–78; Weston, ed., *Good Housekeeping's Complete Wedding Guide*, 19–20; Force, *Your Family* 195; Joyce Jackson, *Joyce Jackson's Guide to Dating* (1955; Englewood Cliffs, NJ: Prentice Hall, 1957), 201–2; Johnson, Randolph, and Pixley, *Looking to Marriage*, 71; Barbara Wilson and the Women's Feature Staff of the *New York Herald Tribune*, *The Brides' School*

Complete Book of Engagement and Wedding Etiquette (New York: Hawthorne Books, 1959), 38.

95. Letter, Beverly George to Larry Everett, Aug. 16, 1946, Folder: Personal Correspondence, 1946, box 1, Beverly Everett Papers (Iowa Women's Archives).

96. Penner, "A Vision of Love and Luxury," 6–7; Rothman, *Hands and Hearts*, 67–75, 83, 274–76. On disruption associated with the wedding, see Arnold van Gennep, *The Rites of Passage*, trans. Monika B. Vizedom and Gabrielle L. Caffee (Chicago: University of Chicago Press, 1960), 116.

97. Weston, ed., *Good Housekeeping's Complete Wedding Guide*, 17–18. For more on the importance of women's magazines during the postwar years, see Walker, *Shaping Our Mothers' World*.

98. Palladino, *Teenagers*, 97–115.

99. On a talk between father and future son-in-law as an out-of-date or seemingly old-fashioned tradition, see Jackson, *Joyce Jackson's Guide to Dating*, 201; Weston, ed., *Good Housekeeping's Complete Wedding Guide*, 19. On the origins of this custom, see Lystra, *Searching the Heart*, 153.

100. Bentley, *Wedding Etiquette Complete*, vii.

101. Breines, *Young, White, and Miserable*, 34, 38.

102. Coontz, *Marriage, A History*, 227; Ehrenreich, *Hearts of Men*, 1–28.

103. Streeter, *Father of the Bride*, 108.

CHAPTER 2

1. *The Golden Chalice*, Produced by US Naval Photographic Center, 66 minutes, MP 464, (Lyndon Baines Johnson [LBJ] Presidential Library), Transfer from Allied Video Master. On the formality of the guests' dress as a contrast to the later, more pronounced informality of 1960s youth, see Kenneth Cmiel, "The Politics of Civility," in *The Sixties: From History to Memory*, David Farber, ed. (Chapel Hill: University of North Carolina Press, 1994), 275–76.

2. Howard, *Brides, Inc.*, 31, 86–89; Jellison, *It's Our Day*, 27–29; Otnes and Pleck, *Cinderella Dreams*, 44–48.

3. Liz Carpenter, *Ruffles and Flourishes: The warm and tender story of a simple girl who found adventure in the White House* (1970; New York: Pocket Books, 1971), 215.

4. Press Conference of Mrs. Lyndon B. Johnson and Miss Luci Baines Johnson (transcript), July 18, 1966, 2, Reference File: Luci's Wedding (1966) (LBJ Library).

5. Helen Thomas, "The White House Says No!" *Boston Herald*, July 28, 1966. In order to keep the details of the dress as secret as possible, Liz Carpenter released a statement just an hour before the wedding. See Press Release, Aug. 6, 1966, Reference File: Luci's Wedding (1966), (LBJ Library).

6. In Rebecca Greer's 1965 *Book for Brides*, she asserted that the financial status of the bride's family determined the size of the wedding. Greer identified four "basic wedding styles." At the highest level was the "Ultra-Formal Wedding,"

the largest and most elaborate. It included the presence of 6–12 attendants, more than 200 guests, a floor-length gown and long train and veil, a church location, and high cost. Luci Johnson's wedding fulfilled the necessary criteria. See Rebecca Greer, *Book for Brides* (New York: Arco Publishing, 1965), 18, 14.

7. The Johnson family denied that tax dollars funded the Johnson/Nugent wedding. To dispel rumors, the family set up a separate account to fund the celebration. See "Three-Ring Wedding," *Time*, Aug. 5, 1966, 7. When asked how much the wedding cost, the White House responded, "Weddings come high now." See Frances Lewine, "Great Society's Wedding Plans," *Los Angeles Times*, July 24, 1966, I1. For an example of a letter expressing outrage at the wedding's price, see Gerald L. Arnholt to Lyndon Johnson, Aug. 9, 1966, Folder: Johnson, Luci (Wedding)—A, box 63, Liz Carpenter Alpha File, White House Social File (WHSF), (LBJ Library).

8. Howard, *Brides, Inc.*, 4–5; Jellison, *It's Our Day*, 76–81; Hanson, *For Richer, For Poorer*, 14, 51; Otnes and Pleck, *Cinderella Dreams*, 45–46, 54.

9. Actual white weddings rarely progressed as smoothly as those publicized in the fictitious settings of advertisements or other forms of mass media. Jellison, *It's Our Day*, 9–11, 17–18, 23–25. See also Hanson, *For Richer, For Poorer*, 20–21, 38–39, 166–67, 175–76; Otnes and Pleck, *Cinderella Dreams*, 42–49.

10. The wedding industry popularized the idea of the bride as "Queen for a day," but this idea of bride as queen seemingly extended throughout the engagement period. See Jellison, *It's Our Day*, 29, 79–81; Mead, *One Perfect Day*, 19–20; Otnes and Pleck, *Cinderella Dreams*. On the average person's sense of a personal relationship with a celebrity, see Richard Schickel, *Intimate Strangers: The Culture of Celebrity in America* (1985; Chicago: Ivan R. Dee, 2000), 4.

11. Carpenter, *Ruffles and Flourishes*, 215; Hanson, *For Richer, For Poorer*, 123–24; Howard, *Brides, Inc.;* Mead, *One Perfect Day*, 59.

12. Cohen, *Consumers' Republic*, 10–11, 141–56, 257–66; Robert M. Collins, "Growth Liberalism in the Sixties: Great Societies at Home and Grand Designs Abroad," in *The Sixties: From History to Memory* (Chapel Hill: University of North Carolina Press, 1994), 13–20; Coontz, *Marriage, A History*, 231–32; Gary Cross, *An All-Consuming Century: Why Consumerism Won in Modern America* (New York: Columbia University Press, 2000), 88–143,146; David Farber, *The Age of Great Dreams: America in the 1960s* (New York: Hill and Wang, 1994), 8–11; Hurley, *Diners, Bowling Alleys, and Trailer Parks*,1–19; Meg Jacobs, *Pocketbook Politics: Economic Citizenship in Twentieth Century America* (Princeton: Princeton University Press, 2005), 249–50; Otnes and Pleck, *Cinderella Dreams*, 7, 9, 44.

13. Gloria Emerson, "Many Years of Careful Planning are Behind Every Girl's Wedding," *New York Times*, June 24, 1960, 18; Barbara Wilson, et al., *Brides' School Complete Book of Engagement and Wedding Etiquette*, 95.

14. Jellison, *It's Our Day*, 21–28 and Otnes and Pleck, *Cinderella Dreams*, 46–49, 54, 174–75. On the influence of media and consumerism on American youth,

see Cohen, *Consumers' Republic*, 319–22; Dominick Cavallo, *A Fiction of the Past: The Sixties in American History* (New York: St. Martin's Press, 1999), 4–5; Gary Cross, *The Cute and the Cool: Wondrous Innocence and Modern American Children's Culture* (New York: Oxford University Press, 2004), 154–56; Kelley Massoni, "'Teena Goes to Market': *Seventeen* Magazine and the Early Construction of the Teen Girl (As) Consumer," *Journal of American Culture* 29 (March 2006): 39–40; Palladino, *Teenagers*, 103–9.

15. J. A. Livington, "Future Boom Tied to Wedding Rings," *Washington Post*, May 27, 1962, A24.

16. U.S. Department of Health, Education, and Welfare, Public Health Division, "Vital Statistics of the United States 1966," Vol. 3, Marriage and Divorce (Washington, C: U.S. Government Printing Office, 1969), 12–13; Lloyd Shearer, "Brides are Big Business," *Parade Magazine*, June 26, 1966, 12.

17. Hanson, *For Richer, For Poorer*, 15.

18. Sam Dawson, "Wedding Bells Ring Out Song of Big Spending," *Jefferson City [Missouri] Post-Tribune*, May 2, 1960, 4; William M. Freeman, "Sales Rise Seen From Marriages," *New York Times*, Dec. 3, 1961, F10; "Hold the Ladder, Dad; Cost of Weddings Soars," *Los Angeles Times*, July 31, 1964, C4; "Merchant Best Man at Wedding," *Los Angeles Times*, Dec. 2, 1966, D16; Martin Tolchin, "The Wedding March is Sweet Music to Many Merchants' Ears," *New York Times*, May 24, 1961, 48; "Wedding Bells, Cash Register Ring Together," *Chicago Tribune*, March 17, 1962, E7.

19. Doris Lewis Smith's copy of *Joys to Remember*, compiled by Frances Youngren (Chicago: Moody Press, 1961). Copy in Dunak's possession. It was not unusual for brides to fill out bride books. They could use the books to keep track of gifts and guests, and *Joys to Remember* included space for photographs and newspaper announcements. Doris Lewis received her bride book from Smith's great aunt, who owned a Christian bookstore.

20. Hanson, *For Richer, For Poorer*, 83.

21. On 1960s prosperity, see Collins, "Growth Liberalism in the Sixties," 11–44.

22. Hanson, *For Richer, For Poorer*,19–23; Jellison, *It's Our Day*, 26–28, 85–88; Otnes and Pleck, *Cinderella Dreams*, 45, 122; Pleck, *Celebrating the Family*, 219–20.

23. Hanson, *For Richer, for Poorer*, 40. See also Otnes and Pleck, *Cinderella Dreams*, 120–22.

24. See Vicki Howard, "American Weddings: Gender, Consumption, and the Business of Brides" (Ph.D. diss., University of Texas, 2000).

25. "Three-Ring Wedding," 19.

26. "It's a Family Affair," *The Long Beach Independent*, July 24, 1966.

27. Marie Smith and Louise Durbin, *White House Brides: A New and Revealing History of Romance and Courtship in the President's Mansion* (Washington, DC: Acropolis Books, 1966), 184.

28. Hanson, *For Richer, For Poorer*, 40.

29. For examples of such announcements, see "Parents Tell Betrothal of Miss Withrow," *Chicago Tribune*, April 9, 1956, B16; "Parents Tell Engagement of Miss Anne Louise Zeddies," *Chicago Tribune*, May 28, 1956, B7. Invitations also suggested parents' central role. Beatrice A. Hunt, owner of Camp Cowassett, in Falmouth, Massachusetts, kept records of wedding invitations sent by camp alumni. Records extended from the 1930s through 1966, and nearly all invitations were sent by parents of the bride. See "Records, ca. 1915–1966," Beatrice A. Hunt Collection (Falmouth Historical Society). Peter Lacey suggests that newspaper announcements emphasized family connections and successes. Peter Lacey, *The Wedding* (New York: Grosset & Dunlap, 1969), 174.

30. On parental investment in their children and concern over their marriages, see Evelyn Mills Duvall, *The Art of Dating* (New York: Association Press, 1967), 233–34.

31. Jackson claimed to be a teenager, but was 40 years old when the *Guide to Dating* first appeared. See Palladino, *Teenagers*, 107–9. Jackson, *Joyce Jackson's Guide to Dating*, 201, 202, vii. For similar advice, see Weston, ed., *Good Housekeeping's Complete Wedding Guide*, 19.

32. On the tradition of asking the bride's father for her hand in marriage, see Otnes and Pleck, *Cinderella Dreams*, 70–71. On advice that it was okay to forgo asking a father's permission, see Greer, *Book for Brides*, 9. For texts that suggested asking a father's permission or familial consent, see Rosalie Brody, *Weddings: What every bride should know about wedding etiquette and arrangements for the formal and informal wedding* (New York: Simon & Schuster, 1963), 1; Emma Aubert Cole, *The Modern Bride Book of Etiquette* (New York: Ziff-Davis, 1961), 80.

33. Johnson, *White House Diary*, 362. Frances Lewine, "Luci Reported Seeking Permission to Marry," *Syracuse Herald-Journal*, Oct. 30, 1965, 1; "Luci's Engagement May Be Told Soon," *Oshkosh Daily Northwestern*, Oct. 30, 1965, 20. Lewine's article was reprinted in *The [Petersburg, Virginia] Progress-Index*, *The Cedar Rapids Gazette*, and numerous other papers around the United States.

34. Douglas B. Cornell, "Newsmen Draw Complete Blank: Secrecy Wraps Visit to LBJ Ranch of Luci and Friend Pat," *Kokomo [Indiana] Tribune*, Oct. 31, 1965, 1; "Luci Seeks Permission to Marry," *Columbus [Nebraska] Daily Telegram*, Oct. 30, 1965, 1.

35. Press Conference of Mrs. Lyndon B. Johnson and Miss Luci Baines Johnson (transcript), July 18, 1966, 3–4, Reference File: Luci's Wedding (1966), (LBJ Library).

36. Otnes and Pleck indicate that the material culture saved from a wedding serves to remind participants of the good times had at the wedding. In this way, memories become sanitized. Luci Johnson might have been participating in an early sanitization of memory as she discussed her father's reaction to news of her potential engagement. See Otnes and Pleck, *Cinderella Dreams*, 16–17.

37. Lady Bird Johnson [Claudia Alta Taylor Johnson], *A White House Diary* (1970; New York: Dell Publishing, 1971), 362.

38. "Three-Ring Wedding," 6.
39. On the typicality of pre-wedding conflict, see Hanson, *For Richer, For Poorer*, 166–67.
40. "Three-Ring Wedding," 19.
41. Louise Hutchinson, "Luci Johnson's Wedding: It's Liz Carpenter's Big Beat," reprinted in the *Abilene Reporter-News*, Aug. 2, 1966. Louise Hutchinson, "Luci Johnson's Wedding: It's Liz Carpenter's Big Beat," *Chicago Tribune*, July 24, 1966, B1, found in Reference File: Luci's Wedding (1966), (LBJ Library).
42. Cora Pohlman to Liz Carpenter, June 1, 1966, Folder: Johnson, Luci (Wedding)—P, box 63, Liz Carpenter Alpha File, WHSF (LBJ Library).
43. Comedienne Edie Adams joked that Luci's wedding was exclusive; only the "the immediate country" was invited. See "Three-Ring Wedding," 19.
44. Carpenter, *Ruffles and Flourishes*, 215; Hutchinson, "Luci Johnson's Wedding: It's Liz Carpenter's Big Beat," B1; Johnson, *A White House Diary*, 432–33; Smith and Durbin, *White House Brides*, 119–24.
45. Carpenter, *Ruffles and Feathers*, 218.
46. "TV Cameras to be Barred at Luci Johnson's Wedding," *New York Times*, June 1, 1966, 50.
47. Val Adams, "Prime Time for Luci," *New York Times*, July 31, 1966, 87.
48. As the self-proclaimed "unpolitical member of a political family," Luci participated in her father's 1964 campaign, acted as a substitute hostess when Mrs. Johnson was unavailable, and participated in various local causes. Smith and Durbin, *White House Brides*, 183.
49. Sister M. Lucilla to Lyndon B. Johnson, June 19, 1966, Folder: Johnson, Luci (Wedding)—L, box 63, Liz Carpenter Alpha File, WHSF (LBJ Library).
50. Schickel, *Intimate Strangers*, 4–5.
51. Pamela R. Frese, ed., *Celebrations of Identity: Multiple Voices in American Ritual Performance* (Westport, CT: Bergin & Garvey, 1993), xv; Frese, "Holy Matrimony," 40; Montemurro, *Something Old, Something Bold*, 12; Otnes and Pleck, *Cinderella Dreams*, 3–4.
52. Carolyn Kitch writes, "If celebrity is a cultural space in which Americans negotiate their values and identities, through which they become something larger than their individual selves, then a celebrity's death is a moment for public discussion of shared ideals and identities." Other significant moments in a celebrity's life—the wedding, for example—might be another moment when the public connected particularly to the celebrity and used expectations of the public enactment of such a rite as a way to express their values and beliefs. See Carolyn Kitch, *Pages from the Past: History and Memory in American Magazines* (Chapel Hill: University of North Carolina Press, 2005), 69, 68. Wendy Leeds-Hurwitz likewise recognized individuals' evaluations of weddings as linked to their own experiences. See Leeds-Hurwitz, *Wedding as Text*, 59.
53. On the long-held views of the link between ritual and community, see van Gennep, *Rites of Passage*, 118–19; Leeds-Hurwitz, *Wedding as Text*, 26–29, 60, 91. On

the sanctioning of individual desire and the conflict produced by this idea, see
Hanson, *For Richer, For Poorer*, 48–49, Howard, *Brides, Inc.*, 92–93; Jellison, *It's
Our Day*, 29.

54. Bailey, *Sex in the Heartland*, 14–16.
55. Mrs. Joy Starr to Luci Johnson, May 31, 1966, Folder: Johnson, Luci
    (Wedding)—S, box 63, Liz Carpenter Alpha File, WHSF (LBJ Library). A review
    for one wedding text, *The Wedding Book* (1964), described the book as a guide
    to instruct the bride and groom on their "responsibilities and obligations to
    each other, to their families and to friends." See "Wedding Guide," *New York
    Times*, Aug. 26, 1964, 42.
56. Weston, ed., *Good Housekeeping's Complete Wedding Guide*, 11; Jellison, *It's Our
    Day*, 29; Wilson et al., *Brides' School Complete Book of Engagement and Wedding
    Etiquette*, 95.
57. Glassie, "Tradition," 405.
58. Laura Kilbane to Luci Johnson, May 29, 1966, Folder: Johnson, Luci
    (Wedding)—K, box 63, Liz Carpenter Alpha File, WHSF (LBJ Library). See
    also Hanson, *For Richer, for Poorer*, 23. On the language increasingly associated
    with the wedding, see Otnes and Pleck, *Cinderella Dreams*, 13–14; Jellison, *It's
    Our Day*, 29. Emily Post, in 1922, wrote specifically about extending invitations
    to friends: "To leave out old friends because they are neither rich nor fashion-
    able . . . shows a want of loyalty and proper feeling . . . " Emily Post, *Etiquette
    in Society, in Business, in Politics, and at Home* (New York: Funk & Wagnalls,
    1922), 314.
59. Laura Kilbane to Luci Johnson, May 29, 1966 and Marsha Wiedler to President
    Johnson, June 6, 1966, Folder: Johnson, Luci (Wedding)—W, box 63, Liz Car-
    penter Alpha File, WHSF (LBJ Library). Such concerns were unfounded. In 1967,
    Lynda Johnson married in the White House; Tricia Nixon followed suit in 1971.
60. Betty Jo Miller to Lyndon B. Johnson, rec. June 3, 1966, Folder: Johnson, Luci
    (Wedding)—M, box 63, Liz Carpenter Alpha File, WHSF, ibid.
61. Leeds-Hurwitz, *Wedding as Text*, 91.
62. Typically, a wedding would take place in the parish church of the bride. See
    Weston, ed., *Good Housekeeping's Complete Wedding Guide*, 43 and Greer, *Book
    for Brides*, 14. See also Cole, *Modern Bride Book of Etiquette*, 129 Hanson, *For
    Richer, For Poorer*, 83; Otnes and Pleck, *Cinderella Dreams*, 109–10; Pleck, *Cel-
    ebrating the Family*, 210–11.
63. "Three-Ring Wedding," 19.
64. Charles R. Sponseller to Luci Johnson, June 22, 1966, Folder: Johnson, Luci
    (Wedding)—S, box 63, Liz Carpenter Alpha File, WHSF (LBJ Library). For
    another letter on the appeal of the Shrine, see Jane Stallard to Luci Johnson,
    June 4, 1966, Folder: Johnson, Luci (Wedding)—S, box 63, Liz Carpenter Alpha
    File, WHSF, ibid.
65. Press Conference of Mrs. Lyndon B. Johnson and Miss Luci Baines Johnson
    (transcript), July 18, 1966, 5, Reference File: Luci's Wedding (1966), ibid. See also

Frances Lewine, "Johnsons Hope to Make Wedding a 'Family Affair,'" *Syracuse Herald Times*, July 24, 1966, 27.

66. It was not unusual for forthcoming weddings to be announced from the pulpit and in the church bulletin or calendar. Interested parties might then attend the ceremony, if they so wished. See Brody, *Weddings*, 28.

67. Minerva B. Kasper to Lady Bird Johnson, June 2, 1966, 1, Folder: Johnson, Luci (Wedding)—K, box 63, Liz Carpenter Alpha File, WHSF (LBJ Library).

68. On feelings of being slighted, see Hanson, *For Richer, For Poorer*, 39. Minerva B. Kasper to Lady Bird Johnson, June 2, 1966, 2. On the coverage Princess Margaret's May 6, 1960 wedding received, see Richard F. Shepard, "TV Networks Set Wide Coverage of Princess Margaret's Nuptials," *New York Times*, March 12, 1960, 43.

69. Cott, *Public Vows*, 1–8, 197. As John Caughey notes, people often feel they enjoy a private relationship with "unmet media figures." These "relationships" continue even "when the TV is turned off, the book closed, or the newspaper thrown away." See John L. Caughey, *Imaginary Social Worlds: A Cultural Approach* (Lincoln: University of Nebraska Press, 1984), 33–54.

70. Mary Williams, *Marriage for Beginners* (New York: Macmillan, 1967), 52.

71. Johnson, *White House Diary*, 434. On the nature of presidential relationships, and particularly the increased "politicization of the personal" during Johnson's terms, see Gil Troy, "Copresident or Codependent? The Rise and Rejection of Presidential Couples since World War II," in *The Presidential Companion: Readings on the First Ladies* Second Edition, Robert Watson and Anthony J. Eksterowicz, eds. (Columbia: University of South Carolina Press, 2006), 258. Carmichael ultimately did not attend the wedding protests, but did send word of his support from Cleveland.

72. Terry Anderson, *The Movement and the Sixties* (New York: Oxford University Press, 1995), 93–108; 251–54; John Morton Blum, *Years of Discord: American Politics and Society, 1961–1974* (New York: Norton, 1991), 270–78; Allen J. Matusow, *The Unraveling of America: A History of Liberalism in the 1960s* (New York: Harper & Row, 1984), 308–44. *Time* magazine recognized "today's youth" as the 1966 Man of the Year. In its coverage of the younger generation, *Time* noted an increased willingness to disagree with political authority and challenge social expectations. See "The Inheritor," *Time*, Jan. 6, 1967, http://www.time.com/time/magazine/article/0,9171,843150,00.html.

73. Smith and Durbin, *White House Brides*, 185. *Good Housekeeping's Complete Wedding Guide* indicated that a bride and groom relied also on the officiating clergyman as they selected the wedding date. See Weston, ed., *Good Housekeeping's Complete Wedding Guide*, 41–43.

74. "Three-Ring Wedding," 21–22.

75. Carpenter, *Ruffles and Flourishes*, 229.

76. For information on the World Friendship Center, see http://wfchiroshima.net/.

77. Barbara Reynolds to Luci Johnson, June 9, 1966, Folder: Johnson, Luci (Wedding)—R, box 63, Liz Carpenter Alpha File, WHSF (LBJ Library).

78. Suzanne Williams to Luci Johnson, June 21, 1966, Folder: Johnson, Luci (Wedding)—W, box 63, Liz Carpenter Alpha File, WHSF, ibid.

79. Liz Carpenter to Barbara Reynolds, June 20, 1966, Folder: Johnson, Luci (Wedding)—R, box 63, Liz Carpenter Alpha File, WHSF, ibid.; Liz Carpenter to Suzanne Williams, June 25, 1966, Folder: Johnson, Luci (Wedding)—W, box 63, Liz Carpenter Alpha File, WHSF, ibid.

80. Barbara Reynolds to Luci Johnson, June 9, 1966, Folder: Johnson, Luci (Wedding)—R, box 63, Liz Carpenter Alpha File, WHSF, ibid.; Suzanne Williams to Luci Johnson, June 21, 1966, Folder: Johnson, Luci (Wedding)—W, box 63, Liz Carpenter Alpha File, WHSF, ibid.

81. Jacob Liebson, Letters to the Editors of the *Times*, "White House Wedding," *New York Times*, Aug. 5, 1966, 23.

82. Carpenter, *Ruffles and Flourishes*, 221.

83. "Three-Ring Wedding," 19. On the growing number of troops in Vietnam, see David L. Anderson, *The Vietnam War* (New York: Palgrave, 2005), 48–49.

84. "Hamilton Passes Draft Physical," *New York Times*, Dec. 14, 1966, A2; "Tells George Hamilton's Draft Status," *The Kansas City Times*, April 13, 1966, 1.

85. Lynda received far more public criticism than Luci. Her relationship with George Hamilton received particular scrutiny. See Curt Pieper to Lynda Johnson, April 12, 1966, Folder: Johnson, Lynda, Criticism-P, box 1204, WHSF, 1963–1969, Alpha File (LBJ Library). Pieper included with his letter a satirical column from the Pennsylvania State University *Daily Collegian*. In the piece, Editorial Editor Mel Ziegler wished for a chance to meet Lynda and demonstrate his love with hopes that they would marry. President Johnson, upon meeting Ziegler and seeing his devotion to Lynda, would be so taken with the young man that he most certainly would postpone his trip to Vietnam, much the same, Ziegler insinuated, as Johnson had done for Nugent and Hamilton. See also D. Hollingworth to Lady Bird Johnson, Nov. 9, 1967, Folder: Johnson, Lynda, Criticism—H, box 1203, WHSF, 1963–1969, Alpha File ibid.; Marianne Winters to Lady Bird Johnson, Feb. 24, 1966, Folder: Johnson, Lynda, Criticism—W, box 1204, WHSF, 1963–1969, Alpha File, ibid.

86. Anonymous to Luci Johnson, May 16, 1966, Folder: Johnson, Lynda, Criticism—Anonymous (Only), 2 of 2, box 1203, WHSF, 1963–1969, Alpha File, *ibid.* For other letters expressing anger over the special privilege received by those close to the Johnson daughters, see Helen G. Martin to Lady Bird Johnson, May 14, 1966, Folder: Johnson, Lynda, Criticism—M, box 1204, WHSF, 1963–1969, Alpha File, ibid. For other letters critiquing the Johnsons wedding spending, see Mr. Gerald L. Arnholt to Lyndon B. Johnson, Folder: Johnson, Luci (Wedding)—A, box 62, WHSF, Liz Carpenter Alpha Files, ibid.; Mrs. G. C. Wilson to President and Mrs. Johnson, Aug. 21, 1966, Folder: Johnson, Lynda, Criticism—W, box 1204, WHSF, 1963–1969, Alpha File, ibid.

87. John Herbers, "Thousands Wait Outside Church," *New York Times*, Aug. 7, 1966, 62.

88. "300 with Hiroshima Placards Fail to Ruin Luci's Big Day," *Chicago Tribune*, Aug. 7, 1966, 6; Herbers, "Thousands Wait Outside Church," 62; Thomas W. Lippman, "Pickets Protest Hiroshima, Vietnam as Luci Is Married," *Washington Post*, Aug. 7, 1966, A3.

89. "300 with Hiroshima Placards Fail to Ruin Luci's Big Day," 6

90. Anderson, *Vietnam War*, 62–64; Anderson, *Movement and the Sixties*, 145–51; Bailey, *Sex in the Heartland*, 80; Edward Morgan, *The 60s Experience: Hard Lessons about Modern America* (Philadelphia: Temple University Press, 1991), 140–57.

91. Helen Thomas, "Big Day Arrives . . . Johnsons Ready," *Long Beach Independent*, Aug. 6, 1966, A8.

92. Johnson, *White House Diary*, 449.

93. Nan Robertson, "Luci Johnson Wed in Capital at Noon," *New York Times*, Aug. 5, 1966, 15.

94. Ibid., 1, 62.

95. Johnson, *White House Diary*, 447.

96. Smith and Durbin, *White House Brides*, 193.

97. Carpenter, *Ruffles and Flourishes*, 230.

98. Johnson, *White House Diary*, 448.

99. Carpenter, *Ruffles and Flourishes*, 231.

100. Ibid., 214.

101. On the emergent view of the personal as political, see Cott, *Public Vows*, 204–5; Alice Echols, *Daring to Be Bad: Radical Feminism in America, 1967–1975* (Minneapolis: University of Minnesota Press, 1989), 16–17; Alice Echols, "Nothing Distant about It: Women's Liberation and Sixties Radicalism," in *The Sixties: From History to Memory*, David Farber, ed. (Chapel Hill: University of North Carolina Press, 1994), 149–67; Sara Evans, *Personal Politics: The Roots of Women's Liberation in the Civil Rights Movement and the New Left* (1979; New York: Vintage Books, 1980), 21, 212–15; Doug Rossinow, "'The Revolution Is about Our Lives': The New Left's Counterculture," in *Imagine Nation: The American Counterculture in the 1960s and 70s,* Peter Braunstein and Michael William Doyle, eds. (New York: Routledge, 2002), 101, 105.

CHAPTER 3

1. Jo Ahern Segal and Elizabeth Alston, "Marriage the New Natural Way," *Look*, June 29, 1971, 46, 45.

2. Ibid., 44.

3. Marcia Seligson, *The Eternal Bliss Machine: America's Way of Wedding* (New York: Bantam Books, 1973), 268, 267.

4. "Marriage the New Natural Way," 46.

5. Jellison, *It's Our Day*, 29–31, 256–58; Seligson, *Eternal Bliss Machine*, 8, 10, 14. On 1960s youth rejection of the American Dream, see Theodore Roszak, *The Making of a Counterculture: Reflections on the Technocratic Society and Its*

Youthful Opposition (1968; Berkeley: University of California Press, 1995), xxv. On the growing focus on authenticity, nature, and the natural environment during the 1970s, see Sam Binkley, *Getting Loose: Lifestyle Consumption in the 1970s* (Durham: Duke University Press, 2007), 4, 165; Charles Reich, *The Greening of America* (New York: Random House, 1970), 219–262; Rossinow, "'The Revolution Is about Our Lives,'" 110; Bruce J. Schulman, *The Seventies: The Great Shift in American Culture, Society, Politics* (Cambridge, MA: Da Capo Press, 2002), 89–90.

6. "Marriage the New Natural Way," 44.

7. On hippie weddings, see Rex Weiner and Deanne Stillman, *Woodstock Census: The Nationwide Survey of the Sixties Generation* (New York: Viking Press, 1979), 21.

8. Anderson, *Movement and the Sixties*, 170–74, 242–43, 248–49; Bailey, *Sex in the Heartland*, 143–45; Farber, *Age of Great Dreams*, 168–69, 174; Matusow, *Unraveling of America*, 275–77, 293, 296–97, 301–02; Morgan, *60s Experience*, 182–83. For contemporary evaluations of hippie appeal, see Reich, *Greening of America*, 223; Winfield W. Salisbury and Frances F. Salisbury, "Youth and the Search for Intimacy," in *The New Sexual Revolution*, Lester A. Kirkendall and Robert N. Whitehurst, eds. (Buffalo: Prometheus Books, 1971), 171; Weiner and Stillman, *Woodstock Census*, 34, 36–37; Leonard Wolf, ed., *Voices from the Love Generation* (Boston: Little, Brown, 1968), xix–xxi, 36–37.

9. Howard Kirschenbaum and Rockwell Stensrud, *The Wedding Book: Alternative Ways to Celebrate Marriage* (New York: Seabury Press, 1974), 68–70; Elizabeth A. Myers, "Burning Bras, Long Hairs, and Dashikis: Personal Politics in American Culture, 1950–1975" (PhD diss., Loyola University Chicago, 2006), 161, 293–94; Rossinow, "'The Revolution Is about Our Lives': The New Left's Counterculture," 105.

10. Sheila Weller, *Girls Like Us: Carole King, Joni Mitchell, Carly Simon—And the Journey of a Generation* (New York: Atria Books, 2008), 212, 213.

11. "Hippie-Bride Without Shoes is Married," *The Derrick [Oil City, Franklin, Clairon, Pennsylvania]*, July 8, 1968, 9. This article also was reprinted in the *Abilene Reporter-News*, July 10, 1968. For a similarly described wedding, see Joan Morrison and Robert K. Morrison, *From Camelot to Kent State: The Sixties Experience in the Words of Those Who Lived It* (1987; New York: Oxford University Press, 2001), 178.

12. Paul Bailey, "Column One," *Commerce [Texas] Journal*, March 27, 1969, 1; "Good Evening," *Bucks County [Pennsylvania] Courier Times*, Aug. 31, 1971, 1; "Quips and Quotes," sent in by Stephanie von Esse, *Tri-City Herald [Washington]*, Dec. 29, 1968, 58; "WBTM Radio Ramblins," *Danville [Virginia] Register*, Dec. 10, 1967, 50. An advertisement for a local pharmacy in Santa Fe featured the following: "Hippie Wedding: Where they give the bride a shower—just before her wedding." Advertisement, *The New Mexican*, Aug. 14, 1970, A3. Sometimes such "jokes" turned more threatening. See Anderson, *Movement*

and the Sixties, 249, 284–85; Alice Echols, Scars of Sweet Paradise: The Life and Times of Janis Joplin (New York: Metropolitan Books, 1999), 150; Weiner and Stillman, Woodstock Census, 47.

13. "Hippie-Bride Without Shoes is Married," 9.

14. Anderson, Movement and the Sixties, 209, 241–42; Roszak, Making of a Counter-culture, 37.

15. Jurate Kazickas, "'As Long as We Both Shall Love,'" Washington Post, Feb. 17, 1971, p. 141.

16. Roberta Price, Huerfano: A Memoir of My Life in the Counterculture (Amherst: University of Massachusetts Press, 2004), 21, 21–27.

17. Kazickas, "'As Long as We Both Shall Love,'" 141.

18. Kirschebaum and Stensrud, Wedding Book, 25.

19. Dan Pavillard, "Editor's Corner," in Ole!, Tucson Daily Citizen Magazine, May 11, 1968, 2; Carol Matzkin, "Who Needs Aisle or Altar?" Corpus Christie Caller Times, July 7, 1968, 6D; Helene Le Gaccia, "For They Have Their Own Thoughts," Delaware County [Pennsylvania] Times, Oct. 9, 1969, 16; "Marriage the New Natural Way," 43–46.

20. Anderson, Movement and the Sixties, 358; Matusow, Unraveling of America, 275–302; Arlene Skolnick, Embattled Paradise: The American Family in an Age of Uncertainty (New York: Basic Books, 1991), 77.

21. Alice Echols, "Hope and Hype in Sixties Haight-Ashbury," in Shaky Ground: The Sixties and Its Aftershocks, Alice Echols, ed. (New York: Columbia University Press, 2002), 30–31.

22. Anderson, Movement and the Sixties, 241–42; Wini Breines, The Great Refusal: Community and Organization in the New Left, 1962–1968 (New York: Praeger Books, 1982), 20; Echols, "Hope and Hype in Sixties Haight-Ashbury," 17–18; Del Earisman, How Now is the Now Generation (Philadelphia: Fortress Press, 1971), 13; Debra Michals, "From 'Consciousness Expansion' to 'Consciousness Rais-ing': Feminism and the Countercultural Politics of the Self," in Imagine Nation: The American Counterculture of the 1960s and 70s, Peter Braunstein and Michael William Doyle, eds. (New York: Routledge, 2002), 45; Timothy Miller, The Hippies and American Values (Knoxville: University of Tennessee Press, 1991), 10–15.

23. Clecak, America's Quest for the Ideal Self, 6–8.

24. Kirschenbaum and Stensrud, Wedding Book, 19, 16. On the need for new wedding styles, see Arisian, New Wedding, 3–4; Kirschenbaum and Stensrud, Wedding Book, 32–33; Seligson, Eternal Bliss Machine, 264–65, 278. On youth's purposeful rebellion, see Doug Rossinow, The Politics of Authenticity: Liberal-ism, Christianity, and the New Left in America (New York: Columbia University Press, 1998), 300–345.

25. On the idea that their parents of the postwar period raised their children to believe they belonged to a new generation, see Coontz, Marriage, A History, 248; Susan J. Douglas, Where the Girls Are: Growing Up Female with the Mass Media (New York: Times Books, 1994), 22, 25; Todd Gitlin, The Sixties: Years of

Hope, Days of Rage (1987; New York: Bantam Books, 1993), 19–20; Roszak, *Making of the Counterculture*, 31; Skolnick, *Embattled Paradise*, 83.

26. Kirschenbaum and Stensrud, *Wedding Book*, 39.

27. Ibid., 19, 23–24; Arthur Dobrin and Kenneth Briggs, *Getting Married the Way You Want* (Englewood Cliffs, NJ: Prentice-Hall, 1974), 5–6, 18.

28. Kirschenbaum and Stensrud, *Wedding Book*, 65.

29. Robert E. Burger, *The Love Contract: Handbook for a Liberated Marriage* (New York: Van Nostrand, 1973), 42, 45–47.

30. Kirschenbaum and Stensrud, *Wedding Book*, 27.

31. Ibid., 27.

32. Gretchen Lemke-Santangelo, *Daughters of Aquarius: Women of the Sixties Counterculture* (Lawrence: University of Kansas Press, 2009), 124.

33. Khoren Arisian, *The New Wedding: Creating Your Own Marriage Ceremony* (New York: Knopf, 1973), 58; Bellah et al., *Habits of the Heart*, 89; Dobrin and Briggs, *Getting Married the Way You Want*, 29–31, 35; Kirschenbaum and Stensrud, *Wedding Book*, 34, 66, 76–77, 89–90, 115–22; Reich, *Greening of America*, 250–51; Seligson, *Eternal Bliss Machine*, 268–69.

34. Timothy Miller, *The 60s Communes: Hippies and Beyond* (Syracuse: Syracuse University Press, 1999), xviii, 67, 202–3.

35. "The Farm," Folder: The Farm—Notes, papers, letters, (Center for Communal Studies); *The Farm Report, Jan–June 1972*, The Farm, ibid.; Oral History with Ina Mae Gaskin, The Farm, 9, ibid.; Michael Traugot, *A Short History of the Farm* (Summertown, TN, 1994), 25, ibid.

36. Burger, *Love Contract*, 48–49, 50.

37. Kirschenbaum and Stensrud, *Wedding Book*, 167.

38. Ibid., 172.

39. Richard J. Israel, "A Note on Counseling Young People Contemplating Inter-Marriage," p. 49, nd, Folder 11, Intermarriage 1970s, Box 15, Series D, Mss Collection 772, Richard J. Israel Papers (American Jewish Archives).

40. Richard Israel, "When Conversion is Not an Option: Helping Couples Write Their Own Marriage Ceremonies," p. 20, *Bamakom* 1, No. 1, Bnai Brith Hillel Foundations, Winter 1973, ibid.

41. Kazickas, "'As Long as We Both Shall Love,'" 141.

42. Arisian, *New Wedding*, 52; Kirschenbaum and Stensrud, *Wedding Book*, 56, 19–20, 126.

43. Linda Merion, "Married at Twin Oaks?" *Leaves of Twin Oaks*, 10, Issue 35, Aug. 1975, Twin Oaks Collection (Center for Communal Studies).

44. Ibid., 11.

45. Ibid.

46. On the desire for personal fulfillment, see Clecak, *America's Quest for the Ideal Self*, 7–8; Arisian, *New Wedding*, 12.

47. Email correspondence from Rockwell Stensrud to Karen Dunak, Jan. 24, 2007, in Dunak's possession.

48. On youth of the 1960s and 1970s as a "generation," see Anderson, *Movement and the Sixties*, 247–59; Delbert L. Earisman, *Hippies in Our Midst: The Rebellion beyond Rebellion* (Minneapolis: Fortress Press, 1968), xi, xiv, 20, 99; Miller, *Hippies and American Values*, 9–10; Reich, *Greening of America*, 4–5; Weiner and Stillman, *Woodstock Census*, 4, 50.

49. Jellison, *It's Our Day*, 41–42. See also Hackstaff, *Marriage in a Culture of Divorce*, 132–33; Earisman, *Hippies in Our Midst*, 39; Rossinow, *Politics of Authenticity*, 300–301, 316–17; Wolf, ed., *Voices from the Love Generation*, 91, 220, 231, and 241.

50. Roszak, *Making of a Counterculture*, 56–57, xxvi.

51. Salisbury and Salisbury, "Youth and the Search for Intimacy," 171.

52. Anderson, *Movement and the Sixties*, 258; Cmiel, "The Politics of Civility," 269–72; Farber, *Age of Great Dreams*, 168–69, 188–89; Reich, *Greening of America*, 4–5, 219–34; Seligson, *Eternal Bliss Machine*, 266; Wolf, ed., *Voices from the Love Generation*, 220.

53. Kirschenbaum and Stensrud, *Wedding Book*, 26.

54. Seligson, *Eternal Bliss Machine*, 264.

55. Price, *Huerfano*, 23.

56. Dobrin and Briggs, *Getting Married the Way You Want*, 30; Kirschenbaum and Stensrud, *Wedding Book*, 68–70; Reich, *Greening of America*, 234–39, 239; Seligson, *Eternal Bliss Machine*, 127. On later reinterpretation of the white gown, see Susanne Friese, "The Wedding Dress: From Use Value to Sacred Object," in *Through the Wardrobe: Women's Relationship with Their Clothes*, Ali Guy, Eileen Green, and Maura Banim Berg, eds. (New York: Oxford University Press, 2001). On emphasis on naturalness in clothing and beauty standards, see Banner, *American Beauty*, 289–90; Kathy Peiss, *Hope in a Jar: The Making of America's Beauty Culture* (New York: Metropolitan Books, 1998), 260–62.

57. David Allyn, *Make Love, Not War: The Sexual Revolution, An Unfettered History* (Boston: Little, Brown, 2000), 100–102; Anderson, *Movement and the Sixties*, 260–61; Patricia Coffin, "The Young Unmarrieds," *Look*, Jan. 26, 1971, 62–65; Farber, *Age of Great Dreams*, 183; Wolf, ed., *Voices from the Love Generation*, 35–36, 91–92, 220, 243–44.

58. Kazickas, "As Long As We Both Shall Love," 141. See also Dobrin and Briggs, *Getting Married the Way You Want*, 19–22; Kirschenbaum and Stensrud, *Wedding Book*, 4.

59. Andrew J. Cherlin, *Marriage, Divorce, Remarriage* (1981; Cambridge, MA: Harvard University Press, 1992), 14–15; Skolnick, *Embattled Paradise*, 90–91.

60. Wolf, *Voices from the Love Generation*, 243.

61. For some parents, the idea of cohabitation before marriage remained an immoral choice. See Morrison and Morrison, *From Camelot to Kent State*, 176. See the 1972 letters exchanged between a young woman, "Pat," and her parents in *Women's Letters: America from the Revolutionary War to the Present*, Lisa Grunwald and Stephen J. Adler, eds. (New York: Dial Press, 2005), 659–62; Beth Bailey's description

of response to Barnard student Linda LeClair's decision to live off campus with her boyfriend. See Bailey, *Sex in the Heartland*, 200–215.

62. While initially available only to married women, many young, unmarried females found doctors willing to prescribe the pill to their single patients. Allyn, *Make Love, Not War*, 33–34, 38–40; Bailey, *Sex in the Heartland*, 9–10, 105–07; Coontz, *Marriage, a History*, 254–55; James Reed, *From Private Vice to Public Virtue: The Birth Control Movement and American Society since 1830* (New York: Basic Books, 1978), 364–65; Ruth Rosen, *The World Split Open: How the Modern Women's Movement Changed America* (New York: Penguin, 2000), 55; Skolnick, *Embattled Paradise*, 88–89; Weiner and Stillman, *Woodstock Census*, 173–75. See also Kirschenbaum and Stensrud, *Wedding Book*, 22–23.

63. Arisian, *New Wedding*, 9–11.

64. Anderson, *Movement and the Sixties*, 312, 314–15, 341–43; Marcia Cohen, *The Sisterhood: The True Story of the Women Who Changed the World* (New York: Simon & Schuster, 1988), 153–57, 163–64; Morgan, *60s Experience*, 225–26; Rosen, *World Split Open*, 84–88; Rossinow, *Politics of Authenticity*, 333; Gayle Graham Yates, *What Women Want: The Ideas of the Movement* (Cambridge: Harvard University Press, 1975), 3–10, 13–20.

65. Kazickas, "As Long As We Both Shall Love," 141.

66. Arisian, *New Wedding*, 3–6, 9–12; Kirschenbaum and Stensrud, *Wedding Book*, 20–23.

67. Kirschenbaum and Stensrud, *Wedding Book*, 26.

68. On the adoption of the personal as political by women's liberationists, see Rosen, *World Split Open*, 102, 113–14, 196–97. On debates between feminists, see Echols, *Daring to Be Bad*, 3–6, 176–78; Evans, *Born for Liberty*, 290, 292–95; Rosen, *World Split Open*, 227–35.

69. Myers, "Burning Bras, Long Hairs, and Dashikis," 285. See also Noreen Connell, "Women and Consumerism," folder 2, Noreen Connell—Consumerism, box 9, Tamiment Collection 106, National Organization for Women—New York City (Tamiment Library).

70. Kirschenbaum and Stensrud, *Wedding Book*, 27.

71. Ibid., 28–29.

72. Ibid., 251.

73. Arisian, *New Wedding*; Carol Newman, *Your Wedding, Your Way: A Guide to Contemporary Wedding Options* (Garden City, NY: Doubleday, 1975).

74. Kirschenbaum and Stensrud, *Wedding Book*, 29.

75. Coontz, *Marriage, a History*, 252; Hackstaff, *Marriage in a Culture of Divorce*, 1, 9, 135–37.

76. Anderson, *Movement and the Sixties*, 336–37; Farber, *Age of Great Dreams*, 255–56; Jellison, *It's Our Day*, 90; Rosen, *World Split Open*, 196–201, 204–5.

77. Robin Morgan, *Going Too Far: The Personal Chronicles of a Feminist* (New York: Random House, 1977), 21–25.

78. Robin Morgan, "Introduction: The Women's Revolution," in *Sisterhood is Powerful: An Anthology of Writings from the Women's Liberation Movement*, ed. Robin Morgan (New York: Random House, 1970), xiv, xv–xviii; Robin Morgan, "Barbarous Rituals," in *Going Too Far*, 107.

79. Morgan, "Barbarous Rituals," in *Going Too Far*, 111.

80. Dorothy Le Sueur, "Individuality for 1970 Brides," *Washington Post*, March 1, 1970, 194, in folder 7, 1970 Newspaper Clippings, box 7, series 7, Articles and Clippings, 1956–1990, Priscilla of Boston Collection (Smithsonian Archives Center). On attention given to the most outrageous weddings, see Hank Burchard, "Motorcycle Wedding," *Washington Post*, Aug. 16, 1971, B1; "I Take Thee, Baby," *Time*, July 4, 1969, http://www.time.com/time/magazine/article/0,9171,840192,00.html; Judith Martin, "The Mod Wedding Scene," *Washington Post*, March 1, 1970, 198; 34–36; "New brides ring out the old traditions," *Business Week*, June 19, 1971, 114. On the rejection of tradition, see Sharen M. Abbott, "Gowns That Reflect You," *Worcester Sunday Telegram*, April 23, 1973, 2A; Dorothy Le Sueur, "Individuality for 1970 Brides," *Washington Post*, March 1, 1970, 194; Judith Martin, "The Mod Wedding Scene," *Washington Post*, March 1, 1970, 198; Bernadine Morris, "Here Comes the Bride—in an Organdy Tent," *New York Times*, Jan. 6, 1967, 52. On "doing your own thing," see Arisian, *New Wedding*, 18; Marian Christy, "Bridal fashions: It's chic to 'do your own thing,'" *Boston Sunday Herald Traveler*, Feb. 15, 1970, 2 in folder 6, 1969 Newspaper Clippings, box 7, series 7: Articles and Clippings, 1956–1990, Priscilla of Boston Collection, ibid.; Dobrin and Briggs, *Getting Married the Way You Want*; Earisman, *Hippies in Our Midst*, 65; Kazickas, "As Long As We Both Shall Love," 141; Miller, *Hippies and American Values*, 5.

81. Cott, *Public Vows*, 1–23; Jellison, *It's Our Day*, 20–21.

CHAPTER 4

1. Anna Quindlen, "*Ms.* Goes to a Wedding," *Ms.*, Dec. 1978, 74–75.

2. Ibid., 73.

3. Ibid.

4. Ibid.

5. Glassie, "Tradition," 408.

6. Quindlen, "*Ms.* Goes to a Wedding," 73. On the expected appearance of feminists during the 1970s, see Rosen, *World Split Open*, 163–64, 230.

7. Kristin Celello, *Making Marriage Work: A History of Marriage and Divorce in the Twentieth-Century United States* (Chapel Hill: University of North Carolina Press, 2009), 105–6, 113–17.

8. Hanson, *For Richer, For Poorer* 14–15; Howard, *Brides, Inc.*, 24–26.

9. Segal and Alston, "Marriage the New Natural Way," 44. On media's propensity to highlight political or cultural activities left of center during the 1960s, see Anderson, *Movement and the Sixties*, 171–74, 218, 241, 361; Bailey, *Sex in the Heartland*, 1–7, 136–38; Farber, *Age of Great Dreams*, 168; Morgan, *60s Experience*, 182–83. On media treatment of hippie weddings, in particular, see Weiner

and Stillman, *Woodstock Census*, 21. "New brides ring out the old traditions,"
114 and "I Take Thee, Baby," *Time*, July 4, 1969, http://www.time.com/time/
magazine/article/0,9171,840192,00.html.

10. For examples of white wedding announcements during the 1970s, see "Chehalis
Couple Marry in Double Ring Ceremony," *Daily Chronicle* [Centralia, Washing-
ton], Sept. 16, 1972, 4; "Harris, Pyles Nuptials Observed," *Middlesboro (Ken-
tucky) Daily News*, July 2, 1974, 2; "Miss Barnert Marries Larry Payne," *Chilli-
cothe (Missouri) Constitution–Tribune*, Jan. 11, 1973, 3; "Miss Lyles, Mr. Melton
Married at St. John's," *Florence (South Carolina) Daily News*, Dec. 30, 1973, 2B;
"Popelar-Daley," *Herald Times Reporter (Manitowic, Wisconsin)*, March 3, 1977,
5; "Wedding Belles," *Times Record (Troy, New York)*, April 1, 1975, 10.

11. Seligson, *Eternal Bliss Machine*, 265–66, 268.

12. On the adoption of countercultural values by those outside the realm of official
counterculture membership, see Binkely, *Getting Loose*, 3–4, 8; Reich, *Greening
of America*, 250–51; Schulman, *Seventies*, 14–17. Stephanie Coontz chronicles the
transformation in the nature of American marriages and identified in the 1970s,
as a shift from survival to self-expression. See Coontz, *Marriage, A History*, 258.
See also Arisian, *New Wedding*; Kirschenbaum and Stensrud, *Wedding Book*.

13. Seligson, *Eternal Bliss Machine*, 2–3.

14. Ibid., 2.

15. Katherine Jellison highlights the wedding's ability to serve as a contrast to the
growing informality of American life. Additionally, she argues that the ceremony provided previously marginalized groups an opportunity to align with the
mainstream, or co-opt elements of mainstream celebration to fit their personal
desires. See Jellison, *It's Our Day*, 45–48, 92–93.

16. Gerri Hirshey, "Popping the Question," *Sunday News Magazine, New York*,
April 16, 1978 in folder 6, box 1, Helen Gurley Brown Papers (Sophia Smith Col-
lection); Helen B. Shaffer, "Marriage: Changing Institution," 765–66, Editorial
Research Reports, No. 13, Vol. II, October 6, 1971, folder 6, box 2, "Families"
Collection, ibid. On no-fault divorce laws, see Celello, *Making Marriage Work*,
119–21; Coontz, *Marriage, A History*, 252; Cott, *Public Vows*, 205; Hendrik Hartog, *Man and Wife in America: A History* (Cambridge, MA: Harvard University
Press, 2000), 3; Jellison, *It's Our Day*, 30–31. On changing views of single life, see
Cherlin, *Marriage, Divorce, Remarriage*, 8–9, 11–12; Clecak, *America's Quest for
the Ideal Self*, 21–22; Coffin, "The Young Unmarrieds," 62–66; Coontz, *Marriage*,
258.

17. U.S. Bureau of the Census, "Table MS-2. Estimated Median Age at First Marriage, by Sex: 1890 to Present," from *Annual Social and Economic Supplement:
2003, Current Population Survey, Current Population Reports*, Series P20-553,
"America's Families and Living Arrangements: 2003" and earlier reports, Sept.
15, 2004, http://www.census.gov/population/socdemo/hh-fam/tabMS-2.pdf.
Seligson reported the following statistic: In 1971, there were 2,196,000 marriages in America, 648,000 more than in 1961. Seligson, *Eternal Bliss Machine*,

2. "Notes from Meeting with E. E. on February 17, 1969," folder 2, box 3, Series 1: Client Files, Estelle Ellis Collection, 1941–1994 (Smithsonian Archives Center).

18. "The *Bride's* Magazine Proposed Advertising and Sales Promotion Program," 1–12, The *Bride's* Magazine Advertising Proposal, March 17, 1969, folder 2, box 3, Series 1: Client Files, Estelle Ellis Collection, 1941–1994, ibid.

19. See Susan B. Carter, ed., *Historical Statistics of the United States: Millennial Edition* (New York: Cambridge University Press, 2006), Table Ae507-513—Marriage and divorce rates: 1920–1995, accessed online, http://bert.lib.indiana. edu:3067/HSUSWeb/table/footnotes.do?id=Ae507-513&footnote=footnote#fn_1. "Notes from Meeting with E. E. on February 17, 1969," folder 2, box 3, Series 1: Client Files, Estelle Ellis Collection, 1941–1994 (Smithsonian Archives Center). Description, Estelle Ellis Collection, 1944-1994, #423, http://americanhistory. si.edu/archives/d7423.htm. This evidence contradicts Chrys Ingraham's assertion that "the magazine nearly disappeared" during the late 1960s and 1970s. See Ingraham, *White Weddings*, 93.

20. "The *Bride's* Magazine Proposed Advertising and Sales Promotion Program," 7, The *Bride's* Magazine Advertising Proposal, March 17, 1969, folder 2 "*Bride's* Magazine Advertising Proposal, 1969," box 3, Series 1: Client Files, Estelle Ellis Collection, 1941–1994 (Smithsonian Archives Center); *Ten Months in a Lifetime*, folder 1 Folder "*Bride's*: Trade literature," box 3, Series 1: Client Files, Estelle Ellis Collection, 1941–1994, ibid.

21. "The *Bride's* Magazine Proposed Advertising and Sales Promotion Program," 3, The *Bride's* Magazine Advertising Proposal, March 17, 1969, folder 2, box 3, Series 1: Client Files, Ellis Collection, 1941–1994, ibid.; "The More Brides, The More *Bride's*," folder 8, "*Bride's* Magazine Trade Ads," box 27, Series 1: Client Files, Estelle Ellis Collection, 1941–1994, ibid.

22. On the propensity to focus on the more radical segments of 1960s and 1970s society, see Jason S. Lantzer, "The Other Side of Campus: Indiana University's Student Right and the Rise of National Conservatism," *Indiana Magazine of History* 101 (June 2005): 153–78.

23. On the Silent Majority, see Anderson, *Movement and the Sixties*, 331; Jefferson Cowie, "Nixon's Class Struggle: Romancing the New Right Worker, 1969–1973," *Labor History* 43 (Aug. 2002): 257–83; Jonathan M. Schoenwald, *A Time for Choosing: The Rise of Modern American Conservatism* (New York: Oxford University Press, 2002); Schulman, *The Seventies*, 37–40.

24. Anna Coffin, "Father and the Bride," *Look*, June 15, 1971; Segal and Alston, "Marriage the New Natural Way," 44.

25. Coffin, "Father and the Bride," 77

26. Ibid., 79, 78. For more on the president's projected role in the wedding, see Jellison, *It's Our Day*, 127

27. "The *Bride's* Magazine Proposed Advertising and Sales Promotion Program," The *Bride's* Magazine Advertising Proposal, March 17, 1969, folder 2, box 3, Series 1: Client Files, Ellis Collection, 1941–1994 (Smithsonian Archives Center);

"Behind the Main Event: Backstage at the White House Preparing for Tricia Nixon's Wedding," *Life*, June 18, 1971, 41–46.

28. A look at any newspaper in the 1970s-era United States yields a plethora of such announcements. See "Candlelight Service Unites Valerie Taylor, Gerald Baker," *Van-Wert (Ohio) Times Bulletin*, Jan. 20, 1971, 9; "Couples Repeat Wedding Vows in Saturday Ceremonies," *Lincoln (Nebraska) Evening Journal*, July 15, 1973, 82; "Miss Claire C. Biron Weds Joseph A. Reinisch," *Lewiston (Maine) Evening Journal*, Aug. 21, 1972, 11; "Miss Wooten Weds Dr. David R. Bird," *The (Burlington, North Carolina) Daily Times-News*, June 18, 1974, 11; "Spencer-Carter Vows Said in Church Rite," *Arcadia (California) Tribune*, Sept. 30, 1973, 6; "Walker Wedding Will Be Today," *Syracuse Herald-American*, May 15, 1977, 35.

29. "The Trousseau," folder 8, "*Bride's* Magazine Trade Ads," box 27, Series 1: Client Files, Estelle Ellis Collection, 1941–1994 (Smithsonian Archives Center).

30. Ibid. Coffin, "Father and the Bride," 76–77. As noted by Beth Bailey, by the late 1960s, it was very possible to look a part of the counterculture without actually taking part in the counterculture. See Bailey, *Sex in the Heartland*, 141.

31. "The Registry," folder 8, "*Bride's* Magazine Trade Ads," box 27, Series 1: Client Files, Estelle Ellis Collection, 1941–1994 (Smithsonian Archives Center).

32. Clecak, *America's Quest for the Ideal Self*, 6–7, 13, 17.

33. Rebecca E. Klatch, *A Generation Divided: The New Left, the New Right, and the 1960s* (Berkeley: University of California Press, 1999), 95; Winfield W. Salisbury and Frances F. Salisbury "Youth and the Search for Intimacy," in *The New Sexual Revolution*, Lester A. Kirkendall and Robert N. Whitehurst, eds. (Buffalo: Prometheus Books, 1971), 170.

34. Helen Thomas, "History Influenced Tricia's Plans," *News Journal [Mansfield, Ohio]*, June 9, 1971, 16.

35. Jellison, *It's Our Day*, 129.

36. Coffin, "Father and the Bride," 76.

37. "New brides ring out the old traditions," 114. Katherine Jellison also points to Tricia as a deviation from the industry's ideal bride. Tricia was slightly older than most brides (age 25) and chose a more sophisticated dress rather than the frilly, girlish "fairy princess" gown popular in years past. See Jellison, *It's Our Day*, 127.

38. Seligson, *Eternal Bliss Machine*, 176.

39. Litwicki, *America's Public Holidays*, 241, 244.

40. Diane K. Shah, "Young Lovers Still Look to Marriage, Family, and Home," *National Observer*, Jan. 26, 1970, np, in folder 3, box 2, "Families" Collection (Sophia Smith Collection).

41. Relying on tradition might help individuals to make sense of changing social or political conditions. Tradition also might provide a more comfortable alternative to creating a new form of celebration. See Swidler, "Culture in Action," 273–86, 273, 279. On the possibility for and normalcy of experimentation during

the 1970s, see Beth Bailey and David Farber, "Introduction," in *America in the Seventies*, Beth Bailey and David Farber, eds. (Lawrence: University Press of Kansas: 2004), 4–7.

42. Joe McCarthy, "Priscilla, Queen of the Wedding Business," *This Week Magazine*, June 1, 1969, 6, in folder 6, 1969 Newspaper Clippings, box 7, Series 7: Articles and Clippings, 1956–1990, Priscilla of Boston Collection (Smithsonian Archives Center); Bernadine Morris, "Bringing the Bride Up to Date," *New York Times*, April 14, 1970, 56; Beverly Maurice, "Boston's Priscilla Speaks Out," *Houston Chronicle, Texas Magazine*, 1970, in folder 7, 1970 newspaper clippings, box 7, Series 7, Articles and Clippings, 1956–1990, Priscilla of Boston Collection (Smithsonian Archives Center).

43. "Priscilla," advertisement, folder 13, Tear Sheets 1970, box 8, Series 6: Tear Sheets, 1950–1994, Priscilla of Boston Collection, ibid.

44. "Priscilla advertisement," *Boston Globe Annual Book for Brides*, Sunday Herald Advertiser, March 4, 1973, B24, folder 10, Newspaper Clippings, 1973, box 7, Series 7, Articles and Clippings, 1956–1990, Priscilla of Boston, Collection, ibid.

45. "Dutch Love Story," folder 15, Tear Sheets, 1973–1974, box 8, Series 6: Tear Sheets, 1950–1994, Priscilla of Boston Collection, ibid.; "Beautiful Brides in Lovely Villages," folder 14, Tear Sheets 1971, box 8, Series 6: Tear Sheets, 1950–1994, Priscilla of Boston Collection, ibid.; "Your Very Own Thing," folder 14, Tear Sheets 1971, box 8, Series 6: Tear Sheets, 1950–1994, Priscilla of Boston Collection, ibid.; Joe McCarthy, "Priscilla, Queen of the Wedding Business," *This Week Magazine*, June 1, 1969, 6–7, in folder 6: 1969 Wedding Clippings, box 7, Series 7, Articles and Clippings, 1956–1990 Priscilla of Boston Collection, ibid.

46. Virginia Bohlin, "The Bride," *Boston Sunday Herald Traveler*, Feb. 15, 1970, 2.

47. "Wedding Dress is Fashion Conscious," *The Progress (Pennsylvania)*, April 26, 1974, 2.

48. Thomas Frank, *The Conquest of Cool: Business Culture, Counterculture, and the Rise of Hip Consumerism* (Chicago: University of Chicago Press, 1997), 104–223; Matusow, *Unraveling of America*, 306–7; Myers, "Burning Bras, Long Hairs, and Dashikis," 294–96; Salisbury and Salisbury, "Youth and the Search for Intimacy," 171.

49. Elizabeth Brenner, "Wedding costs soaring, too, but couples aren't scrimping," *Chicago Tribune*, June 24, 1980, C1.

50. Jennifer Seder, "Marriage Proposals," *Los Angeles Times*, Jan. 19, 1979, G1.

51. Hanson, *For Richer, For Poorer*, 105.

52. On the power of the "Middle American," see "Man and Woman of the Year: The Middle American," *Time*, Jan. 5, 1970, http://www.time.com/time/magazine/article/0,9171,943113,00.html; "Backstage at a White House Wedding: Behind the Main Event," *Life*, June 18, 1971, 45.

53. Kammen, *Mystic Chords of Memory*, 4–5, 10, 620; Newman, *Your Wedding, Your Way*, 16.

54. "Priscilla Kidder . . . the Wedding Queen," *Boston Sunday Globe*, Feb. 26, 1967, in folder 4, 1967 Newspaper Clippings, box 7, Series 7, Articles and Clippings, 1956–1990, Priscilla of Boston Collection (Smithsonian Archives Center).

55. Shah, "Young Lovers Still Look to Marriage, Family, and Home," np.

56. "The Bride's World Remains Traditional," *The Odessa American*, April 25, 1973, 20. For a similar perspective, see "Modern Brides Ready for Marital Challenge," *The Progress [Pennsylvania]*, April 26, 1974, 2.

57. John R. Gillis reported that the *New York Times* declared a "return to tradition" as late as 1988. See Gillis, *World of their Own Making*, 150.

58. Newman, *Your Wedding, Your Way*, 16.

59. *US Magazine*, June 12, 1979, in folder 14, Newspaper Clippings 1979, box 7, Series 7, Articles and Clippings, 1956–1990, Priscilla of Boston Collection (Smithsonian Archives Center).

60. *The Middlesex News*, Aug. 26, 1979, folder 14, Newspaper Clippings 1979, box 7, Series 7, Articles and Clippings, 1956–1990, Priscilla of Boston Collection, ibid.

61. *The Patriot Ledger*, Oct. 14, 1978, folder 13, Newspaper Clippings 1978, box 7, Series 7, Articles and Clippings, 1956–1990, Priscilla of Boston, Collection, ibid.

62. Jennifer Seder, "Marriage Proposals," *Los Angeles Times*, Jan. 19, 1979, G1, G6.

63. Daniel Marcus, *Happy Days and Wonder Years: The Fifties and Sixties in Contemporary Cultural Politics* (New Brunswick: Rutgers University Press, 2004), 2–3.

64. Carol Troy, "Here Comes the Bride!" *New York Times*, June 3, 1979, SM23.

65. Seder, "Marriage Proposals," G1.

66. Douglas, *Where the Girls Are*, 245–47.

67. Jellison, *It's Our Day*, 131–33; Otnes and Pleck, *Cinderella Dreams* 50.

68. George W. Knight, *Wedding Ceremony Idea Book: How to Plan a Unique and Memorable Wedding Ceremony* (Brentwood, TN: J.M. Productions, 1984), 5.

69. Bellah et al., *Habits of the Heart*, 93, 89–99.

70. *Modern Bride* editors with Stephanie H. Dahl, *Modern Bride: Guide to Your Wedding and Marriage* (New York: Ballantine Books, 1984), xiv.

71. Ibid., xiv.

72. Ellen Freudenheim, *The Executive Bride: A Ten-Week Wedding Planner* (New York: Bantam Books, 1985), 4.

73. Ibid.

74. Kirschenbaum and Stensrud, *Wedding Book*, 22–24; Seligson, *Eternal Bliss Machine*, 264–68.

75. "Marriage the New Natural Way," 46.

76. David M. Potter, "American Individualism in the Twentieth Century," in *History and American Society: Essays of David M. Potter*, Don E. Fehrenbacher, ed. (New York: Oxford University Press, 1973), 257–59, 275–76.

77. Skolnick, *Embattled Paradise*, 97.

78. Email correspondence from Rockewell Stensrud to Karen Dunak, Jan. 23, 2007, in Dunak's possession.

79. Litwicki, *American Public Holidays*, 244.

CHAPTER 5

1. Michael C. Botkin, "A Gay Affair; The Wedding Comes Off, Amid Criticism, But to the Delight of Thousands," *Gay Community News*, Oct. 18–Oct. 24, 1987, 16; Carl M. Cannon, "Homosexuals Stage Mass 'Wedding' Hundreds of Gays Exchange Vows, Protest Tax Laws," *Miami Herald*, October 11, 1987, 6A; "Homosexuals Stage Mass 'Wedding' Ceremony on Mall," *Fredericksburg News Post*, Oct. 12, 2987, C7; George Chauncey, *Why Marriage? The History Shaping Today's Debate over Gay Equality* (New York: Basic Books, 2004), 119.

2. Botkin, "A Gay Affair," 16; "Gays Stage Mass Wedding," *Galveston Daily News*, Oct. 11, 1987, C6.

3. Carl M. Cannon, "Homosexuals Stage Mass 'Wedding' Hundreds of Gays Exchange Vows, Protest Tax Laws," *Miami Herald*, October 11, 1987, 6A; "Homosexuals Stage Mass 'Wedding' Ceremony on Mall," *Fredericksburg News Post*, Oct. 12, 1987, C7. On Reverend Troy Perry and the Metropolitan Community Church, see Chauncey, *Why Marriage?* 91; John Howard, "Protest and Protestantism: Early Lesbian and Gay Institution Building in Mississippi," in *Modern American Queer History*, Allida M. Black, ed. (Philadelphia: Temple University Press, 2001), 206–8; Melissa M. Wilcox, "Of Markets and Missions: The Early History of the Universal Fellowship of Metropolitan Community Churches," *Religion and American Culture* 11 (Winter 2001): 83–108.

4. Sue Hyde, "1987 and 2007: United Then, United Now," Oct. 11, 2007, http://www.thetaskforce.org/blog/20071011-sue-hyde-united-then-united-now.

5. Cannon, "Homosexuals Stage Mass 'Wedding' Hundreds of Gays Exchange Vows, Protest Tax Laws," 6A.

6. Botkin, "A Gay Affair," 16.

7. On the implicitly political nature of same-sex weddings, see Douglas C. Haldeman, "Ceremonies and Religion in Same-Sex Marriage," in *On the Road to Same-Sex Marriage: A Supportive Guide to Psychological, Political, and Legal Issues*, Robert Cabaj and David W. Purcell, eds. (San Francisco: Jossey-Bass Publishers, 1998), 145.

8. Mary Bernstein and Renate Reimann, "Queer Families and the Politics of Visibility," in *Queer Families, Queer Politics: Challenging Culture and the State*, Mary Bernstein and Renate Reimann, eds. (New York: Columbia University Press, 2001), 8; Ingraham, *White Weddings*, 166.

9. On African American postwar efforts to personalize the wedding, see Dunak, "Ceremony and Citizenship," 402–24.

10. Allan Berube, *Coming Out under Fire: The History of Gay Men and Women in World War Two* (New York: Free Press, 1990), 5–7, 34–44, 98–106, 228–79; George Chauncey, *Gay New York: Gender, Urban Culture, and the Making of the Gay Male World, 1890–1940* (New York: Basic Books, 1994), 33–45, 65–76; D'Emilio and Freedman, *Intimate Matters*, 121–30; David Eisenbach, *Gay Power: An American Revolution* (New York: Carroll & Graf Publishers, 2006), 2–5;

Lillian Faderman, *Odd Girls and Twilight Lovers: A History of Lesbian Life in Twentieth-Century America* (New York: Columbia University Press, 1991); Thomas A. Foster, ed., *Long Before Stonewall: Histories of Same-Sex Sexuality in Early America* (New York: New York University Press, 2007); Nancy Garden, *Hear Us Out! Lesbian and Gay Stories of Struggle, Progress, and Hope, 1950 to the Present* (New York: Farrar Straus Giroux, 2007); E. Anthony Rotundo, *American Manhood: Transformations in Masculinity from the Revolution to the Modern Era* (New York: Basic Books, 1993), 75–91; Andrea Weiss and Greta Schiller, *Before Stonewall: The Making of a Gay and Lesbian Community* (Tallahassee, FL: Naiad Press, 1988), 12–17.

11. Berube, *Coming Out under Fire*, 5–7, 34–44, 98–106, 228–79; Margot Canaday, *The Straight State: Sexuality and Citizenship in Twentieth-Century America* (Princeton: Princeton University Press, 2009); K. A. Cuordileone, "'Politics in an Age of Anxiety': Cold War Political Culture and the Crisis in American Masculinity," *Journal of American History* 87 (Sept. 2000): 515–45; D'Emilio and Freedman, *Intimate Matters*, 288–95; John D'Emilio, *Sexual Politics, Sexual Communities: The Making of a Homosexual Minority in the United States* (Chicago: University of Chicago Press, 1983), 23–33, 40–53; Eisenbach, *Gay Power*, 2–5; David K. Johnson, *The Lavender Scare: The Cold War Persecution of Gays and Lesbians in the Federal Government* (Chicago: University of Chicago Press, 2004); Mintz and Kellogg, *Domestic Revolutions*, 180–81; Weiss and Schiller, *Before Stonewall*, 30–39, 43–47.

12. D'Emilio, *Sexual Politics, Sexual Communities*, 40–45.

13. Ibid., 24, 37–38.

14. Chauncey, *Why Marriage?* 24–29; Martin Meeker, *Contacts Desired: Gay and Lesbian Communications and Community, 1940s–1970s* (Chicago: University of Chicago Press, 2006), 8–9.

15. Eric Marcus, *Together Forever: Gay and Lesbian Marriage* (New York: Anchor Books, 1998), xii. This view continued well beyond the 1950s and 1960s. See Mary Mendola, *The Mendola Report: A New Look at Gay Couples* (New York: Crown Publishers, 1980), 42.

16. Even the earliest gay political magazine noted the presence of gay "married" couples within the homosexual community. Michael Warner, *The Trouble with Normal: Sex, Politics, and the Ethics of Queer Life* (New York: Free Press, 1999), 87–89; Chauncey, *Why Marriage?* 87–88.

17. Hermann Stoessel, "The Decline and Fall of Marriage, *ONE*, VII (April 1959): 6–7, *ONE* Collection (Kinsey Institute Library).

18. Jim Egan, "Homosexual Marriage: Fact or Fancy?" *ONE*, VII (Dec. 1959): 6–7, *ONE* Collection, ibid.

19. Randy Lloyd, "Let's Push Homophile Marriage," *ONE*, XI (June 1963): 5, 7–8, 8, *ONE* Collection, ibid.

20. Ibid., 10.

21. Chauncey, *Why Marriage?* 88.

22. Robert Cabaj, "History of Gay Acceptance and Relationships," in *On the Road to Same-Sex Marriage: A Supportive Guide to Psychological, Political, and Legal Issues*, Robert Cabaj and David W. Purcell, eds. (San Francisco: Jossey-Bass Publishers, 1998), 11–12; D'Emilio, *Sexual Politics, Sexual Communities*, 33–37, 52–125, 185–86; Eisenbach, *Gay Power*,19–25; Garden, *Hear Us Out!* 48–49; Weiss and Schiller, *Before Stonewall*, 48–49, 53.

23. Brett Beemyn, "The Silence is Broken: A History of the First Lesbian, Gay, and Bisexual College Student Groups," *Journal of the History of Sexuality* 12 (April 2003): 217–20; Michael Bronski, "Over the Rainbow: Gay-Movement Organizes Obsessed with Fighting for Same-Sex Marriage Seem to Have Forgotten Their Roots in a Quest for a More Liberated World, One They Shared with Feminists Who Viewed Marriage as Hopelessly Patriarchal," in *I Do, I Don't: Queers on Marriage*, Greg Wharton and Ian Philips, eds. (San Francisco: Suspect Thought Press, 2004), 48–49; D'Emilio and Freedman, *Intimate Matters*, 318–19; John D'Emilio, "Placing Gay in the Sixties," in John D'Emilio, *The World Turned: Essays on Gay History, Politics, and Culture* (Durham: Duke University Press, 2002), 30; D'Emilio, *Sexual Politics, Sexual Communities*, 144–75, 223–33; Weiss and Schiller, *Before Stonewall*, 61–67.

24. D'Emilio, *Sexual Politics, Sexual Communities*, 138–44; Eisenbach, *Gay Power*, 19, 34–35, 59–64, 80–81; Weiss and Schiller, *Before Stonewall*, 56–60. For an example of such a story, see "The Homosexual: Newly Visible, Newly Understood," *Time*, Oct. 31, 1969.

25. Jack Starr, "The Homosexual Couple," *Look*, Jan. 26, 1971, 69.

26. Ibid., 70; Pascoe, *What Comes Naturally*, 299, n42, 387; Warner, *Trouble with Normal*, 87.

27. Starr, "The Homosexual Couple," 71. D'Emilio, *Sexual Politics, Sexual Communities*, 192–95; Haldeman, "Ceremonies and Religion in Same-Sex Marriage," 149–51; John Howard, "Protest and Protestantism: Early Lesbian and Gay Institution Building in Mississippi," in *Modern American Queer History*, Allida M. Black, ed. (Philadelphia: Temple University Press, 2001), 198–223; Garden, *Hear Us Out!* 50–52; Wilcox, "Of Markets and Missions," 83–108.

28. Chauncey, *Why Marriage?* 93–94. I use quotation marks around marriage and married to differentiate from formal, licensed, heterosexual unions. In no way do I aim to minimize these relationships.

29. Mendola, *The Mendola Report*, 5–9. Oral history collections also speak to the existence of long-term same-sex coupling, both in the years before and after Stonewall. See Marcy Adelman, ed., *Long Time Passing: Lives of Older Lesbians* (Boston: Alyson Publications, 1986); Marcus, *Together Forever*; Keith Vacha, *Quiet Fire: Memoirs of Older Gay Men*, ed. Cassie Damewood (Trumansburg, NY: Crossing Press, 1985).

30. Mendola, *The Mendola Report*, 36–37, 43.

31. Chauncey, *Why Marriage?* 94.

32. Ibid., 88–111; Eisenbach, *Gay Power*, ix; Mark D. Jordan, *Blessing Same-Sex Unions: The Perils of Queer Romance and the Confusion of Christian Marriage* (Chicago: University of Chicago Press, 2005), 52; Gil Kudrin, "Love: An AIDS Odyssey," in *I Do, I Don't: Queers on Marriage*, Greg Wharton and Ian Philips, eds (San Francisco: Suspect Thought Press, 2004), 195–97; Mintz and Kellogg, *Domestic Revolutions*, 235; Warner, *Trouble with Normal*, 84.

33. Haldeman, "Ceremonies and Religion in Same-Sex Marriage," 143. On the 1993 march, see Barbara J. Cox, "Same-Sex Marriage and Choice-of-Law: If We Marry in Hawaii, Are We Still Married When We Return Home?" *Wisconsin Law Review* 1033 (1994): 1035–36.

34. Letter to the Editor, E. Donald Wright, "Millenium March was a Terrific Day," *Syracuse Herald Journal*, May 18, 2000, 12.

35. Christopher Bram, "Delicate Monsters: Talking with Myself about Gay Marriage," in *I Do, I Don't: Queers on Marriage*, Greg Wharton and Ian Philips, eds. (San Francisco: Suspect Thought Press, 2004), 41.

36. Tess Ayers and Paul Brown, *The Essential Guide to Lesbian and Gay Weddings* (New York: HarperSanFrancisco, 1994), 6.

37. Ibid., 109, 31.

38. Ibid., xiii.

39. Ibid., xiv.

40. Tess Ayers and Paul Brown, *The Essential Guide to Lesbian and Gay Weddings* (1994; New York: Alyson Books, 1999); Sheri Venema, "Gay Wedding Announcements a Growing Trend," Jan. 5, 2003, http://www.womensenews.org/article.cfm/dyn/aid/1170/context/archive; "Same-Sex Wedding Announcement Forces Change at Kansas City Star," June 3, 2009, WDAF-TV, http://www.fox4kc.com/wdaf-story-marriage-announcement-060309,0,5807537.story. For an early example of media support, see Chris Nealon, "Washington Paper Celebrates Les/Gay Unions" *Gay Community News*, Dec. 22, 1990, 6. On increased visibility of same-sex relationships, see Bernstein and Reimann, "Queer Families and the Politics of Visibility," 1–5; David W. Purcell, "Current Trends in Same-Sex Marriage," in *On the Road to Same-Sex Marriage: A Supportive Guide to Psychological, Political, and Legal Issues*, Robert Cabaj and David W. Purcell, eds. (San Francisco: Jossey-Bass Publishers, 1998), 29–31; Suzanna Danuta Walters, *All the Rage: The Story of Gay Visibility in America* (Chicago: University of Chicago Press, 2001).

41. William C. Symonds and Jessi Hempel, "The Gay Marriage Dividend," *Business Week*, May 24, 2004, 50.

42. David Walker, "Gay Weddings: Growing Opportunity?" *Photo District News*, April 2, 2009, http://www.pdnonline.com/pdn/content_display/features/featured-in-print/e3ie2b23ab2b6e7cd3470e26c7f9e1f7109; Ayers and Brown, *Essential Guide to Lesbian and Gay Weddings* (1994), 5.

43. Ibid., 16; Kari Huus, "For Same-Sex Pairs, Festivities Begin," MSNBC.com, March 12, 2004, http://money.cnn.com/2005/05/20/pf/weddings/; Jonathan

Finer, "At Expo, Few Disagreements on Gay Marriage: Wedding Planners Foresee Expanded Market in Mass," *Washington Post*, May 3, 2004, A03; Julie Flaherty, "Freedom to Marry, and to Spend on It," *New York Times*, May 16, 2004, 2; Ingraham, *White Weddings*, 165; Jellison, *It's Our Day*, 104–05; Diane Marder, "Gay, Lesbian Wedding Market Embraced," *Philadelphia Inquirer*, April 3, 2002, http://articles.philly.com/2002-04-03/news/25339460_1_les-bian-couples-gay-community-domestic-partner-benefits; Mead, *One Perfect Day*, 228; Sasha Talcott, "Gay Couples Rewriting Wedding Etiquette," *Boston Globe*, March 21, 2004, B6. On marketplace attention to the queer consumer, see Dan Baker, "A History in Ads: The Growth of the Gay and Lesbian Market," in *Homo Economics: Capitalism, Community, and Lesbian and Gay Life*, Amy Gluckman and Betsy Reed, eds. (New York: Routledge, 1997), 19; Grant Lukenbill, *Untold Millions: Secret Truths About Marketing to Gay and Lesbian Consumers* (New York: Harrington Park Press, 1999), 23–4; 169–71; 175–76; Lisa Penaloza, "We're Here, We're Queer, and We're Going Shopping! A Critical Perspective on the Accommodation of Gays and Lesbians in the U.S. Marketplace," in *Gays, Lesbians, and Consumer Behavior: Theory, Practice, and Research Issues in Marketing*, ed. Daniel Wardlow (New York: Harrington Park Press, 1996), 25–26.

44. Maggie Daniels and Carrie Loveless, *Wedding Planning and Management: Consultancy for Diverse Clients* (Boston: Butterworth-Heinemann, 2007), 65.

45. Walker, "Gay Weddings: Growing Opportunity?"; "Gay Weddings Could Boost California Economy by $370 Million," *Advocate*, June 3, 2008.

46. Grace Wong, "Ka-ching! Wedding price tag nears $30K," CNN Money.com, May 20, 2005, http://money.cnn.com/2005/05/20/pf/weddings/; Mead, *One Perfect Day*, 23–27.

47. Daniels and Loveless, *Wedding Planning and Management*, 65.

48. Ayers and Brown, *Essential Guide to Lesbian and Gay Weddings* (1994), xiv, 109; Lex T., "Visions of Happily Ever After," Jan. 7, 2003, Human Rights Campaign, Marriage & Relationship Recognition, "Your Stories," http://www.hrc.org/issues/3773.htm.

49. Haldeman, "Ceremonies and Religion in Same-Sex Marriage," 145, 162.

50. Chauncey, *Why Marriage?* 129. For more on the importance of the term "marriage," see Daniel R. Pinello, *America's Struggle for Same-Sex Marriage* (New York: Cambridge University Press, 2006), 8.

51. Bella English, "Fully Engaged," *Boston Globe*, Feb. 4, 2004; Meg Stone, "Choosing Family," in *I Do, I Don't: Queers on Marriage*, Greg Wharton and Ian Philips, eds. (San Francisco: Suspect Thought Press, 2004), 324.

52. Jordan, *Blessing Same-Sex Unions*, 87.

53. "Gay Weddings," Episodes 6 and 8, Discs 1 and 2. Bravo TV, 2002. DVD. NBC/Ventura, 2004.

54. "Gay Weddings," Interview Scott and Harley, Disc 2. Bravo TV, 2002. DVD. NBC/Ventura, 2004.

55. "How Can I Involve Family in My Commitment Ceremony," Nov. 5, 2001, http://www.hrc.org/issues/4623.htm.

56. "Gay Weddings," Episodes 1, Disc 1 and Episode 6, Disc 2. Bravo TV, 2002. DVD. NBC/Ventura, 2004.

57. Ayers and Brown, *Essential Guide to Lesbian and Gay Weddings*, 64.

58. Cox, "A (Personal) Essay on Same-Sex Marriage," *National Journal of Sexual Orientation Law* 1.1 (1995): 87–89.

59. Kath Weston, *Families We Choose: Lesbians, Gays, Kinship* (New York: Columbia University Press, 1991), 103–36.

60. Stone, "Choosing Family," 324.

61. Lewin, "Weddings without Marriages," 48.

62. Haldeman, "Ceremonies and Religion in Same-Sex Marriage," 157.

63. Anne Campbell, "A Queer Wedding Indeed," in *I Do, I Don't: Queers on Marriage*, Greg Wharton and Ian Philips, eds. (San Francisco: Suspect Thought Press, 2004), 72.

64. Warner, *Trouble with Normal*, 100. See also Lewin, "Weddings without Marriages," 46.

65. Haldeman, "Ceremonies and Religion in Same-Sex Marriage," 154, 162.

66. Warner, *Trouble with Normal*, 115–16.

67. "Gay Weddings," Bravo TV, 2003, Episode 2, Disc 1.

68. Haldeman, "Ceremonies and Religion in Same-Sex Marriage," 162.

69. Douglas Carl, "Counseling Same-Sex Couples," in *Same-Sex Marriage: The Moral and Legal Debate*, Robert M. Baird and Stuart E. Rosenbaum, eds. (Amherst, NY: Prometheus Books, 1997), 45–46; Lewin, "Weddings without Marriages," 51.

70. Haldeman, "Ceremonies and Religion in Same-Sex Marriage," 157.

71. Amie M. Evans, "Happily Ever After," in *I Do, I Don't: Queers on Marriage*, Greg Wharton and Ian Philips, eds. (San Francisco: Suspect Thought Press, 2004), 128–30.

72. Ibid., 130.

73. Bernstein and Reimann, "Queer Families and the Politics of Visibility," 3; Lewin, "Weddings without Marriages," 45.

74. "Speaking Out; On Lesbian and Gay Weddings and the Urge to Smash Blenders," *Gay Community News*, Sept. 20–Sept. 26, 1987, 5.

75. S. Bear Bergman "Forget Marriage, Have a Wedding," in *I Do, I Don't: Queers on Marriage*, Greg Wharton and Ian Philips, eds. (San Francisco: Suspect Thought Press, 2004), 29, 30.

76. Chauncey, *Why Marriage?* 143.

77. "Betty" in *Word is Out: Stories of Some of Our Lives* (San Francisco: New Glide Publications, 1978), 213. Cabaj, "History of Gay Acceptance and Relationships," 20; Chauncey, *Why Marriage?* 32–33; D'Emilio, *Sexual Politics, Sexual Communities*, 176–77, 195, 235; and D'Emilio and Freedman, *Intimate Matters*, 320–23.

78. Ayers and Brown, *Essential Guide to Lesbian and Gay Weddings*, 29, 32, 34.

79. Warner, *Trouble with Normal*, 132.

80. Haldeman, "Ceremonies and Religion in Same-Sex Marriage," 159.

81. David McConnell, Untitled Essay, in *I Do, I Don't: Queers on Marriage*, Greg Wharton and Ian Philips, eds. (San Francisco: Suspect Thought Press, 2004), 219.

82. Cox, "A (Personal) Essay on Same-Sex Marriage," 89; Lewin, "Weddings without Marriages," 47, 51.

83. Ayers and Brown, *Essential Guide to Lesbian and Gay Weddings*, 122.

84. Cox, "A (Personal) Essay on Same-Sex Marriage," 28.

85. Warner, *Trouble with Normal*, 132–33.

86. Lewin, "Weddings Without Marriages," 47.

87. Leslea Newman, "The Butch That I Marry," in *I Do, I Don't: Queers on Marriage*, Greg Wharton and Ian Philips, eds. (San Francisco: Suspect Thought Press, 2004), 248.

88. Jordan, *Blessing Same-Sex Unions*, 143.

89. Haldeman, "Ceremonies and Religion in Same-Sex Marriage," 145–55; Jordan, *Blessing Same-Sex Unions*, 153.

90. Haldeman, "Ceremonies and Religion in Same-Sex Marriage," 159.

91. Lewin, "Weddings Without Marriages," 48.

92. Edwin Brent Jones and Edward Lee Reynolds, "Wedding Plans #1," March 4, 2005, Guy Dads blog, http://guydads.blogspot.com/2005/03/wedding-plans-1. html; Jones and Reynolds, "Weddings Update #2, April 14, 2005, Guy Dads blog, http://guydads.blogspot.com/2005/04/wedding-update-2.html; Jones and Reynolds, "The wedding schedule with program notes," June 24, 2005, Guy Dads blog, http://guydads.blogspot.com/search?q=the+wedding+schedule+w ith+program+notes; Jones and Reynolds, "Menu for the Wedding Reception," June 16, 2005, Guy Dads blog, http://guydads.blogspot.com/2005/06/menu-for-wedding-reception.html; Jones and Reynolds, "Third Meeting with the Rabbi," May 2, 2005, Guy Dads blog, http://guydads.blogspot.com/2005_05_01_archive. html.

93. Jones and Reynolds, "Shalom!" June 21, 2005, Guy Dads Blog, http://guydads. blogspot.com/2005/06/shalom.html.

94. Jones and Reynolds, "Catching up on the news," Guy Dads blog, Aug. 29, 2005, http://guydads.blogspot.com/2005_08_01_archive.html; Jones and Reynolds, "Gay mail," Guy Dads blog, Sept. 28, 2005, http://guydads.blogspot. com/2005_09_01_archive.html.

95. Jones and Reynolds, "Our legal gay wedding," Guy Dads blog, Oct. 20, 2008, http://guydads.blogspot.com/2008/10/our-legal-gay-wedding.html.

96. Joe Garofoli, "Same-sex marriage poll finds majority approve," *San Francisco Chronicle*, Feb. 29, 2012, http://www.sfgate.com/cgi-bin/article.cgi?f=/ c/a/2012/02/29/MNGN1NDIRP.DTL.

97. Anna Quindlen, "The Same People," *Newsweek*, June 9, 2008, http://www.the-dailybeast.com/newsweek/2008/05/31/the-same-people.html.

CONCLUSION

1. Cindy Clark, "Kate Middleton's Wedding Dress is a 'Triumph,'" *USA Today*, April 29, 2011, http://www.usatoday.com/life/people/2011-04-29-kates-dress_N.htm; Wendy Koch, "Royal Wedding Ceremony Follows Tradition," *USA Today*, April 29, 2011, http://www.usatoday.com/life/people/2011-04-29-royal-wedding-program_N.htm; James Poniewozik, "Will and Kate Colonize American TV, for a Morning," *Time*, April 29, 2011, http://entertainment.time.com/2011/04/29/will-and-kate-colonize-american-tv-for-a-morning/.

2. Marjorie Connelly, "Royal Wedding is Drawing a Yawn From Many Americans," *New York Times*, April 22, 2011, http://www.nytimes.com/2011/04/23/world/europe/23royals.html; Poniewozik, "Will and Kate Colonize American TV, for a Morning"; Kathryn Shattuck, "Get Your Royal Wedding Fix on TV," *New York Times*, April 28, 2011, http://artsbeat.blogs.nytimes.com/2011/04/28/get-your-royal-wedding-fix-on-tv/.

3. "A Party of Royal Proportions," April 14, 2011, http://disneyweddingsblog.com/walt-disney-world-resort/a-party-of-royal-proportions/.

4. Craig Wilson, "Americans Gear Up for Royal Wedding Spectacle," *USA Today*, April 27, 2011, http://www.usatoday.com/life/people/2011-04-27-royal-wedding-Americans-watch_n.htm.

5. Ibid.

6. Conan, "Paul Bettany Interview, 05/02/11," *Conan* video, 7:07. May 2, 2011. http://teamcoco.com/video/10803/fans.

7. http://whyamericansshouldcareabouttheroyalwedding.com/.

8. Shattuck, "Get Your Royal Wedding Fix on TV."

9. Connelly, "Royal Wedding is Drawing a Yawn From Many Americans."

10. Rebecca Adams, "Royal Wedding vs. Kim Kardashian's Wedding: By the Numbers," *Huffington Post*, April 28, 2012, http://www.huffingtonpost.com/2012/04/27/royal-wedding-vs-kardashian_n_1459827.html; Allison Corneau, "More Than 20 Million Viewers Watch Kim Kardashian's TV Wedding," *US Weekly*, Oct. 11, 2011, http://www.usmagazine.com/entertainment/news/more-than-10-million-viewers-watch-kim-kardashians-tv-wedding-20111110; "Criticisms About Kim Kardashian's Wedding Surface," *Hollywood Reporter*, Aug. 20, 2011, http://www.hollywoodreporter.com/news/kim-kardashian-criticisms-wedding-surface-225637; Rebecca Ford and Lauren Schutte, "Kim Kardashian's Divorce: 10 Signs the Marriage was One Big Hoax All Along," Oct. 31, 2011, *Hollywood Reporter*, http://www.hollywoodreporter.com/news/kim-kardashian-divorce-kris-humphries-media-publicity-255371.

11. Susan J. Douglas, *The Rise of Enlightened Sexism: How Pop Culture Took Us from Girl Power to Girls Gone Wild* (New York: St. Martin's Press, 2010), 19, 189–95.

12. Deb Riechmann, "Jenna Bush's Wedding is Low-Key Affair at Ranch," *USA Today*, May 12, 2008, http://www.usatoday.com/life/people/2008-05-10-bush-wedding_N.htm.

13. "Jenna Bush's Wedding Album," *People*, May 12, 2008, http://www.people.com/people/gallery/0,,20199244,00.html#20454736.

14. Riechmann, "Jenna Bush's Wedding is Low-Key Affair at Ranch."

15. Frank Newport, "Bush Job Approval at 28%, Lowest of His Administration," GALLUP, April 11, 2008, www.gallup.com/poll/106426/bush-job-approval-28-lowest-administration.aspx; Riechmann, "Jenna Bush's Wedding is Low-Key Affair at Ranch."

16. Stephen M. Silverman, "President on Jenna Bush's Wedding: A Mother-Daughter Event," *People*, Feb. 20, 2008, http://www.people.com/people/article/0,,20178975,00.html.

17. Julia Reed, "Jenna Bush: Texas I Do's," *Vogue*, May 2008, http://www.vogue.com/magazine/article/jenna-bush-texas-i-dos/.

18. Ingraham, *White Weddings*, 20; The Knot: http://wedding.theknot.com/wedding-planning.aspx.

19. Jane Zhang, "I Do . . . for Less," *Wall Street Journal*, June 8, 2009, http://online.wsj.com/article/SB10001424052970203353904574145520680497830.html.

20. Lauren Drell, "Pinterest: Behind the Design of an Addictive Visual Network," *Mashable*, Dec. 16, 2011, http://mashable.com/2011/12/16/pinterest-design/; Douglas MacMillan, "Why Image-Sharing Network Pinterest is Hot," *Bloomberg Businessweek*, Nov. 17, 2011, http://www.businessweek.com/magazine/why-imagesharing-network-pinterest-is-hot-11172011.html.

21. John and Sherry Petersik, younghouselove.com, "The Blog Begins," Sept. 24, 2007, http://www.younghouselove.com/2007/09/the-blog-begins/; younghouselove.com, "Our Wedding," http://www.younghouselove.com/wedding-album/.

22. Sara Cotner, 2000dollarwedding.com, "From Conception to Reception," July 21, 2008, http://2000dollarwedding.com/2008/07/from-conception-to-reception.html.

23. Meg Keene, *A Practical Wedding: Creative Ideas for Planning a Beautiful, Affordable, and Meaningful Celebration* (Boston: Da Capo Books, 2012), 65–68.

24. Ibid., 121–42.

25. Ibid., 152.

26. Lisa Selin Davis, "All but the Ring: Why Some Couples Don't Wed," *Time*, May 29, 2009, http://www.time.com/time/magazine/article/0,9171,1898346,00.html

27. Elizabeth Pleck, *Not Just Roommates: Cohabitation after the Sexual Revolution* (Chicago: University of Chicago Press, 2012), 229–32.

28. Davis, "All but the Ring"; Gellar, *Here Comes the Bride*, 8–9.

29. Belinda Luscombe, "Who Needs Marriage? A Changing Institution," *Time*, Nov. 18, 2010, www.time.com/time/magazine/article/0,9171,203116,00.html.

BIBLIOGRAPHY

ARCHIVAL COLLECTIONS

American Jewish Archives (Cincinnati, Ohio)

Center for Communal Studies, University of Southern Indiana (Evansville, Indiana)

Center for the Study of History and Memory, Indiana University (Bloomington, Indiana)

Falmouth Historical Society (Falmouth, Massachusetts)

Iowa Women's Archives, University of Iowa (Iowa City, Iowa)

Kinsey Institute for Research in Sex, Gender, and Reproduction, Indiana University (Bloomington, Indiana)

Lyndon Baines Johnson Presidential Library, University of Texas (Austin, Texas)

Smithsonian Institute, National Museum of American History Archives Center (Washington, DC)

Sophia Smith Collection, Smith College (Northampton, Massachusetts)

Tamiment Library, New York University (New York, New York)

University Archives, University of Missouri (Columbia, Missouri)

FILMS

The Best Years of Our Lives. Dir. William Wyler. DVD. 1946. MGM, 2000.

Bride Wars. Dir. Gary Winnick. DVD. 2009. Twentieth Century Fox, 2009.

Father of the Bride. Dir. Vicente Minnelli. 1950. DVD. Warner Home Video, 2003.

The Golden Chalice. Produced by U.S. Naval Photographic Center. 66 minutes. MP 464. LBJ Library, Austin, Texas. Transferred from Allied Video Master.

SOURCES

Adelman, Marcy, ed. *Long Time Passing: Lives of Older Lesbians*. Boston: Alyson Publications, Inc., 1986.

Allyn, David. *Make Love, Not War: The Sexual Revolution, an Unfettered History*. New York: Little, Brown, 2000.

Anderson, David L. *The Vietnam War*. New York: Palgrave, 2005.

Anderson, Terry. "The New American Revolution: The Movement and Business." In *The Sixties: From History to Memory*, ed. David Farber. Chapel Hill: University of North Carolina Press, 1994.

———. *The Movement and the Sixties*. New York: Oxford University Press, 1996.

Arisian, Khoren. *The New Wedding: Creating Your Own Marriage Ceremony*. New York: Knopf, 1973.

Arlitt, Ada Hart. "The Wedding and Honeymoon," in *Modern Marriage and Family Living*, ed. Morris Fishbein and Ruby Jo Reeves Kennedy, 177–86. New York: Oxford University Press, 1957.

Ayers, Tess, and Paul Brown. *The Essential Guide to Lesbian and Gay Weddings*. New York: HarperSanFrancisco, 1994.

———. *The Essential Guide to Lesbian and Gay Weddings*. 1994; New York: Alyson Books, 1999.

Bailey, Beth. *From Front Porch to Back Seat*. Baltimore: Johns Hopkins University Press, 1988.

———. *Sex in the Heartland*. Cambridge, MA: Harvard University Press, 1999.

Bailey, Beth and David Farber, eds. *America in the Seventies*. Lawrence: University Press of Kansas, 2004.

Bailey, Beth and David Farber. "Introduction." In *America in the Seventies*, ed. Beth Bailey and David Farber. Lawrence: University Press of Kansas, 2004.

Baird, Robert M. and Stuart E. Rosenbaum, eds. *Same-Sex Marriage: The Moral and Legal Debate*. Amherst, NY: Prometheus Books, 1997.

Baker, Dan. "A History in Ads: The Growth of the Gay and Lesbian Market." In *Homo Economics: Capitalism, Community, and Lesbian and Gay Life*, ed. Amy Gluckman and Betsy Reed, 11–20. New York: Routledge, 1997.

Baker, Margaret. *Wedding Customs and Folklore*. 1972; Vancouver: David & Charles, 1977.

Banner, Lois. *American Beauty*. New York: Knopf, 1983.

Beemyn, Brett. "The Silence is Broken: A History of the First Lesbian, Gay, and Bisexual College Student Groups." *Journal of the History of Sexuality* 12 (April 2003): 205–23.

Bellah, Robert N., Richard Madsen, William M. Sullivan, Ann Swidler, and Steven M. Tipton, eds. *Habits of the Heart: Individualism and Commitment in American Life*. Berkeley: University of California Press, 1985.

Benkov, Laura. *Reinventing the Family: The Emerging Story of Lesbian and Gay Parents*. New York: Crown Publishers, 1994.

Bentley, Marguerite (Mrs. Logan Bentley). *Wedding Etiquette Complete*. Philadelphia: The John C. Winston Company, 1947.

Bergman, S. Bear. "Forget Marriage, Have a Wedding." In *I Do, I Don't: Queers on Marriage*, ed. Greg Wharton and Ian Philips, 29–31. San Francisco: Suspect Thought Press, 2004.

Bernstein, Mary and Renate Reimann. "Queer Families and the Politics of Visibility." In *Queer Families, Queer Politics: Challenging Culture and the State*, ed. Mary Bernstein and Renate Reimann, 1–17. New York: Columbia University Press, 2001.

Bernstein, Mary and Renate Reimann, eds. *Queer Families, Queer Politics: Challenging Culture and the State*. New York: Columbia University Press, 2001.

Berube, Allan. *Coming Out under Fire: The History of Gay Men and Women in World War Two*. New York: Free Press, 1990.

Best, Amy L. *Prom Night: Youth, Schools, and Popular Culture*. New York: Routledge, 2000.

Binkley, Sam. *Getting Loose: Lifestyle Consumption in the 1970s*. Durham: Duke University Press, 2007.

Black, Allida M., ed. *Modern American Queer History*. Philadelphia: Temple University Press, 2001.

Blum, John Morton. *V Was for Victory: Politics and American Culture during World War II*. New York: Harcourt Brace, 1976.

———. *Years of Discord: American Politics and Society, 1961–1974*. New York: Norton, 1991.

Blumin, Philip and Pepper Schwartz. *American Couples: Money, Work, Sex*. New York: Morrow, 1983.

Bodnar, John. *The Transplanted: A History of Immigrants in Urban America*. Bloomington: Indiana University Press, 1985.

Boroff, David. *Campus U.S.A.: Portraits of American Colleges in Action*. New York: Harper & Brothers, 1958.

———. "Jewish Teenage Culture." *Annals of the American Academy of Political and Social Science* 338 (Nov. 1961): 79–90.

Bram, Christopher. "Delicate Monsters: Talking with Myself about Gay Marriage." In *I Do, I Don't: Queers on Marriage*, ed. Greg Wharton and Ian Philips, 41–43. San Francisco: Suspect Thought Press, 2004.

Breines, Wini. *The Great Refusal: Community and Organization in the New Left, 1962–1968*. New York: Praeger Books, 1982.

———. *Young, White, and Miserable: Growing Up Female in the Fifties*. Boston: Beacon Books, 1992.

Bremner, Robert H. and Gary W. Reichard, eds. *Reshaping America: Society and Institutions, 1945–1960*. Columbus: Ohio State University Press, 1982.

Brewer, Susan A. *Why America Fights: Patriotism and War Propaganda from the Philippines to Iraq*. New York: Oxford University Press, 2009.

Brinkley, Alan. "The Illusion of Unity in Cold War Culture." In *Rethinking Cold War Culture*, d. Peter J. Kuznick and James Gilbert, 61–73. Washington, DC: Smithsonian Institution Press, 2001.

Brody, Rosalie. *Weddings: What every bride should know about wedding etiquette and arrangements for the formal and informal wedding*. New York: Simon & Schuster, 1963.

Bronski, Michael. "Over the Rainbow: Gay-Movement Organizes Obsessed with Fighting for Same-Sex Marriage Seem to Have Forgotten Their Roots in a Quest for a More Liberated World, One They Shared with Feminists Who Viewed Marriage as Hopelessly Patriarchal." In *I Do, I Don't: Queers on Marriage*, ed. Greg Wharton and Ian Philips, 48–52. San Francisco: Suspect Thought Press, 2004.

Burger, Robert E. *The Love Contract: Handbook for a Liberated Marriage*. New York: Van Nostrand, 1973.

Burgess, Ernest W. and Paul Wallin. *Engagement and Marriage*. Chicago: J. B. Lippincott, 1953.

Bussel, Rachel Kramer. "Marriage: Thanks, but No Thanks." In *I Do, I Don't: Queers on Marriage*, ed. Greg Wharton and Ian Philips, 64–66. San Francisco: Suspect Thought Press, 2004.

Cabaj, Robert P. "History of Gay Acceptance and Relationships." In *On the Road to Same-Sex Marriage: A Supportive Guide to Psychological, Political, and Legal Issues*, ed. Robert P. Cabaj and David W. Purcell, 1–28. San Francisco: Jossey-Bass Publishers, 1998.

Cabaj, Robert P. and David W. Purcell, eds. *On the Road to Same-Sex Marriage: A Supportive Guide to Psychological, Political, and Legal Issues*. San Francisco: Jossey-Bass Publishers, 1998

Campbell, Anne. "A Queer Wedding Indeed." In *I Do, I Don't: Queers on Marriage*, ed. Greg Wharton and Ian Philips, 71–73. San Francisco: Suspect Thought Press, 2004.

Campbell, Patricia J. *Sex Education Books for Young Adults, 1892–1979*. New York: R. R. Bowker Company, 1979.

Canaday, Margot. *The Straight State: Sexuality and Citizenship in Twentieth-Century America*. Princeton: Princeton University Press, 2009.

Carpenter, Liz. *Ruffles and Flourishes: The warm and tender story of a simple girl who found adventure in the White House*. 1970; New York: Pocket Books, 1971.

Carter, Susan B., ed. *Historical Statistics of the United States: Millennial Edition*. New York: Cambridge University Press, 2006.

Caughey, John L. *Imaginary Social Worlds: A Cultural Approach*. Lincoln: University of Nebraska Press, 1984.

Cavallo, Dominick. *A Fiction of the Past: The Sixties in American History*. New York: St. Martin's Press, 1999.

Celello, Kristin. *Making Marriage Work: A History of Marriage and Divorce in the Twentieth-Century United States*. Chapel Hill: University of North Carolina Press, 2009.

Chauncey, George. *Gay New York: Gender, Urban Culture, and the Making of the Gay Male World, 1890–1940*. New York: Basic Books, 1994.

———. *Why Marriage? The History Shaping Today's Debate over Gay Equality*. New York: Basic Books, 2004.

Cherlin, Andrew J. *Marriage, Divorce, Remarriage*. 1981; Cambridge, MA: Harvard University Press, 1992.

Clark, Michael D. *The American Discovery of Tradition, 1865–1942*. Baton Rouge: Louisiana State University, 2005.

Clecak, Peter. *America's Quest for the Ideal Self: Dissent and Fulfillment in the 60s and 70s*. New York: Oxford University Press, 1983.

Cmiel, Kenneth. "The Politics of Civility." In *The Sixties: From History to Memory*, ed. David Farber, 263–90. Chapel Hill: University of North Carolina Press, 1994.

Cohen, Lizabeth. *A Consumers' Republic: The Politics of Consumption in Postwar America.* New York: Knopf, 2003.

Cohen, Marcia. *The Sisterhood: The True Story of the Women Who Changed the World.* New York: Simon & Schuster, 1988.

Cole, Emma Aubert. *The Modern Bride Book of Etiquette.* New York: Ziff-Davis, 1961.

Collins, Robert M. "Growth Liberalism in the Sixties: Great Societies at Home and Grand Designs Abroad." In *The Sixties: From History to Memory*, ed. David Farber, 11–45. Chapel Hill: University of North Carolina Press, 1994.

———. *More: The Politics of Economic Growth in Postwar America.* New York: Oxford University Press, 2000.

Coontz, Stephanie. *Marriage, a History: From Obedience to Intimacy or How Love Conquered Marriage.* New York: Viking, 2005.

———. *The Way We Never Were: American Families and the Nostalgia Trap.* New York: Basic Books, 1992.

———. *The Social Origins of Private Life: A History of American Families, 1600–1900.* New York: Verso, 1988.

Corral, Jill and Lisa Miya Jervis, eds. *Young Wives' Tales: New Adventures in Love and Partnership.* Seattle, WA: Seal Press, 2001.

Cott, Nancy. *Public Vows: A History of Marriage and the Nation.* Cambridge, MA: Harvard University Press, 2000.

Cowie, Jefferson. "Nixon's Class Struggle: Romancing the New Right Worker, 1969–1973." *Labor History* 43 (Aug. 2002): 257–83.

Cox, Barbara J. "A (Personal) Essay on Same-Sex Marriage." *National Journal of Sexual Orientation Law* 1.1 (1995): 87–89.

———. "Same-Sex Marriage and Choice-of-Law: If We Marry in Hawaii, Are We Still Married When We Return Home?" *Wisconsin Law Review* 1033 (1994): 1062–1118.

Crawford, John E. and Luther E. Woodward. *Better Ways of Growing Up: Psychology and Mental Health for Youth.* Philadelphia: Muhlenberg Press, 1948.

Cross, Gary. *An All-Consuming Century: Why Consumerism Won in Modern America.* New York: Columbia University Press, 2000.

———. *The Cute and the Cool: Wondrous Innocence and Modern American Children's Culture.* New York: Oxford University Press, 2004.

Cuordileone, K. A. "'Politics in an Age of Anxiety': Cold War Political Culture and the Crisis in American Masculinity." *Journal of American History* 87 (Sept. 2000): 515–45.

Curran, Colleen, ed. *Altared: Bridezillas, Bewilderment, Big Love, Breakups, and What Women Really Think about Contemporary Weddings.* New York: Vintage, 2007.

Daniels, Maggie and Carrie Loveless. *Wedding Planning and Management: Consultancy for Diverse Clients.* Boston: Butterworth-Heinemann, 2007.

Davis, Rebecca L. *More Perfect Unions: The American Search for Marital Bliss.* Cambridge, MA: Harvard University Press, 2010.

D'Emilio, John. *Sexual Politics, Sexual Communities: The Making of a Homosexual Minority in the United States.* Chicago: University of Chicago Press, 1983.

———. "Placing Gay in the Sixties." In *The World Turned: Essays on Gay History, Politics, and Culture*, ed. John D'Emilio, 23–44. Durham: Duke University Press, 2002.

D'Emilio, John, ed. *The World Turned: Essays on Gay History, Politics, and Culture.* Durham: Duke University Press, 2002.

D'Emilio, John and Estelle B. Freedman. *Intimate Matters: A History of Sexuality in America.* 1988; Chicago: University of Chicago Press, 1997.

DePaulo, Bella. *Singled Out: How Singles Are Stereotyped, Stigmatized, and Ignored, and Still Living Happily Ever After.* New York: St. Martin's Press, 2006.

Devlin, Rachel. *Relative Intimacy: Fathers, Adolescent Daughters, and Postwar American Culture.* Chapel Hill: University of North Carolina Press, 2005.

Diamond, Etan. *Souls of the City: Religion and the Search for Community in Postwar America.* Bloomington: Indiana University Press, 2003.

Dobrin, Arthur and Kenneth Briggs. *Getting Married the Way You Want.* Englewood Cliffs, NJ: Prentice-Hall, 1974.

Douglas Carl. "Counseling Same-Sex Couples." In *Same-Sex Marriage: The Moral and Legal Debate,* ed. Robert M. Baird and Stuart E. Rosenbaum, 44–54. Amherst, NY: Prometheus Books, 1997.

Douglas, Susan J. *Where the Girls Are: Growing Up Female with the Mass Media.* New York: Times Books, 1994.

———. *The Rise of Enlightened Sexism: How Pop Culture Took Us from Girl Power to Girls Gone Wild.* New York: St. Martin's Press, 2010.

Dunak, Karen M. "Ceremony and Citizenship: African American Weddings, 1945–60." *Gender & History* 21 (Aug. 2009): 402–24.

Duvall, Evelyn Mills. *The Art of Dating.* New York: Association Press, 1967.

Duvall, Evelyn. "Courtship and Engagement." In *Modern Marriage and Family Living,* eds. Morris Fishbein and Ruby Jo Reeves Kennedy, 144–57. New York: Oxford University Press, 1957.

Earisman, Del. *How Now Is the Now Generation?* Philadelphia: Fortress Press, 1971.

Earisman, Delbert L. *Hippies in Our Midst: The Rebellion beyond Rebellion.* Philadelphia: Fortress Press, 1968.

Echols, Alice. *Daring to Be Bad: Radical Feminism in America, 1967–1975.* Minneapolis: University of Minnesota Press, 1989.

———. "Nothing Distant about It: Women's Liberation and Sixties Radicalism." In *The Sixties: From History to Memory*, ed. David Farber, 149–74. Chapel Hill: University of North Carolina Press, 1994.

———. *Scars of Sweet Paradise: The Life and Times of Janis Joplin.* New York: Metropolitan Books, 1999.

———. "Hope and Hype in Sixties Haight-Ashbury." In *Shaky Ground: The Sixties and Its Aftershocks*, ed. Alice Echols, 17–50. New York: Columbia University Press, 2002.

Echols, Alice, ed. *Shaky Ground: The Sixties and Its Aftershocks.* New York: Columbia University Press, 2002.

Ehrenreich, Barbara. *The Hearts of Men: American Dreams and the Flight from Commitment*. New York: Anchor Books, 1983.

———. *Fear of Falling: The Inner Life of the Middle Class*. New York: Pantheon Books, 1989.

Eisenbach, David. *Gay Power: An American Revolution*. New York: Carroll & Graf, 2006.

Eisler, Benita. *Private Lives: Men and Women of the Fifties*. Danbury, CT: Franklin Watts, 1986.

Evans, Amie M. "Happily Ever After." In *I Do, I Don't: Queers on Marriage*, ed. Greg Wharton and Ian Philips, 128–31. San Francisco: Suspect Thought Press, 2004.

Evans, Sara. *Personal Politics: The Roots of Women's Liberation in the Civil Rights Movement and the New Left*. 1979; New York: Vintage Books, 1980.

———. *Born for Liberty: A History of Women in America*. 1989; New York: Free Press, 1997.

Farber, David. *The Age of Great Dreams: America in the 1960s*. New York: Hill and Wang, 1994.

Farber, David, ed. *The Sixties: From History to Memory*. Chapel Hill: University of North Carolina Press, 1994.

Fehrenbacher, Don E., ed. *History and American Society: Essays of David M. Potter*. New York: Oxford University Press, 1973.

Fishbein, Morris and Ruby Jo Reeves Kennedy, eds. *Modern Marriage and Family Living*. New York: Oxford University Press, 1957.

Force, Elizabeth S. *Your Family: Today and Tomorrow*. New York: Harcourt, Brace, 1955.

Foster, Frances Smith, ed. *Love and Marriage in Early African America*. Lebanon, NH: University Press of New England, 2008.

Foster, Thomas A., ed. *Long Before Stonewall: Histories of Same-Sex Sexuality in Early America*. New York: New York University Press, 2007.

Frank, Thomas. *The Conquest of Cool: Business Culture, Counterculture, and the Rise of Hip Consumerism*. Chicago: University of Chicago Press, 1997.

Fraser, Steve and Gary Gerstle, eds. *The Rise and Fall of the New Deal Order, 1930–1980*. Princeton: Princeton University Press, 1989.

Frese, Pamela R., ed. *Celebrations of Identity: Multiple Voices in American Ritual Performance*. Westport, CT: Bergin & Garvey, 1993.

Frese, Pamela Rae. "Holy Matrimony: A Symbolic Analysis of the American Wedding Ritual." Ph.D. diss., University of Virginia, 1982.

Freudenheim, Ellen. *The Executive Bride: A Ten-Week Wedding Planner*. New York: Bantam Books, 1985.

Friedman, Barbara G. *From the Battlefront to the Bridal Suite: Media Coverage of British War Brides, 1942–1946*. Columbia: University of Missouri Press, 2007.

Friese, Susanne. "The Wedding Dress: From Use Value to Sacred Object." In *Through the Wardrobe: Women's Relationship with Their Clothes*, ed. Ali Guy, Eileen Green, and Maura Banim Berg, 53–79. New York: Oxford University Press, 2001.

Fussell, Betty Harper. *My Kitchen Wars*. New York: North Point Press, 1999.

Garden, Nancy. *Hear Us Out! Lesbian and Gay Stories of Struggle, Progress, and Hope, 1950 to the Present*. New York: Farrar Straus Giroux, 2007.

Gellar, Jaclyn. *Here Comes the Bride: Women, Weddings, and the Marriage Mystique*. New York: Falls Walls Eight Windows, 2001.

van Gennep, Arnold. *The Rites of Passage*. Trans. Monika B. Vizedom and Gabrielle L. Caffee. Chicago: University of Chicago Press, 1960.

Gerstle, Gary. *American Crucible: Race and Nation in the Twentieth Century*. Princeton: Princeton University Press, 2001.

Gillis, John R. *A World of Their Own Making: Myth, Ritual, and the Quest for Family Values*. New York: Basic Books, 1996.

Gitlin, Todd. *The Sixties: Years of Hope, Days of Rage*. 1987; New York: Bantam Books, 1993.

Glassberg, David. *American Historical Pageantry: The Uses of Tradition in the Early Twentieth Century*. Chapel Hill: University of North Carolina Press, 1990.

Glassie, Henry. "Tradition." *Journal of American Folklore* 108 (Autumn 1995): 369–95.

Gluckman, Amy and Betsy Reed, eds. *Homo Economics: Capitalism, Community, and Lesbian and Gay Life*. New York: Routledge, 1997.

Graebner, William. *Coming of Age in Buffalo: Youth and Authority in Postwar America*. Philadelphia: Temple University Press, 1993.

Greer, Rebecca. *Book for Brides*. New York: Arco Publishing, 1965.

Grunwald, Lisa and Stephen J. Adler, eds. *Women's Letters: America from the Revolutionary War to the Present*. New York: Dial Press, 2005.

Hackstaff, Karla B. *Marriage in a Culture of Divorce*. Philadelphia: Temple University Press, 1999.

Haldeman, Douglas C. "Ceremonies and Religion in Same-Sex Marriage." In *On the Road to Same-Sex Marriage: A Supportive Guide to Psychological, Political, and Legal Issues*, ed. Robert P. Cabaj and David W. Purcell, 141–64. San Francisco: Jossey-Bass Publishers, 1998.

Hanson, Kitty. *For Richer, For Poorer*. New York: Abelard-Schuman, 1967.

Hartmann, Susan M. *The Home Front and Beyond: American Women in the 1940s*. Boston: Twayne, 1982.

Hartog, Hendrik. *Man and Wife in America: A History*. Cambridge, MA: Harvard University Press, 2000.

Harvey, Brett. *The Fifties: A Woman's Oral History*. New York: HarperPerennial, 1994.

Hegarty, Marilyn. *Victory Girls, Khaki Wackies, and Patriotutes: The Regulation of Female Sexuality during World War II*. New York: New York University Press, 2007.

Hobsbawn, Eric. "Introduction: Inventing Traditions." In *The Invention of Tradition*, ed. Eric Hobsbawm and Terence Ranger, 1–14. Cambridge: University of Cambridge Press, 1983.

Howard, John. "Protest and Protestantism: Early Lesbian and Gay Institution Building in Mississippi." In *Modern American Queer History*, ed. Allida M. Black, 198–223. Philadelphia: Temple University Press, 2001.

Howard, Vicki. *Brides, Inc.: American Weddings and the Business of Tradition*. Philadelphia: University of Pennsylvania Press, 2006.

Howard, Vicki Jo. "American Weddings: Gender, Consumption, and the Business of Brides." PhD diss., University of Texas, 2000.

Hurley, Andrew. *Diners, Bowling Alleys, and Trailer Parks: Chasing the American Dream in Postwar Consumer Culture*. New York: Basic Books, 2002.

Ingraham, Chrys. *White Weddings: Romancing Heterosexuality in Popular Culture*. New York: Routledge, 1999.

Jackson, Joyce. *Joyce Jackson's Guide to Dating*. 1955; Englewood Cliffs, NJ: Prentice Hall, 1957.

Jackson, Kenneth T. *Crabgrass Frontier: The Suburbanization of the United States*. New York: Oxford University Press, 1985.

Jacobs, Meg. *Pocketbook Politics: Economic Citizenship in Twentieth Century America*. Princeton: Princeton University Press, 2005.

Jellison, Katherine. "From the Farmhouse Parlor to the Pink Barn: The Commercialization of Weddings in the Rural Midwest." *Iowa Heritage Illustrated* 77 (Summer 1996): 50–65.

———. *It's Our Day: America's Love Affair with the White Wedding, 1945–2005*. Lawrence: University Press of Kansas, 2008.

Johnson, David K. *The Lavender Scare: The Cold War Persecution of Gays and Lesbians in the Federal Government*. Chicago: University of Chicago Press, 2004.

Johnson, Lady Bird [Claudia Alta Taylor Johnson]. *A White House Diary*. 1970; New York: Dell Publishing, 1971.

Johnson, Roswell H., Helen Randolph, and Erma Pixley. *Looking to Marriage*. 1943; New York: Allyn and Bacon, 1945.

Jordan, Mark D. *Blessing Same-Sex Unions: The Perils of Queer Romance and the Confusion of Christian Marriage*. Chicago: University of Chicago Press, 2005.

Kammen, Michael G. *The Mystic Chords of Memory: The Transformation of Tradition in American Culture*. New York: Knopf, 1991.

Keene, Meg. *A Practical Wedding: Creative Ideas for Planning a Beautiful, Affordable, and Meaningful Celebration*. Boston: Da Capo Books, 2012.

Kern, Stephen. *The Culture of Love: Victorians to Moderns*. Cambridge, MA: Harvard University Press, 1992.

Kidd, Virginia Venable. "Happily Ever After and Other Relationship Styles: Rhetorical Visions of Interpersonal Relations in Popular Magazines, 1951–1972." PhD diss., University of Minnesota, 1974.

Kirkendall, Lester A. "Too Young to Marry?" Public Affairs Pamphlet, no. 236, 1956. In *Teen Love, Teen Marriage*, ed. Jules Saltman, 74–104. New York: Grosset & Dunlap, 1966.

Kirkendall, Lester A. and Robert N. Whitehurst, eds. *The New Sexual Revolution*. New York: Donald W. Brown, 1971.

Kirschenbaum, Howard and Rockwell Stensrud. *The Wedding Book: Alternative Ways to Celebrate Marriage*. New York: Seabury Press, 1974.

Kitch, Carolyn. *Pages from the Past: History and Memory in American Magazines.* Chapel Hill: University of North Carolina Press, 2005.

Klatch, Rebecca E. *A Generation Divided: The New Left, the New Right, and the 1960s.* Berkeley: University of California Press, 1999.

Knight, George W. *Wedding Ceremony Idea Book: How to Plan a Unique and Memorable Wedding Ceremony.* Brentwood, TN: JM Productions, 1984.

Kudrin, Gil. "Love: An AIDS Odyssey." In *I Do, I Don't: Queers on Marriage,* ed. Greg Wharton and Ian Philips, 195–97. San Francisco: Suspect Thought Press, 2004.

Kutulas, Judy. "'That's the Way I've Always Heard It Should Be': Baby Boomers, 1970s Singer-Songwriters, and Romantic Relationships." *Journal of American History* 97 (Dec. 2010): 682–702.

Kuznick, Peter J. and James Gilbert, eds. *Rethinking Cold War Culture.* Washington, DC: Smithsonian Institution Press, 2001.

Lacey, Peter. *The Wedding.* New York: Grosset & Dunlap, 1969.

Lantzer, Jason S. "The Other Side of Campus: Indiana University's Student Right and the Rise of National Conservatism." *Indiana Magazine of History* 101 (June 2005): 153–78.

Leeds-Hurwitz, Wendy. *Wedding as Text: Communicating Cultural Identities through Ritual.* Mahwah, NJ: Lawrence Erlbaum Associates, 2002.

Leff, Mark H. "The Politics of Sacrifice on the American Homefront in World War II." *Journal of American History* 77 (March 1991): 397–418.

LeMasters, E. E. *Modern Courtship and Marriage.* New York: Macmillan, 1957.

Lemke-Santangelo, Gretchen. *Daughters of Aquarius: Women of the Sixties Counterculture.* Lawrence: University of Kansas Press, 2009.

Leuca, Mary. *Romanian Americans in Lake County, Indiana: An Ethnic Heritage Curriculum Project.* West Lafayette, IN: Purdue University, 1978.

Lewin, Ellen. "Weddings Without Marriages: Making Sense of Lesbian and Gay Commitment Rituals." In *Queer Families, Queer Politics: Challenging Culture and the State,* ed. Mary Bernstein and Renate Reimann, 44–51. New York: Columbia University Press, 2001.

Lipsett, Linda Otto. *To Love and to Cherish: Brides Remembered.* San Francisco: Quilt Digest Press, 1989.

Litoff, Judy Barrett and David C. Smith, eds. *Since You Went Away: World War II Letters from American Women on the Home Front.* Oxford University Press: New York, 1991.

Litoff, Judy Barrett, David C. Smith, Barbara Wooddall Taylor, and Charles E. Smith. *Miss You: The World War II Letters of Barbara Wooddall Taylor and Charles E. Taylor.* Athens: University of Georgia Press, 1990.

Litwicki, Ellen M. *America's Public Holidays, 1865–1920.* Washington, DC: Smithsonian Institution Press, 2000.

Lukenbill, Grant. *Untold Millions: Secret Truths about Marketing to Gay and Lesbian Consumers.* New York: Harrington Park Press, 1999.

Lystra, Karen. *Searching the Heart: Women, Men, and Romantic Love in Nineteenth-Century America.* New York: Oxford University Press, 1989.

Marcus, Daniel. *Happy Days and Wonder Years: The Fifties and Sixties in Contemporary Cultural Politics*. New Brunswick: Rutgers University Press, 2004.

Marcus, Eric. *Together Forever: Gay and Lesbian Marriage*. New York: Anchor Books, 1998.

Marling, Karal Ann. *As Seen on TV: The Visual Culture of Everyday Life in the 1950s*. Cambridge, MA: Harvard University Press, 1994.

Massoni, Kelley. "'Teena Goes to Market': *Seventeen* Magazine and the Early Construction of the Teen Girl (As) Consumer." *Journal of American Culture* 29 (March 2006): 31–42.

Matusow, Allen J. *The Unraveling of America: A History of Liberalism in the 1960s*. New York: Harper & Row, 1984.

May, Elaine Tyler. *Homeward Bound: American Families in the Cold War Era*. New York: Basic Books, 1988.

McClay, Wilfred M. *The Masterless: Self and Society in Modern America*. Chapel Hill: University of North Carolina Press, 1994.

McComb, Mary C. *Great Depression and the Middle Class: Experts, Collegiate Youth, and Business Ideology, 1929–1941*. New York: Routledge, 2006.

McConnell, David. Untitled essay in *I Do, I Don't: Queers on Marriage*, ed. Greg Wharton and Ian Philips, 219–20. San Francisco: Suspect Thought Press, 2004.

McGovern, Eleanor. *Uphill: A Personal Story*. Boston: Houghton Mifflin, 1974.

Mead, Rebecca. *One Perfect Day: The Selling of the American Wedding*. New York: Penguin Press, 2007.

Meeker, Martin. *Contacts Desired: Gay and Lesbian Communications and Community, 1940s–1970s*. Chicago: University of Chicago Press, 2006.

Mendola, Mary. *The Mendola Report: A New Look at Gay Couples*. New York: Crown Publishers, 1980.

Merrill, Francis E. *Courtship and Marriage: A Study in Social Relationships*. New York: William Sloane Associates, 1949.

Meyerowitz, Joanne, ed. *Not June Cleaver: Women and Gender in Postwar America, 1945–1960*. Philadelphia: Temple University Press, 1994.

Michals, Debra. "From 'Consciousness Expansion' to 'Consciousness Raising': Feminism and the Countercultural Politics of the Self." In *Imagine Nation: The American Counterculture of the 1960s and 70s*, ed. Peter Braunstein and Michael William Doyle, 41–68. New York: Routledge, 2002.

Miller, Timothy. *The Hippies and American Values*. Knoxville: University of Tennessee Press, 1991.

———. *The 60s Communes: Hippies and Beyond*. Syracuse: Syracuse University Press, 1999.

Mintz, Steven and Helen Kellogg. *Domestic Revolutions: A Social History of American Family*. New York: Free Press, 1988.

Modell, John. *Into One's Own: From Youth to Adulthood in the United States, 1920–1975*. Berkeley: University of California Press, 1989.

Modern Bride editors with Stephanie H. Dahl. *Modern Bride: Guide to Your Wedding and Marriage*. New York: Ballantine Books, 1984.

Monsarrat, Ann. *And the Bride Wore . . . The Story of the White Wedding*. New York: Dodd, Mead & Company, 1973.

Montemurro, Beth. *Something Old, Something Bold: Bridal Showers and Bachelorette Parties*. New Brunswick: Rutgers University Press, 2006.

Morgan, Edward P. *The 60s Experience: Hard Lessons about Modern America*. Philadelphia: Temple University Press, 1991.

Morgan, Robin. "Introduction: The Women's Revolution." In *Sisterhood is Powerful: An Anthology of Writings from the Women's Liberation Movement*, ed. Robin Morgan, xiii–xli. New York: Random House, 1970.

———. *Going Too Far: The Personal Chronicles of a Feminist*. New York: Random House, 1977.

Morgan, Robin, ed. *Sisterhood is Powerful: An Anthology of Writings from the Women's Liberation Movement*. New York: Random House, 1970.

Morrison, Joan and Robert K. Morrison. *From Camelot to Kent State: The Sixties Experience in the Words of Those Who Lived It*. 1987; New York: Oxford University Press, 2001.

Myers, Elizabeth A. "Burning Bras, Long Hairs, and Dashikis: Personal Politics in American Culture, 1950–1975." PhD diss., Loyola University Chicago, 2006.

Nardi, Peter, David Sanders, and Judd Marmor, eds. *Growing Up before Stonewall: Life Stories of Some Gay Men*. New York: Routledge, 1994.

Neisser, Edith G. *When Children Start Dating*. Chicago: Science Research Associates, 1951.

Newman, Carol. *Your Wedding, Your Way: A Guide to Contemporary Wedding Options*. Garden City, NY: Doubleday, 1975.

Newman, Leslea. "The Butch That I Marry." In *I Do, I Don't: Queers on Marriage*, ed. Greg Wharton and Ian Philips, 247–49. San Francisco: Suspect Thought Press, 2004.

Nickles, Shelley. "More is Better: Mass Consumption, Gender, and Class Identity in Postwar America." *American Quarterly* 54 (Dec. 2002): 581–622.

Nissenbaum, Stephen. *The Battle for Christmas: A Cultural History of America's Most Cherished Holiday*. New York: Vintage, 1997.

Norfleet, Barbara. *Wedding*. New York: Simon & Schuster, 1979.

Otnes, Cele C. and Elizabeth H. Pleck. *Cinderella Dreams: The Allure of the Lavish Wedding*. Berkeley: University of California Press, 2003.

Palladino, Grace. *Teenagers: An American History*. New York: Basic Books, 1996.

Pascoe, Peggy. *What Comes Naturally: Miscegenation Law and the Making of Race in America*. New York: Oxford University Press, 2009.

Paul, Pamela. *The Starter Marriage and the Future of Matrimony*. New York: Random House, 2003.

Penaloza, Lisa. "We're Here, We're Queer, and We're Going Shopping! A Critical Perspective on the Accommodation of Gays and Lesbians in the U.S. Marketplace."

In *Gays, Lesbians, and Consumer Behavior: Theory, Practice, and Research Issues in Marketing*, ed. Daniel Wardlow, 9–42. New York: Harrington Park Press, 1996.

Peiss, Kathy. *Hope in a Jar: The Making of America's Beauty Culture*. New York: Metropolitan Books, 1998.

Penner, Barbara. "'A Vision of Love and Luxury': The Commercialization of Nineteenth-Century American Weddings." *Winterthur Portfolio* 39 (Spring 2004): 1–20.

Pierce, Wellington G. *Youth Comes of Age*. New York: McGraw-Hill, 1948.

Pinello, Daniel R. *America's Struggle for Same-Sex Marriage*. New York: Cambridge University Press, 2006.

Plant, Rebecca Jo. *Mom: The Transformation of Motherhood in Modern America*. Chicago: University of Chicago Press, 2010.

Pleck, Elizabeth. *Celebrating the Family: Ethnicity, Consumer Culture, and Family Values*. Cambridge: Harvard University, 2000.

———. "The Making of the Domestic Occasion: The History of Thanksgiving in the United States." *Journal of Social History* 32 (Summer 1999): 773–89.

———. *Not Just Roommates: Cohabitation after the Sexual Revolution*. Chicago: University of Chicago Press, 2012.

Post, Emily. *Etiquette in Society, in Business, in Politics, and at Home*. New York: Funk & Wagnalls, 1922.

Potter, David. *People of Plenty: Economic Abundance and the American Character*. 1958; Chicago: University of Chicago Press, 1954.

Potter, David M. "American Individualism in the Twentieth Century." In *History and American Society: Essays of David M. Potter*, ed. Don E. Fehrenbacher, 256–76. New York: Oxford University Press, 1973.

Price, Roberta. *Huerfano: A Memoir of My Life in the Counterculture*. Amherst: University of Massachusetts Press, 2004.

Purcell, David W. "Current Trends in Same-Sex Marriage." In *On the Road to Same-Sex Marriage: A Supportive Guide to Psychological, Political, and Legal Issues*, ed. Robert P. Cabaj and David W. Purcell, 29–40. San Francisco: Jossey-Bass Publishers, 1998.

Rauch, Jonathan. *Gay Marriage: Why It Is Good for Gays, Good for Straights, and Good for America*. New York: Henry Holt, 2004.

Reed, James. *From Private Vice to Public Virtue: The Birth Control Movement and American Society since 1830*. New York: Basic Books, 1978.

Reich, Charles. *The Greening of America*. New York: Random House, 1970.

Riley, Glenda. *Divorce: An American Tradition*. New York: Oxford University Press, 1991.

Roberts, Nancy. "A Gift to Share." In *Long Time Passing: Lives of Older Lesbians*, ed. Marcy Adelman, 94–108. Boston: Alyson Publications, 1986.

Rosen, Ruth. *The World Split Open: How the Modern Women's Movement Changed America*. New York: Penguin, 2000.

Rossinow, Doug. *The Politics of Authenticity: Liberalism, Christianity, and the New Left in America*. New York: Columbia University Press, 1998.

————. 'The Revolution Is about Our Lives': The New Left's Counterculture." In *Imagine Nation: The American Counterculture in the 1960s and 70s*, ed. Peter Braunstein and Michael William Doyle, 99–124. New York: Routledge, 2002.

Roszak, Theodore. *The Making of a Counterculture: Reflections on the Technocratic Society and Its Youthful Opposition*. 1968; Berkeley: University of California Press, 1995.

Rothenberg, Paula. *Invisible Privilege: A Memoir about Race, Class, and Gender*. Lawrence: University Press of Kansas, 2000.

Rothman, Ellen. *Hands and Hearts: A History of Courtship in America*. Cambridge, MA: Harvard University Press, 1987.

Rotundo, E. Anthony. *American Manhood: Transformations in Masculinity from the Revolution to the Modern Era*. New York: Basic Books, 1993.

Ru, Leila J. "Romantic Friendship." In *Modern American Queer History*, ed. Allida M. Black, 13–23. Philadelphia: Temple University Press, 2001.

Sadler, William S. *Courtship and Love*. New York: Macmillan, 1953.

Salisbury, Winfield W. and Frances F. Salisbury. "Youth and the Search for Intimacy." In *The New Sexual Revolution*, ed. Lester A. Kirkendall and Robert N. Whitehurst, 169–82. Buffalo: Prometheus Books, 1971.

Saltman, Jules, ed. *Teen Love, Teen Marriage*. New York: Grosset & Dunlap, 1966.

Schaffer, Stephanie Slocum. *America in the Seventies*. Syracuse: Syracuse University Press, 2003.

Schicke, Richard. *Intimate Strangers: The Culture of Celebrity in America*. 1985; Chicago: Ivan R. Dee, 2000.

Schmidt, Leigh Eric. *Consumer Rites: The Buying & Selling of American Holidays*. Princeton: Princeton University Press, 1995.

Schoenwald, Jonathan M. *A Time for Choosing: The Rise of Modern American Conservatism*. New York: Oxford University Press, 2001.

Schreier, Sandy. *Hollywood Gets Married*. New York: Clarkson Potter, 2002.

Schrum, Kelly. *Some Wore Bobby Sox: The Emergence of Teenage Girls' Culture, 1920–1945*. New York: Palgrave, 2004.

Schulman, Bruce J. *The Seventies: The Great Shift in American Culture, Society, Politics*. Cambridge, MA: Da Capo Press, 2002.

Seligson, Marcia. *The Eternal Bliss Machine: America's Way of Wedding*. New York: Bantam Books, 1973.

Shanley, Mary Lyndon. "Just Marriage: On the Public Importance of Private Unions." In *Just Marriage*, ed. Joshua Cohen and Deborah Chasman, 3–32. New York: Oxford, 2004.

Simmons, Christina. *Making Marriage Modern: Women's Sexuality from the Progressive Era to World War II*. New York: Oxford University Press, 2009.

Sirjamaki, John. "American Culture and Family Life." In *Modern Marriage and Family Living*, ed. Morris Fishbein and Ruby Jo Reeves Kennedy, 37–49. New York: Oxford University Press, 1957.

Skolnick, Arlene. *Embattled Paradise: The American Family in an Age of Uncertainty*. New York: Basic Books, 1991.

Smith, Judith E. *Visions of Belonging: Family Stories, Popular Culture, and Postwar Democracy, 1940–1960.* New York: Columbia University Press, 2004.

Smith, Marie and Louise Durbin. *White House Brides: A New and Revealing History of Romance and Courtship in the President's Mansion.* Washington, DC: Acropolis Books, 1966.

Smith-Rosenberg, Carroll. "The Female World of Love and Ritual: Relations between Women in Nineteenth-Century America." In *Disorderly Conduct: Visions of Gender in Victorian America*, ed. Carroll Smith-Rosenberg, 53–76. New York: Knopf, 1985.

Spigel, Lynn. *Welcome to the Dreamhouse: Popular Media and Postwar Suburbs.* Durham: Duke University Press, 2001.

Stambolian, George. *Male Fantasies/Gay Realities: Interviews with Ten Men.* New York: SeaHorse Press, 1984.

Stern, Gail F., ed. *Something Old, Something New: Ethnic Weddings in America.* Philadelphia: Balch Institute for Ethnic Studies, 1987.

Stone, Hannah M. and Abraham Stone. *A Marriage Manual: A Practical Guidebook to Sex and Marriage.* 1935; New York: Simon & Schuster, 1953.

Stone, Meg. "Choosing Family." In *I Do, I Don't: Queers on Marriage*, ed. Greg Wharton and Ian Philips, 324–25. San Francisco: Suspect Thought Press, 2004.

Streeter, Edward. *Father of the Bride.* New York: Simon & Schuster, 1948.

Susman, Warren I., ed. *Culture as History: The Transformation of American Society in the Twentieth Century.* New York: Pantheon Books, 1984.

Swidler, Ann. "Culture in Action: Symbols and Strategies." *American Sociological Review* 51 (April 1986): 273–86.

Traugot, Michael. *A Short History of the Farm.* Summertown, TN, 1994.

Troy, Gil. "Copresident or Codependent? The Rise and Rejection of Presidential Couples since World War II." In *The Presidential Companion: Readings on the First Ladies.* 2nd edition, ed. Robert P. Watson and Anthony J. Eksterowicz, 252–72. Columbia: University of South Carolina Press, 2006.

U.S. Bureau of the Census. "Table MS-2. Estimated Median Age at First Marriage, by Sex: 1890 to Present." From *Annual Social and Economic Supplement: 2003, Current Population Survey, Current Population Reports.* Series P20-553. "America's Families and Living Arrangements: 2003" and earlier reports. Sept. 15, 2004. http://www.census.gov/population/socdemo/hh-fam/tabMS-2.pdf.

U.S. Department of Health, Education, and Welfare, Public Health Division. "Vital Statistics of the United States 1966." Vol. 3, *Marriage and Divorce.* Washington, DC: U.S. Government Printing Office, 1969.

Vacha, Keith. *Quiet Fire: Memoirs of Older Gay Men*, ed. Cassie Damewood. Trumansburg, NY: Crossing Press, 1985.

Walker, Nancy A. *Shaping Our Mothers' World: American Women's Magazines.* Jackson: University Press of Mississippi, 2000.

Walters, Suzanna Danuta. *All the Rage: The Story of Gay Visibility in America.* Chicago: University of Chicago Press, 2001.

Warner, Michael. *The Trouble with Normal: Sex, Politics, and the Ethics of Queer Life.* New York: Free Press, 1999.

Weiner, Rex and Deanne Stillman. *Woodstock Census: The Nationwide Survey of the Sixties Generation.* New York: Viking Press, 1979.

Weiss, Andrea and Greta Schiller. *Before Stonewall: The Making of a Gay and Lesbian Community.* Tallahassee, FL: Naiad Press, 1988.

Weiss, Jessica. *To Have and To Hold: Marriage, the Baby Boom, and Social Change.* Chicago: University of Chicago Press, 2001.

Weller, Sheila. *Girls like Us: Carole King, Joni Mitchell, Carly Simon—And the Journey of a Generation.* New York: Atria Books, 2008.

Weston, Elizabeth Stewart, ed. *Good Housekeeping's Complete Wedding Guide.* Garden City, NY: Hanover House Books, 1957.

Weston, Kath. *Families We Choose: Lesbians, Gays, Kinship.* New York: Columbia University Press, 1991.

Wharton, Greg and Ian Philips, eds. *I Do, I Don't: Queers on Marriage.* San Francisco: Suspect Thought Press, 2004.

Wicoff, Kamy. *I Do But I Don't: Why the Way We Marry Matters.* Cambridge, MA: Da Capo Press, 2006.

Wilcox, Melissa M. "Of Markets and Missions: The Early History of the Universal Fellowship of Metropolitan Community Churches." *Religion and American Culture* 11 (Winter 2001): 83–108.

Williams, Mary. *Marriage for Beginners.* New York: Macmillan, 1967.

Williams, Thomas E. "Rural America in an Urban Age, 1945–1960." In *Reshaping America: Society and Institutions*, ed. Robert H. Bremmer and Gary W. Reichard, 147–62. Columbus: Ohio State University Press, 1982.

Wilson, Barbara, and the Women's Feature Staff of the New York Herald Tribune. *The Brides' School Complete Book of Engagement and Wedding Etiquette.* New York: Hawthorne Books, 1959.

Winchell, Meghan K. *Good Girls, Good Food, Good Fun: The Story of USO Hostesses during World War II.* Chapel Hill: University of North Carolina Press, 2008.

Wolf, Leonard, ed. *Voices from the Love Generation.* Boston: Little, Brown and Co., 1968.

Woods, Marjorie Binford. *Your Wedding: How to Plan and Enjoy It.* 1942; Indianapolis: Bobbs-Merrill Company, 1949.

Word is Out: Stories of Some of Our Lives. Documentary film. San Francisco: New Glide Publications, 1978.

Wuthnow, Robert. *After Heaven: Spirituality in America since the 1950s.* Berkeley: University of California Press, 1998.

Yalom, Marilyn. *A History of the Wife.* New York: HarperCollins, 2001.

Yankelovich, Daniel. *New Rules: Searching for Self-Fulfillment in a World Turned Upside Down.* New York: Random House, 1981.

Yates, Gayle Graham. *What Women Want: The Ideas of the Movement.* Cambridge, MA: Harvard University Press, 1975.

INDEX

Government, 8, 21, 64, 66, 96, 101, 116, 139, 151, 157, 165
Great Depression, 19, 23
Grooms, 5, 7, 9–10, 16, 18, 20, 26–31, 34, 36–38, 40, 42–43, 45, 49, 50–53, 57–59, 62, 66, 69, 71–73, 76–77, 79, 81, 100–101, 103, 105–14, 117–26, 131–34, 136, 138, 146–50, 159, 161, 175–77, 181; increased participation of, 9, 38, 76, 81–97, 113, 116, 127–28; as limited in wedding influence, 2–3, 14–15, 41
"Guy Dads," 164

Haight-Ashbury, 78–79, 81, 94
Hager, Harry, 172–75
Hanson, Kitty, 49–51, 53, 105–6, 119, 122
Harper's, 140, 142
Hathaway, Anne, 1
Hippies, 78–79, 91–92, 131
Hiroshima World Friendship Center, 65
Homosexuality, 314–68; and inequality, 139–43, 160; policing of, 139–41; visibility of, 142, 146–49, 166–67
Hope chest, 37
Howard, Vicki, 6
Hudson, Kate, 1
Human Be-In, January 1967, 78
Human Rights Campaign, 152, 165
Humphries, Kris, 172

Individualism: as celebrated in weddings, 6–8, 10, 27–30, 36, 41–42, 46–47, 57–59, 63, 2, 77, 82–86, 89–93, 96, 101, 104–7, 113, 116–21, 126–33, 138, 150, 160, 172–74, 180; as hallmark of postwar culture, 20–22, 25–26, 112–14, 174, 180
Ingraham, Chrys, 175
Internal Revenue Service, 136

The J, 165–66
Jackson, Joyce, 53
Johnson, Lady Bird, 54, 56; as mother of the bride, 52, 62, 111; response to protestors, 64, 70–71
Johnson, Luci, 10, 44–49, 51–52, 54–56, 71–74, 112–13, 116–17, 127, 173–74; and Catholicism, 59–62; criticism of, 56–59, 62–70; as typical bride, 44–47, 57, 60, 65–67
Johnson, Lynda, 62, 68, 72, 116
Johnson, Lyndon B., 45, 57–59, 62–63, 72; criticism of, 64–65, 67–70; as father-of-the-bride, 54, 71

Jones, Edwin Brent, 164–66
Judaism. *See* Religion
Junkin, Carey, 136

Kardashian, Kim, 172
Keene, Meg, 177–79
Kelly, Grace, 31
Kidder, Priscilla, 71, 112, 118–20, 122–23, 125
Kinsey, Alfred, 139
Kirkendall, Lester A., 31–32, 92
Kirschenbaum, Howard, 82–84, 88, 92, 97
The Knot, 175–77
Krovatin, Gerald, 103, 105

Lambda Legal, 150
Liberation, politics of, 77, 81–83, 92, 94–98, 101, 124, 127, 142–44
Look, 75–78, 81–82, 106, 110–11, 113, 116, 131, 142
Los Angeles Times, 122, 126
Love, 7, 11, 13, 21, 24, 2, 31–32, 43, 63, 77, 80, 84–87, 90, 92, 95, 97, 118, 123, 127, 130, 133, 135–36, 140, 143–47, 154, 157–58, 163, 165–66, 168
The Love Contract, 84

The Making of a Counterculture, 91
Malme, Karen, 151, 155
Marriage, 4, 8–9, 11, 20–25, 29–34, 36–38, 40–43, 47, 49, 53, 98–99, 108, 123–25, 128, 150; as conveying adulthood, 15, 30–31, 43, 103; critiques and rejections of, 116, 129, 143; and homosexuality, 134–68; instructional texts, 22, 25, 30–32, 40–42, 84, 87; and rights of citizenship, 8, 23, 63, 100–101, 136–39, 142–46, 149–51, 157–59, 162, 164–68; and sex, 25, 30, 71, 86–87, 93–94; views of, expressed in weddings, 6, 8, 10–11, 27, 29, 81–82, 85–86, 88–97, 100, 103–4, 106, 114, 116, 118, 128–35, 150–51, 154–57
Mattachine Society, 139–40
McConnell, Mike, 142–42
Media, 21–22, 56, 78, 80–81, 96, 101, 147, 151; influence on the wedding, 10, 16, 25–31, 34, 42–43, 48, 57–58, 100, 106, 109–110, 112–15, 119, 122–24, 175–79; and response to weddings, 4–5, 49–55, 100, 105–8, 117, 131, 170–74
Mendola, Mary, 143–44
The Mendola Report, 143–44
Middleton, Catherine (Kate), 169–71
Mitchell, Joni, 79
Modern Bride, 122, 128–29

ABOUT THE AUTHOR

Karen Dunak is Assistant Professor of History at Muskingum University in New Concord, Ohio.